J.K. LASSER PRO™
NEW STRATEGIES FOR COLLEGE FUNDING
An Advisor's Guide

J.K. LASSER PRO™
NEW STRATEGIES FOR
COLLEGE FUNDING
An Advisor's Guide

Raymond D. Loewe, CLU, ChFC
with
KC Dempster, ChFC

John Wiley & Sons, Inc.

Microsoft Excel is a registered trademark of Microsoft Corporation.

Library of Congress Cataloging-in-Publication Data:

Loewe, Raymond D.
    J.K. Lasser pro new strategies for college funding : an advisor's guide / Raymond Loewe.
       p.   cm. — (J.K. Lasser pro series)
    Includes index.
    ISBN 0-471-21989-4 (cloth / CD-ROM : alk. paper)
    1. College costs—United States—Handbooks, manuals, etc.
  2. Finance, Personal—United States—Handbooks, manuals, etc.
  I. Title: New strategies for college funding.   II. Title.   III. Series.
  LB2342 .L54   2002
  378.3'0973—dc21   2001008390

Printed in the United States of America

10 9 8 7 6 5 4 3 2 1

ABOUT THE
CD-ROM

Introduction

The spreadsheets on the enclosed CD-ROM are saved in Microsoft® Excel 2000. In order to use the spreadsheets, you will need to have the software capable of reading Microsoft® Excel files.

System Requirements

- IBM PC or compatible computer
- CD-ROM drive
- Windows 95 or later
- Microsoft Excel 2000

For users who do not have Microsoft® Excel on their computers you can download the free viewer from the Microsoft web site. The URL for the viewer is *http://office.microsoft.com/downloads/2000/xlviewer.aspx*

Note: The *Microsoft Excel 97/2000 Viewer* is recommended for use with a stand-alone computer that does not have Microsoft Excel installed. This product allows the user to open and view Excel 97 and Excel 2000 spreadsheet files. The viewer is not suitable for use on a server.

Using the Files

Loading Files

To use the spreadsheet files, launch your spreadsheet program. Select **File, Open** from the pull-down menu. Select the appropriate drive and directory. A list of files should appear. If you do not see a list of files in the directory, you need to select **Microsoft Excel Files (*.XLS)** under **Files of Type.** Double click on the file you want to open. Edit the file according to your needs.

Printing Files

If you want to print the files, select **File, Print** from the pull-down menu.

Saving Files

When you have finished editing a file, you should save it under a new file name by selecting **File, Save As** from the pull-down menu.

User Assistance

If you need assistance with installation or if you have a damaged CD-ROM, please contact Wiley Technical Support at:

Phone: (212) 850-6753
Fax: (212) 850-6800 (Attention: Wiley Technical Support)
Email: *techhelp@wiley.com*
URL: *www.wiley.com/techsupport*

To place additional orders or to request information about other Wiley products, please call (800) 225-5945.

Contents

Acknowledgments

When we began this book project, we knew it was going to be an intense experience because of the deadline we set for ourselves. We agreed to have it completely written in two-and-a-half months. As with most projects, we seriously underestimated the intricacies and difficulties, not only of two people combining different work styles but also of continuing to run the daily business affairs while writing a book.

Needless to say, the deadlines could not have been met without the considerable and valuable support of several people. Our thanks to Milt Eisenhardt who designed the Life Insurance Funded College Plans that we illustrated in the book. Milt who is also know locally as The College Money Coach™ was also instrumental in feeding us information from his current counseling endeavors that was very helpful.

We cannot overlook the valuable help of our attorney and friend, Abby Nason Cohler. Abby helped us with our many legal questions even when we gave her emergency deadlines.

Christine Lindstrom was always ready to do research and any other task we asked of her in order to provide the best information possible to our readers.

And Mary Miller was the pillar who held the business together while our attention was elsewhere. She and her assistant Chris Crosby kept us on track for the client-related things we had to do, and shouldered the burden when we had to go back to writing mode.

We are very thankful for our team and could not have completed this book without their support and hard work.

Introduction

O ver the past twenty-three years we have helped tens of thousands of parents deal with their college problems. During that period we learned some significant lessons, especially regarding designing and implementing college savings plans. The most important of these lessons deal with the following three issues:

- College is a retirement problem.

- College savings plans must be flexible and dynamic.

- Two-way communication between the planner and the parent is extremely critical in both the design and implementation stages.

College Is a Retirement Problem

First let us look at the retirement problem. If you do not believe that college is a subset of the retirement problem, visualize the following:

- Lots of loans are available for college, but who will lend you money for retirement? If you do not pay off your college loans prior to retirement, how will this impact your ability to retire?

- There may be financial aid available to help you pay for college. But where is the financial aid to help you during retirement?

- How old will you be when your youngest child graduates from college? After you have wiped out all your savings, borrowed on your house, and perhaps taken money out of your retirement program, are there leftover retirement funds for you?

Why is the retirement link so important? The retirement problem creates a conflict between saving for college and saving for retirement. This is a dilemma many parents face. They try to decide between saving for retirement and reaping the tax advantages of a retirement plan, or saving for college. If they save for college, should they use one of the new Section 529 Plans that give tremendous tax advantages? What about the fact that they severely penalize the ability to use this money for other things such as retirement if the kids do not go to college?

A clear example of how the college versus retirement savings dilemma can pop up is the experience of the Allen family. Brad and Kathleen Allen had two children in high school. They had been saving money for years. Most of it was in retirement accounts such as their 401(k) plan and IRAs. But they also had some mutual fund accounts outside their retirement accounts.

When we met the Allens, they asked us to help them settle on a college budget that would still allow them to meet their retirement goals. They provided us with all their investment data. Using some proprietary software and their answers to some additional questions such as their desired annual income at retirement, their life expectancy, and their expected pension and social security income, we were able to show Brad and Kathleen that they were a little short of their annual retirement income goal. They decided that they were comfortable with the slightly lower income level.

The next question was how they planned to pay for college. The response was that the nonqualified savings was their college savings account. The interactive feature of the software allowed us to immediately remove those funds from the analysis and show them the impact it had on their projected retirement income. Suddenly it was 18 percent less!

As a result of this analysis and meeting, we were able to help the Allens balance their retirement savings and college expenditures. However, they did have to ask their daughter to compromise on her college choices. If they had built their college savings plan better in the beginning, they could have restructured things to achieve a better college/retirement scenario.

Retirement also limits the time horizon for dealing with the college problem. If a client has a retirement date in mind, he or she needs to be out of college debt by this date. This may require increasing the amount the client saves for college or increasing the out-of-pocket contribution during the college years to limit college loans.

All these issues create dilemmas for parents and planners. There is no question that college and retirement are linked. A good college plan must take into account retirement issues. Sometimes the best savings plan is a plan that is flexible enough to shift from college to retirement and back again if necessary.

College Savings Plans Must Be Flexible and Dynamic

A college savings plan needs to be flexible and dynamic because family circumstances often change significantly during the college savings period. Also, legislative changes in recent years have had significant impact on college savings plans. Despite the best planning, our experience with college savings plans has taught us that they may need to change dramatically as many as three or four times during the college savings cycle. Perhaps the best example can be demonstrated by a story:

Let us look at the situation of Ken and Mary Christine. Ken and Mary were newlyweds when we first met them. Mary was pregnant with their first child, and they decided that they wanted to set up a college savings plan. Ken and Mary had met when they were both students at Yale University. It was important to them that their child benefit from the same type of educational experience that they had. They wanted the best for their child, regardless of cost.

We sat down with Ken and Mary, forecasted the future costs of an Ivy League school, and came up with a savings plan involving a significant monthly expenditure. Ken and Mary were not planning on financial aid. They both had great careers. Mary planned to continue her career after the birth of their child.

Two years later Mary was pregnant again. This time triplets were on the way. Although Ken and Mary wanted to provide the best for all their children, they could not afford to prefund an Ivy League education for four children. Also, Mary decided that her career would have to take a backseat to four children. She knew that although she may resume her career at a later date, the loss of five or more years of workplace experience would have a significant impact on her future earning potential.

In looking at Ken's and Mary's situation a number of things changed. The amount of savings per child would have to be drastically reduced. Lower income potential and four children in college at the same time meant that need-based financial aid was now a significant factor. Their plan needed radical changes. College goals were amended, funding amounts changed, and savings vehicles and account titling needed to be rethought to take financial aid into account.

Lifestyle circumstances, both short term and long term, will influence a college-funding plan. For example, loss of income, changes in family size, divorce, private school enrollment, children not attending college, or discovering a child's special needs all have an impact. Plans need to be flexible.

Legislative changes can also have a significant effect on the need for flexibility in developing college savings plans. Perhaps the best example is to look at Uniform Gifts to Minors Accounts (UGMA) or custodial accounts. The UGMA or custodial account was often used in the past as a vehicle for college savings. There were many reasons: UGMA accounts were easy to use, they were effective in isolating an account for the benefit of a specific child, and they offered significant tax benefits. Many financial planners frequently recommended them as college planning vehicles.

Then Congress enacted the "Kiddie Tax." Suddenly custodial accounts became dramatically less desirable. But parents were trapped. According to the UGMA laws, they had made an irrevocable gift to their children and found they could not legally make changes to account titling or withdraw money from the accounts unless it was to be used for that child and for something that was not a normal parental responsibility.

The complication was that while Congress changed the tax laws, they did not change the financial aid rules. Custodial accounts continued to have a negative effect on financial aid. Many college plans were locked into a rigid structure. Good planning became not so good planning just because Congress changed the law.

Congress can change laws at any time. Sometimes laws expire. One of the great opportunities today involves the decision to use Section 529 Plans. There are many good reasons why they should be used as a college planning tool. But the law creating all the benefits expires in 2011. It is hoped that Congress will make the tax benefits of Section 529 Plans permanent, but no one really knows what will happen. This does not necessarily mean that Section 529 Plans should be written off, but all college savings plans need to be flexible and have an appropriate exit strategy in case changes are necessary.

Two-Way Communication between Planner and Parent Is Critical

One of the most difficult parts of the college plan is setting meaningful goals and translating those goals into a meaningful plan. We have found the use of interactive software to be an extremely useful tool in helping parents set and fine-tune those goals. The College Money College Savings Toolbox™ contains three tools to help you communicate interactively with parents. They are in the form of Microsoft® Excel spreadsheet templates. These spreadsheets use time-sensitive data. Therefore, the enclosed CD-ROM will be useful in re-creating the illustrations in this book. To work effectively, however, these spreadsheet templates need to be updated annually because college costs, inflation rates, and financial aid rules change. Please visit *www. wiley.com/go/loewe* to order current templates at a substantially reduced cost.

Figure I.1 summarizes each tool in the College Money College Savings Toolbox.™ See Appendixes B, D, and E for instructions on installing the tools on your computer, with helpful tips and comments.

The College Savings Calculator™ is the first tool to use when designing a long-term college savings plan. It allows parents to get a feel for future college costs in five general cost categories (state, state nonresident, medium, high, Ivy League) across four geographical regions and to project the monthly savings required to meet these costs. The magnitude of these costs will spur a serious parent to take action. Armed with this information a parent can begin to plan:

- The college cost class he or she is willing to prefund
- Whether or not to cost share with the student

When setting up a long-term college funding plan, we really cannot accurately predict future financial aid. However, we can guess at the likelihood of future financial aid and build in flexibility. The College Financial Aid Test™ is the tool to use. Any good savings plan will balance the benefits of:

- Financial aid
- Tax savings
- Control of money

The College Financial Aid Test™ should be used for initial target planning and then used periodically to enhance plan features as college gets closer and financial aid gets more predictable.

The College Funding Integrator™ helps parents to quantify their college funding obligation for their entire family by:

- Projecting future college costs for each student
- Projecting total family college costs
- Planning a funding package consisting of
  — Fixed or increasing savings
  — A "pay-as-you-go" component during college
  — A parent borrowing and repayment plan

This interactive model helps parents refine their plan by allowing "what if" changes such as

- College types to adjust costs
- Savings and "pay-as-you-go" commitments
- Pre- and postfunding time periods

The College Funding Integrator™ displays changes graphically, making this program an extremely effective college planning tool.

FIGURE I.1 The College Money College Savings Toolbox

What This Book Does

This book demonstrates how we help parents design savings plans for college. These proven techniques can help you design better plans and be more successful in implementing them. The book lays out a complete step-by-step system for designing a plan. It starts by helping you get really good data about parents' educational goals for their children. It helps you quantify the risk they are willing to take and helps you build a college cost forecast that quantifies the problem. Next it helps you sift through the myriad college planning tools, including those created by recent legislation. The end result is an extremely effective plan.

In each step, we show you

- What we do

- What you need to know to do it the right way

- Why we do it the way we do it (our rationale)

- How we do it effectively

How This Book Is Organized

Part I of this book is built around quantifying the college problem for each parent you counsel. Parents need to make choices during the goal-setting stage, including

- Which types of colleges they wish to include

- Whether or not to realistically plan on financial aid

- Whether planned cost sharing with the student should be part of the plan

- How to best define their planning time horizon

Do not underestimate the importance of this section. Very often, the goals that parents initially state are not really their true goals. The college problem is so complex that parents usually do not understand the implications of these initial goals and the drastic effects that college-planning decisions will have on their ability to retire later. Carefully exploring these implications is critical to the process.

Part I not only gives you the facts and tools you need to assemble this part of the plan but also gives you the tools and techniques to communicate effectively with parents.

- Chapters 1 and 2 deal with helping parents select the most appropriate college cost type and projecting future college costs.

- Chapters 3 and 4 deal with the financial aid system. The discussion there helps you explore to what degree allowances for financial aid should be incorporated into the plan.

- Chapters 5 and 6 incorporate college-planning time horizons into the planning process.

At the end of Part I you will have all the tools you need to quantify the college problem for your client's family and communicate that problem effectively and motivationally to your client.

Part II deals with tools and products you need to implement the plan. There are a number of unique vehicles for college planning, including

- The Coverdell Education Savings Account (formerly the Education IRA)

- State-sponsored Section 529 Plans including

  — Tuition savings plans

  — Prepaid tuition plans

Furthermore, they include some not-so-unique vehicles that can be adapted to college planning, such as

- The Simple Plan™—a parent-owned mutual fund portfolio

- Overfunded life insurance; fixed, variable, and indexed

- Overfunded retirement plans in conjunction with federal Parent Loan for Undergraduate Students (PLUS) loans

- Savings bonds

Choosing the right vehicle and product requires carefully balancing income tax strategies, financial aid strategies, and control of money issues. Chapters 7, 8, and 9 deal with these issues.

Part III helps you put the plan together and build in appropriate exit strategies to give your plan the flexibility it needs to have. Chapter 10 offers case studies to help you assemble your plans effectively. Chapter 10 also demonstrates how you can make the planning process easier for parents to accept by breaking the planning process into two phases, a feasibility study and a plan design phase. Finally, Part III demonstrates by example the importance of building in exit strategies. Parents will truly appreciate your attention to exit strategies. Such strategies add flexibility to your plans that sets them apart from your competition.

PART

I

Quantifying the College Problem and Communicating with Parents

Putting Together the College Cost Forecast
(Understanding College Costs and Inflation)

"Why do parents not save for college?" Reporters and other financial advisors frequently ask this question. Here are some of the answers.

- Some parents are overwhelmed by the sheer magnitude of the numbers. Because they cannot possibly meet the savings requirements, they adopt the "Ostrich Plan," bury their heads in the sand and do not do anything.

- Many parents look at the time framework. College seems so far away that they assume that there is plenty of time.

- Some wait to see if their children are college material, or wait to see how motivated their students are before they plan their college commitment.

- And most parents start with very good intentions. But life events such as an unexpectedly high car repair bill, braces for the children, a medical emergency, or a more costly than expected family vacation, get in the way. And what parent has not experienced the extraordinary expenses of raising children that often shoot holes in their college plan, leaving it interrupted or abandoned?

In any case, a proper plan, one that sets realistic goals and builds in contingencies for life events and expenses, will work. It all begins with the advisor helping to set the stage the right way.

The planning starts by setting realistic goals. Realistic goals begin with an understanding of college costs and college inflation. Understanding these two critical elements also allows us to develop a sound, forecasting model to project college costs into the future.

In this chapter, we are going to help you understand the components of the cost of college, give you a history of college inflation, and create a college cost forecasting model you can use to help parents plan effectively. Creating the model involves five steps:

Step 1: Develop college cost categories.

Step 2: Create a list of benchmark colleges for each category.

Step 3: Determine base costs for next year.

Step 4: Determine the appropriate inflation factors.

Step 5: Build future cost tables.

Understanding College Costs

College is expensive. Most parents know that college is expensive. Yet most parents and advisors underestimate college costs. The cost of college is made up of a number of components. They all add up, so it is important not to overlook any of them.

- The first component of college cost is tuition. Although tuition costs may seem easy to ascertain, they are often not. Some colleges actually show tuition on a per-credit basis, and parents and planners need to dig out the number of credits required per year. Sometimes tuition is buried in a comprehensive cost along with room and board and the other costs of college.

- Component number two is fees. Most colleges charge a required general fee. This is different from special fees such as a health insurance fee that may be optional.

- The third component, room and board, is usually based on a room in the college dormitory and a meal plan in the on-campus dining hall. Although living in an off-campus apartment or living at home and commuting can reduce the cost of room and board, other costs such as increased transportation may be incurred.

- Finally books, transportation, laundry money, and other personal expenses must also be included. Most parents also inform us that personal expenses are severely underestimated by colleges. Because of this we include an additional component parents call "pizza money" to cover such things as entertainment, fraternity or sorority dues, and extra spending money parents slip their students periodically.

When helping parents forecast the cost of college as part of a college savings plan, it is usually a good idea to include all of these costs. Parents can make decisions later, if necessary, to cut costs by choosing to have students live at home or off campus.

As we indicated previously, a number of colleges do not break down costs. Instead they use a comprehensive fee. This comprehensive fee is supposed to include everything. Nevertheless, parents who have gone through the college process tell us to still add an allowance for "pizza money."

Good Information Is Difficult to Get

One would think that it would be relatively easy to get good college cost information, but it is not. For the last twenty years we have been putting together a college cost forecast. We have found that the information on college costs is inconsistent among various sources and often not available until late in the year.

For example, tuition and fees at many state colleges are set by state legislatures and are not finalized until May or June of the academic year. Bills are usually payable in July or August. This often causes stress for parents in planning funding, especially when there are pockets of significant cost increases as there were for the 2001–2002 academic year. As we indicated above, some colleges list their costs by component, others lump many costs together as a comprehensive fee, and yet others list only some of the component costs and leave it to parents and students to fill in the gaps with their own estimates. In addition, many college guidebooks contain last year's cost data or estimates for the current year for at least some of the colleges they list. All these facts make it difficult to compile consistent data for a good college cost forecast.

We have usually found that the best place to get current data is from the college Web site, the college catalog, or a call to the admissions department. Even these sources are sometimes inconsistent, making it difficult to find specific data. Sometimes, for example, college costs are listed on Web sites under financial aid, sometimes under admissions, and sometimes in other places. Many times verbal data from the admissions department does not agree with Web site data.

Using Today's College Costs to Forecast Future College Costs

Because information is so inconsistent among colleges, and because some colleges can have substantial one-time cost increases, we have found that it is most helpful to parents to build a college cost forecast around a set of college cost categories rather than around specific colleges. For example:

- State colleges (residents)
- State colleges (nonresident costs)
- Medium-priced private colleges
- High-priced private colleges
- Very-high-priced colleges (Ivy League)

We have also noted that there are some cost differences across regions. To account for these regional differences, we have broken costs down by the following regions:

- Northeast
- South
- Midwest
- West

Finally, we have found it important to attach typical colleges to each category, so that parents and students can relate better. This has led us to develop a list of benchmark colleges by cost category and by region as an effective device to help parents grasp college costs as part of a forecasting tool.

Table 1.1 denotes the benchmark colleges we have chosen for the 2001–2002 college cost forecast and shows the cost breakdown for each school.

TABLE 1.1 Benchmark College Costs for the School Year Ending June 2002

College	Type	Tuition and Fees	Room and Board	Other	Pizza	Total	Region
Rutgers	Low	$6,652	$6,852	$2,893	$2,100	$18,497	Northeast
Rutgers (Nonresident)	Medium/Low	$10,688	$6,852	$2,893	$2,100	$22,533	Northeast
Lycoming College	Medium	$19,404	$5,376	$2,200	$2,100	$29,080	Northeast
American Univ.	High/Medium	$22,478	$8,829	$1,900	$2,100	$35,307	Northeast
Univ. of Pennsylvania	High—Ivy League	$26,630	$8,244	$2,336	$2,100	$39,310	Northeast
Ohio State Univ.	Low	$4,788	$5,807	$3,129	$2,100	$15,824	Midwest
Ohio State Univ. (NR)	Medium/Low	$13,554	$5,807	$3,129	$2,100	$24,590	Midwest

TABLE 1.1 Benchmark College Costs for the
School Year Ending June 2002 *(Continued)*

College	Type	Tuition and Fees	Room and Board	Other	Pizza	Total	Region
Cornell College (IA)	Medium	$20,250	$5,600	$2,000	$2,100	$29,950	Midwest
Kenyon College	High/Medium	$27,550	$4,580	$1,600	$2,100	$35,830	Midwest
Northwestern University	High—Ivy League	$25,839	$7,752	$2,655	$2,100	$38,346	Midwest
Univ. of North Carolina	Low	$3,184	$5,930	$2,460	$2,100	$13,674	South
U of N Carolina (NR)	Medium/Low	$12,350	$5,930	$2,960	$2,100	$23,340	South
University of Richmond	Medium	$22,570	$4,730	$2,100	$2,100	$31,500	South
Univ. of Miami	High/Medium	$23,462	$7,940	$3,050	$2,100	$36,552	South
Duke University	High—Ivy League	$26,810	$7,648	$2,332	$2,100	$38,890	South
U of Washington	Low	$3,983	$6,378	$3,381	$2,100	$15,842	West
U of Washington (NR)	Medium/Low	$13,258	$6,378	$3,381	$2,100	$25,117	West
University of Denver	Medium	$22,037	$3,748	$2,250	$2,100	$30,135	West
California Inst of Tech	High/Medium	$21,120	$6,543	$4,482	$2,100	$34,245	West
Stanford University	High—Ivy League	$25,917	$8,030	$2,400	$2,100	$38,447	West

The costs in Table 1.1 are today's real college costs. They are reflective of what a student would pay today, including all the component parts. Parents need to see these costs and understand their validity before they will buy into your forecast of future college costs because when we adjust these costs for inflation, we are going to see some very large numbers.

Understanding College Inflation

College inflation obviously is important in making projections. What is not so obvious is that it also may dictate how clients need to invest for college. Any good investment plan needs to stay ahead of inflation and taxes. The fact that college inflation has been consistently higher than normal inflation makes a college cost forecast scary and calls for a more aggressive investment strategy.

Table 1.2 is a history of college inflation and the Consumer Price Index (CPI). A quick look at Table 1.2 shows a dramatic range of college inflation numbers, from a high of 14.35 percent in 1982 to a low of 3.60 percent in 1973. The source of these numbers is the College Board, a trade association of colleges. Unfortunately, the college inflation numbers are based on tuition, room, and board. Normally increases in room and board charges would tend to follow CPI. Because college inflation has been almost always higher than CPI, this may actually understate the rise in tuition.

CPI figures for this analysis come from the Department of Labor, Bureau of Labor Statistics. We used numbers representing all urban consumers for all items and we used mid-year data, from July 1 to June 30 each year, to better coincide with college inflation numbers. This is important because college inflation is based on an academic year.

TABLE 1.2 History of College Inflation versus CPI

Year	College Inflation	CPI	Difference
2000	4.77%	3.66%	1.11%
1999	4.24%	2.14%	2.10%
1998	4.77%	1.68%	3.09%
1997	4.62%	2.23%	2.39%
1996	5.05%	2.95%	2.10%
1995	5.32%	2.76%	2.56%
1994	5.44%	2.77%	2.67%
1993	5.99%	2.78%	3.21%
1992	5.79%	3.16%	2.63%
1991	7.61%	4.45%	3.16%
1990	7.83%	4.81%	3.02%
1989	8.61%	4.99%	3.62%
1988	7.89%	4.16%	3.73%
1987	7.39%	3.90%	3.49%
1986	8.02%	1.61%	6.41%
1985	8.15%	3.55%	4.60%
1984	8.03%	4.14%	3.89%
1983	9.78%	2.44%	7.34%
1982	14.35%	6.48%	7.87%
1981	13.95%	10.73%	3.22%
1980	12.00%	13.22%	−1.22%
1979	9.05%	11.27%	−2.22%
1978	7.37%	7.74%	−0.37%
1977	8.10%	6.72%	1.38%
1976	9.27%	5.43%	3.84%

TABLE 1.2 History of College Inflation versus CPI *(Continued)*

Year	College Inflation	CPI	Difference
1975	7.20%	9.65%	−2.45%
1974	5.93%	11.53%	−5.60%
1973	3.60%	5.73%	−2.13%
1972	6.07%	3.04%	3.03%
1971	8.60%	4.37%	4.23%
Average	**7.49%**	**5.14%**	**2.36%**

For the past ten years, college inflation has been subsiding, averaging about 5.86 percent. At first blush, this appears to be good news for parents of young children. Yet when we examine CPI figures, we find that the news is not really good. For the same ten-year period, CPI has averaged 2.86 percent. This leaves a gap of 2.50 percent, demonstrating that college inflation is running almost double CPI. In recent years, CPI has been kept low by good government fiscal and monetary policy. Nevertheless, our experience indicates that nothing is forever. Someday inflation will rise again and college inflation will probably rise with it, but at a higher level.

Table 1.3 is an analysis of college inflation and CPI looking at five-year increments. This is useful for you as an advisor to see patterns better. It is also helpful in developing some averages for forecasting purposes.

TABLE 1.3 College Inflation versus CPI Period Averages

Average	College Inflation	CPI	Difference
Last 5 years	4.69%	2.53%	2.16%
Last 10 years	5.36%	2.86%	2.50%
Last 15 years	6.22%	3.20%	3.02%
Last 20 years	7.38%	3.77%	3.61%
Last 25 years	7.74%	4.79%	2.94%
Last 30 years	7.49%	5.14%	2.36%

Averages help us remove peaks and valleys from the system. Earlier in our discussion of college costs, we decided to use cost categories. Individual colleges can experience a wide range of cost increases that are not representative of the long haul. For example, for the 2001–2002 academic year, a number of colleges had increases substantially above the average, 4.77 percent.

- Clemson proposed a whopping big 42 percent increase for in-state residents, likely an attempt to get the state to ante up more funding. Their actual increase according to data on their Web site was only 2.8 percent.

- According to their Web site, Iowa State University increased tuition by 7.6 percent.

- University of Minnesota raised tuition by 11.4 percent.

These schools represent only a few that either considered or actually raised tuition above average college inflation. If we had chosen any of the above schools as the basis for a college cost projection, we would have had a distorted forecast.

Completing the College Forecast Model

Our last step is to use college cost and inflation data to build a forecasting model. There are many ways to do this, and over the last twenty-two years we have experimented with several. The model with the best predictive results has been a dynamic model. In other words, each year we update the base college costs and inflation data. By doing this, we give parents good target numbers in the early years and hone in with more accurate numbers as we get closer to college. Because we believe that a good college plan should be reviewed and fine-tuned annually, this type of forecasting is extremely effective. Although we could use actual annual inflation in a reverse pattern, we find that averages work effectively and simplify our model. Tables 1.4, 1.5, 1.6, and 1.7 were built in the following manner:

- For each region we used the benchmark college costs for each type of cost category as next year's base college cost.

- We then broke down the total college cost for each benchmark college into two cost groups:

  — Tuition, fees, room, and board

  — Other costs, including personal expenses, books, and "pizza money"

- Next, we inflated tuition, fees, room, and board using a college inflation factor. (Remember the College Board college inflation figures included room and board.) We inflated other costs using a CPI inflation factor.

- Finally, we developed a college inflation factor using the average college inflation numbers for the last five years to predict college costs for the next five years, the last ten years for years five through ten, and the twenty-five-year average for years ten through twenty-five. CPI inflation factors are similarly constructed. Using these averages in a dynamic model allowed us to weight short- and long-term inflation factors appropriately.

TABLE 1.4 The College Savings Calculator™—College Cost Projections (Northeast)

Base Year: 2001					College Cost Region: Northeast	

		←————————— Base-Year Data —————————→				
College Type		1	2	3	4	5
College Description		Low	Low/Med	Medium	Med/High	High
Base-Year Tuition, Fees,						
Room, and Board		$13,504	$17,540	$24,780	$31,307	$34,874
Base-Year Other Costs		$4,993	$4,993	$4,300	$4,000	$4,436

			←————————— College Cost Projections —————————→				
			1	2	3	4	5
			Low	Low/Med	Medium	Med/High	High
	Inflation	Inflation					
	Rate	Rate	Total	Total	Total	Total	Total
Year	Tuition	Other	Costs	Costs	Costs	Costs	Costs
2001	Base-Year Data		$18,497	$22,533	$29,080	$35,307	$39,310
2002	4.69%	2.53%	$19,257	$23,482	$30,351	$36,877	$41,058
2003	4.69%	2.53%	$20,049	$24,473	$31,679	$38,518	$42,885
2004	4.69%	2.53%	$20,876	$25,507	$33,068	$40,233	$44,796
2005	4.69%	2.53%	$21,739	$26,588	$34,518	$42,027	$46,794
2006	4.69%	2.53%	$22,640	$27,715	$36,035	$43,903	$48,883
2007	5.36%	2.86%	$23,712	$29,059	$37,844	$46,143	$51,377
2008	5.36%	2.86%	$24,837	$30,471	$39,747	$48,499	$54,001
2009	5.36%	2.86%	$26,019	$31,955	$41,749	$50,979	$56,763
2010	5.36%	2.86%	$27,259	$33,514	$43,854	$53,588	$59,668
2011	5.36%	2.86%	$28,562	$35,151	$46,068	$56,333	$62,726
2012	7.74%	4.79%	$30,580	$37,679	$49,467	$60,537	$67,408
2013	7.74%	4.79%	$32,744	$40,392	$53,120	$65,059	$72,444
2014	7.74%	4.79%	$35,066	$43,306	$57,048	$69,923	$77,860
2015	7.74%	4.79%	$37,558	$46,436	$61,271	$75,155	$83,687
2016	7.74%	4.79%	$40,232	$49,796	$65,811	$80,784	$89,955
2017	7.74%	4.79%	$43,102	$53,406	$70,693	$86,839	$96,699
2018	7.74%	4.79%	$46,182	$57,283	$75,943	$93,353	$103,953
2019	7.74%	4.79%	$49,489	$61,448	$81,588	$100,361	$111,758
2020	7.74%	4.79%	$53,038	$65,923	$87,659	$107,901	$120,155
2021	7.74%	4.79%	$56,848	$70,730	$94,189	$116,013	$129,190
2022	7.74%	4.79%	$60,940	$75,895	$101,211	$124,742	$138,912
2023	7.74%	4.79%	$65,333	$81,445	$108,764	$134,135	$149,373
2024	7.74%	4.79%	$70,050	$87,409	$116,888	$144,242	$160,629
2025	7.74%	4.79%	$75,117	$93,818	$125,626	$155,117	$172,741
2026	7.74%	4.79%	$80,558	$100,707	$135,026	$166,820	$185,775
2027	7.74%	4.79%	$86,403	$108,110	$145,138	$179,415	$199,802
2028	7.74%	4.79%	$92,681	$116,067	$156,016	$192,969	$214,898
2029	7.74%	4.79%	$99,425	$124,621	$167,718	$207,556	$231,144
2030	7.74%	4.79%	$106,671	$133,815	$180,309	$223,255	$248,629
2031	7.74%	4.79%	$114,456	$143,700	$193,855	$240,151	$267,447
2032	7.74%	4.79%	$122,821	$154,327	$208,430	$258,336	$287,701
2033	7.74%	4.79%	$131,809	$165,753	$224,112	$277,909	$309,501
2034	7.74%	4.79%	$141,468	$178,038	$240,985	$298,977	$332,966
2035	7.74%	4.79%	$151,849	$191,247	$259,142	$321,654	$358,223
2036	7.74%	4.79%	$163,005	$205,451	$278,681	$346,063	$385,409
2037	7.74%	4.79%	$174,997	$220,726	$299,706	$372,338	$414,674
2038	7.74%	4.79%	$187,886	$237,153	$322,332	$400,622	$446,176
2039	7.74%	4.79%	$201,742	$254,820	$346,682	$431,069	$480,088
2040	7.74%	4.79%	$216,637	$273,821	$372,888	$463,845	$516,594
2041	7.74%	4.79%	$232,650	$294,257	$401,091	$499,129	$555,893
2042	7.74%	4.79%	$249,866	$316,239	$431,446	$537,114	$598,201
2043	7.74%	4.79%	$268,376	$339,883	$464,116	$578,008	$643,748
2044	7.74%	4.79%	$288,279	$365,318	$499,279	$622,033	$692,784
2045	7.74%	4.79%	$309,680	$392,679	$537,128	$669,431	$745,577
2046	7.74%	4.79%	$332,694	$422,113	$577,867	$720,461	$802,415

Source: College Money © 1997–2000. Version 2002 (Book).b.

TABLE 1.5 The College Savings Calculator™—College Cost Projections (South)

Base Year: 2001   **College Cost Region: South**

College Type College Description			Base-Year Data				
			1 Low	2 Low/Med	3 Medium	4 Med/High	5 High
Base-Year Tuition, Fees, Room, and Board			$9,114	$18,280	$27,300	$31,402	$34,458
Base-Year Other Costs			$4,560	$5,060	$4,200	$5,150	$4,432

			College Cost Projections				
			1 Low	2 Low/Med	3 Medium	4 Med/High	5 High
Year	Inflation Rate Tuition	Inflation Rate Other	Total Costs	Total Costs	Total Costs	Total Costs	Total Costs
2001 Base-Year Data			$13,674	$23,340	$31,500	$36,552	$38,890
2002	4.69%	2.53%	$14,217	$24,325	$32,887	$38,155	$40,618
2003	4.69%	2.53%	$14,783	$25,354	$34,336	$39,831	$42,425
2004	4.69%	2.53%	$15,373	$26,429	$35,851	$41,582	$44,314
2005	4.69%	2.53%	$15,988	$27,550	$37,435	$43,412	$46,290
2006	4.69%	2.53%	$16,629	$28,722	$39,091	$45,326	$48,355
2007	5.36%	2.86%	$17,391	$30,118	$41,067	$47,609	$50,821
2008	5.36%	2.86%	$18,190	$31,585	$43,145	$50,011	$53,416
2009	5.36%	2.86%	$19,028	$33,126	$45,332	$52,537	$56,146
2010	5.36%	2.86%	$19,907	$34,745	$47,632	$55,194	$59,019
2011	5.36%	2.86%	$20,829	$36,447	$50,052	$57,989	$62,041
2012	7.74%	4.79%	$22,266	$39,072	$53,762	$62,277	$66,671
2013	7.74%	4.79%	$23,804	$41,891	$57,752	$66,887	$71,649
2014	7.74%	4.79%	$25,453	$44,918	$62,043	$71,844	$77,005
2015	7.74%	4.79%	$27,221	$48,169	$66,656	$77,173	$82,766
2016	7.74%	4.79%	$29,115	$51,661	$71,618	$82,905	$88,963
2017	7.74%	4.79%	$31,146	$55,411	$76,954	$89,068	$95,630
2018	7.74%	4.79%	$33,323	$59,440	$82,693	$95,696	$102,802
2019	7.74%	4.79%	$35,658	$63,768	$88,866	$102,824	$110,518
2020	7.74%	4.79%	$38,162	$68,419	$95,506	$110,490	$118,819
2021	7.74%	4.79%	$40,847	$73,415	$102,648	$118,736	$127,751
2022	7.74%	4.79%	$43,727	$78,784	$110,331	$127,605	$137,362
2023	7.74%	4.79%	$46,816	$84,553	$118,595	$137,145	$147,703
2024	7.74%	4.79%	$50,131	$90,753	$127,487	$147,407	$158,830
2025	7.74%	4.79%	$53,687	$97,416	$137,052	$158,446	$170,803
2026	7.74%	4.79%	$57,502	$104,577	$147,343	$170,322	$183,688
2027	7.74%	4.79%	$61,597	$112,275	$158,415	$183,098	$197,554
2028	7.74%	4.79%	$65,991	$120,549	$170,329	$196,843	$212,476
2029	7.74%	4.79%	$70,708	$129,443	$183,147	$211,632	$228,535
2030	7.74%	4.79%	$75,771	$139,005	$196,940	$227,544	$245,818
2031	7.74%	4.79%	$81,206	$149,285	$211,782	$244,664	$264,419
2032	7.74%	4.79%	$87,041	$160,337	$227,753	$263,086	$284,440
2033	7.74%	4.79%	$93,307	$172,221	$244,940	$282,909	$305,988
2034	7.74%	4.79%	$100,034	$184,999	$263,436	$304,240	$329,181
2035	7.74%	4.79%	$107,258	$198,740	$283,341	$327,194	$354,146
2036	7.74%	4.79%	$115,017	$213,516	$304,763	$351,896	$381,018
2037	7.74%	4.79%	$123,349	$229,406	$327,818	$378,480	$409,943
2038	7.74%	4.79%	$132,300	$246,496	$352,632	$407,089	$441,080
2039	7.74%	4.79%	$141,914	$264,876	$379,340	$437,880	$474,598
2040	7.74%	4.79%	$152,243	$284,645	$408,086	$471,019	$510,679
2041	7.74%	4.79%	$163,339	$305,909	$439,027	$506,687	$549,522
2042	7.74%	4.79%	$175,261	$328,781	$472,331	$545,077	$591,338
2043	7.74%	4.79%	$188,071	$353,385	$508,180	$586,398	$636,355
2044	7.74%	4.79%	$201,836	$379,852	$546,770	$630,875	$684,819
2045	7.74%	4.79%	$216,629	$408,326	$588,310	$678,750	$736,997
2046	7.74%	4.79%	$232,527	$438,958	$633,027	$730,284	$793,172

Source: College Money © 1997–2000. Version 2002 (Book).b.

TABLE 1.6 The College Savings Calculator™—College Cost Projections (Midwest)

Base Year: 2001					College Cost Region: Midwest

			<-----------	Base-Year Data		----------->
College Type			1	2	3	4	5
College Description			Low	Low/Med	Medium	Med/High	High
Base-Year Tuition, Fees, Room, and Board			$10,595	$19,361	$25,850	$32,130	$33,591
Base-Year Other Costs			$5,229	$5,229	$4,100	$3,700	$4,755

			<-----------		College Cost Projections		----------->
			1	2	3	4	5
			Low	Low/Med	Medium	Med/High	High
Year	Inflation Rate Tuition	Inflation Rate Other	Total Costs	Total Costs	Total Costs	Total Costs	Total Costs
2001	Base-Year Data		$15,824	$24,590	$29,950	$35,830	$38,346
2002	4.69%	2.53%	$16,453	$25,630	$31,266	$37,431	$40,042
2003	4.69%	2.53%	$17,109	$26,717	$32,642	$39,104	$41,815
2004	4.69%	2.53%	$17,793	$27,851	$34,080	$40,854	$43,668
2005	4.69%	2.53%	$18,506	$29,036	$35,583	$42,684	$45,605
2006	4.69%	2.53%	$19,249	$30,273	$37,154	$44,598	$47,631
2007	5.36%	2.86%	$20,133	$31,747	$39,029	$46,883	$50,049
2008	5.36%	2.86%	$21,059	$33,296	$41,001	$49,288	$52,593
2009	5.36%	2.86%	$22,031	$34,924	$43,076	$51,819	$55,269
2010	5.36%	2.86%	$23,051	$36,635	$45,258	$54,483	$58,085
2011	5.36%	2.86%	$24,120	$38,433	$47,554	$57,286	$61,047
2012	7.74%	4.79%	$25,785	$41,205	$51,075	$61,575	$65,587
2013	7.74%	4.79%	$27,569	$44,182	$54,861	$66,189	$70,469
2014	7.74%	4.79%	$29,481	$47,379	$58,932	$71,153	$75,720
2015	7.74%	4.79%	$31,531	$50,812	$63,309	$76,494	$81,367
2016	7.74%	4.79%	$33,728	$54,501	$68,017	$82,239	$87,441
2017	7.74%	4.79%	$36,083	$58,463	$73,079	$88,422	$93,974
2018	7.74%	4.79%	$38,608	$62,719	$78,524	$95,073	$101,002
2019	7.74%	4.79%	$41,316	$67,292	$84,380	$102,230	$108,561
2020	7.74%	4.79%	$44,220	$72,206	$90,678	$109,932	$116,693
2021	7.74%	4.79%	$47,334	$77,485	$97,452	$118,219	$125,442
2022	7.74%	4.79%	$50,675	$83,158	$104,739	$127,137	$134,854
2023	7.74%	4.79%	$54,259	$89,255	$112,578	$136,734	$144,980
2024	7.74%	4.79%	$58,104	$95,807	$121,010	$147,062	$155,875
2025	7.74%	4.79%	$62,230	$102,849	$130,082	$158,177	$167,597
2026	7.74%	4.79%	$66,657	$110,419	$139,841	$170,139	$180,210
2027	7.74%	4.79%	$71,408	$118,555	$150,341	$183,014	$193,782
2028	7.74%	4.79%	$76,507	$127,301	$161,638	$196,871	$208,386
2029	7.74%	4.79%	$81,980	$136,703	$173,792	$211,785	$224,101
2030	7.74%	4.79%	$87,855	$146,812	$186,870	$227,838	$241,012
2031	7.74%	4.79%	$94,163	$157,680	$200,943	$245,116	$259,212
2032	7.74%	4.79%	$100,934	$169,365	$216,085	$263,715	$278,797
2033	7.74%	4.79%	$108,206	$181,930	$232,380	$283,735	$299,876
2034	7.74%	4.79%	$116,014	$195,441	$249,915	$305,286	$322,562
2035	7.74%	4.79%	$124,399	$209,970	$268,785	$328,485	$346,978
2036	7.74%	4.79%	$133,404	$225,595	$289,093	$353,458	$373,257
2037	7.74%	4.79%	$143,076	$242,398	$310,949	$380,342	$401,542
2038	7.74%	4.79%	$153,466	$260,471	$334,471	$409,284	$431,987
2039	7.74%	4.79%	$164,627	$279,910	$359,787	$440,441	$464,758
2040	7.74%	4.79%	$176,617	$300,817	$387,035	$473,985	$500,032
2041	7.74%	4.79%	$189,499	$323,307	$416,362	$510,099	$538,003
2042	7.74%	4.79%	$203,340	$347,499	$447,929	$548,979	$578,877
2043	7.74%	4.79%	$218,212	$373,523	$481,907	$590,839	$622,877
2044	7.74%	4.79%	$234,194	$401,519	$518,481	$635,909	$670,244
2045	7.74%	4.79%	$251,370	$431,638	$557,851	$684,434	$721,236
2046	7.74%	4.79%	$269,828	$464,042	$600,231	$736,682	$776,131

Source: College Money © 1997–2000. Version 2002 (Book).b.

TABLE 1.7 The College Savings Calculator™—College Cost Projections (West)

Base Year: 2001   **College Cost Region: West**

			1	2	Base-Year Data 3	4	5
College Type			1	2	3	4	5
College Description			Low	Low/Med	Medium	Med/High	High
Base-Year Tuition, Fees, Room, and Board			$10,361	$19,636	$25,785	$27,663	$33,947
Base-Year Other Costs			$5,481	$5,481	$4,350	$6,582	$4,500

			1	2	College Cost Projections 3	4	5
			Low	Low/Med	Medium	Med/High	High
Year	Inflation Rate Tuition	Inflation Rate Other	Total Costs	Total Costs	Total Costs	Total Costs	Total Costs
2001	Base-Year Data		$15,842	$25,117	$30,135	$34,245	$38,447
2002	4.69%	2.53%	$16,467	$26,177	$31,454	$35,709	$40,153
2003	4.69%	2.53%	$17,118	$27,283	$32,833	$37,238	$41,937
2004	4.69%	2.53%	$17,796	$28,438	$34,275	$38,835	$43,801
2005	4.69%	2.53%	$18,503	$29,645	$35,781	$40,504	$45,751
2006	4.69%	2.53%	$19,240	$30,904	$37,355	$42,246	$47,789
2007	5.36%	2.86%	$20,116	$32,405	$39,234	$44,324	$50,223
2008	5.36%	2.86%	$21,035	$33,982	$41,210	$46,508	$52,784
2009	5.36%	2.86%	$21,998	$35,639	$43,289	$48,803	$55,478
2010	5.36%	2.86%	$23,008	$37,381	$45,475	$51,216	$58,313
2011	5.36%	2.86%	$24,067	$39,210	$47,774	$53,752	$61,296
2012	7.74%	4.79%	$25,718	$42,033	$51,303	$57,657	$65,865
2013	7.74%	4.79%	$27,487	$45,064	$55,096	$61,853	$70,778
2014	7.74%	4.79%	$29,382	$48,318	$59,175	$66,360	$76,064
2015	7.74%	4.79%	$31,413	$51,814	$63,560	$71,202	$81,749
2016	7.74%	4.79%	$33,589	$55,568	$68,275	$76,405	$87,864
2017	7.74%	4.79%	$35,921	$59,600	$73,345	$81,996	$94,442
2018	7.74%	4.79%	$38,421	$63,932	$78,798	$88,004	$101,519
2019	7.74%	4.79%	$41,101	$68,585	$84,661	$94,461	$109,132
2020	7.74%	4.79%	$43,974	$73,585	$90,967	$101,400	$117,323
2021	7.74%	4.79%	$47,055	$78,956	$97,750	$108,859	$126,135
2022	7.74%	4.79%	$50,358	$84,728	$105,044	$116,876	$135,617
2023	7.74%	4.79%	$53,901	$90,929	$112,890	$125,494	$145,818
2024	7.74%	4.79%	$57,702	$97,594	$121,330	$134,758	$156,795
2025	7.74%	4.79%	$61,778	$104,757	$130,409	$144,718	$168,606
2026	7.74%	4.79%	$66,152	$112,455	$140,175	$155,425	$181,316
2027	7.74%	4.79%	$70,844	$120,729	$150,681	$166,938	$194,993
2028	7.74%	4.79%	$75,879	$129,623	$161,984	$179,317	$209,711
2029	7.74%	4.79%	$81,283	$139,183	$174,144	$192,628	$225,551
2030	7.74%	4.79%	$87,081	$149,461	$187,227	$206,942	$242,597
2031	7.74%	4.79%	$93,305	$160,511	$201,303	$222,335	$260,943
2032	7.74%	4.79%	$99,986	$172,390	$216,449	$238,889	$280,688
2033	7.74%	4.79%	$107,158	$185,163	$232,746	$256,693	$301,939
2034	7.74%	4.79%	$114,858	$198,897	$250,283	$275,842	$324,811
2035	7.74%	4.79%	$123,125	$213,665	$269,153	$296,438	$349,430
2036	7.74%	4.79%	$132,002	$229,546	$289,460	$318,592	$375,929
2037	7.74%	4.79%	$141,535	$246,624	$311,313	$342,423	$404,453
2038	7.74%	4.79%	$151,773	$264,991	$334,831	$368,057	$435,156
2039	7.74%	4.79%	$162,768	$284,745	$360,141	$395,634	$468,206
2040	7.74%	4.79%	$174,579	$305,991	$387,381	$425,301	$503,784
2041	7.74%	4.79%	$187,265	$328,843	$416,698	$457,219	$542,083
2042	7.74%	4.79%	$200,894	$353,424	$448,251	$491,558	$583,312
2043	7.74%	4.79%	$215,536	$379,865	$482,213	$528,504	$627,698
2044	7.74%	4.79%	$231,268	$408,309	$518,768	$568,257	$675,481
2045	7.74%	4.79%	$248,171	$438,907	$558,115	$611,030	$726,924
2046	7.74%	4.79%	$266,335	$471,826	$600,468	$657,056	$782,307

Source: College Money © 1997–2000. Version 2002 (Book).b.

Again, there are many different forecasting techniques that we could have used to construct our college forecast tables, but we have found this method effective. It allows us to predict college costs over the long-term with reasonable accuracy. It also helps us make short-term adjustment to handle spikes in college inflation. Using this model most effectively, however, requires annual updates and annual client reviews.

Using the Forecast Tables

What we have accomplished so far is to generate a table for each of the four geographic regions projecting future college costs by college cost category. By examining each table, you can see what inflation factors were used in making projections. These tables would prove awkward to use, however, in an interview with a parent. This is especially true if the parent wanted to explore several college cost options.

In order to make this data user-friendly, we recast the data in these tables into twenty separate tables, one for each of the benchmark colleges we established. These tables are located in Appendix A. In addition, we did some calculations for you so that you do not need to do them in front of the client. We totaled the four-year college bill for you, and we calculated the annual savings required to pay the bill at three different interest or growth rates. Table 1.8 is a reproduction of one of these pages for your review.

Here is how easy these tables are to use:

Your client, Bob Jones, wishes to have his daughter attend Duke University. Duke is a southern region, Ivy League cost-category college. His daughter will begin college in 2014.

By finding the first year of college, 2014, in column one of the table, we locate the appropriate data row. Going across the row we identify the data that our client needs:

- Freshman year cost = $77,005

- Sophomore year cost = $82,766

- Junior year cost = $88,963

- Senior year cost = $95,630

- Total college cost = $344,363

- Annual savings required at 8% = $1,059

If the client decides he needs information on other colleges, it is easy to get the data by consulting the appropriate table.

TABLE 1.8 The College Savings Calculator™—Projected College Costs and Savings Required

Assumptions:

Planned Savings Starts in September	2002
Planned Withdrawals Begin in September	Freshman Year
Geographic Region (1 = Northeast, 2 = Midwest, 3 = South, 4 = West)	**3 South**
Cost Categories (1 = Low, 2 = Med/Low, 3 = Medium, 4 = Med/High, 5 = High)	**5 Ivy League**
Benchmark College:	**Duke University**
Projected After-Tax Growth Rates on Savings Deposits	8.00% 9.00% 7.00%

Notes:

Assume Funding through August of the Last Year of College

College Costs are total costs based on college budget bill plus misc. costs reported by parents.

Cost Categories—1 Low for State schools (in-state resident), 5 High for Ivy League, 2–4 Medium range for Private

Projected Freshman Year	Projected Freshman Cost	Projected Sophomore Cost	Projected Junior Cost	Projected Senior Cost	Projected Four-Year Cost	Approx. Mo. Savings Req. 8.00%	Approx. Mo. Savings Req. 9.00%	Approx. Mo. Savings Req. 7.00%
2002						n/a	n/a	n/a
2003	$42,425	$44,314	$46,290	$48,355	$181,384	$2,890	$2,874	$2,907
2004	$44,314	$46,290	$48,355	$50,821	$189,780	$2,418	$2,392	$2,445
2005	$46,290	$48,355	$50,821	$53,416	$198,882	$2,083	$2,049	$2,117
2006	$48,355	$50,821	$53,416	$56,146	$208,738	$1,833	$1,794	$1,874
2007	$50,821	$53,416	$56,146	$59,019	$219,402	$1,642	$1,597	$1,687
2008	$53,416	$56,146	$59,019	$62,041	$230,622	$1,487	$1,438	$1,537
2009	$56,146	$59,019	$62,041	$66,671	$243,877	$1,368	$1,315	$1,422
2010	$59,019	$62,041	$66,671	$71,649	$259,380	$1,275	$1,218	$1,334
2011	$62,041	$66,671	$71,649	$77,005	$277,366	$1,203	$1,142	$1,266
2012	$66,671	$71,649	$77,005	$82,766	$298,091	$1,148	$1,083	$1,215
2013	$71,649	$77,005	$82,766	$88,963	$320,383	$1,100	$1,032	$1,172
2014	$77,005	$82,766	$88,963	$95,630	$344,363	$1,059	$986	$1,135
2015	$82,766	$88,963	$95,630	$102,802	$370,160	$1,022	$946	$1,103
2016	$88,963	$95,630	$102,802	$110,518	$397,912	$991	$911	$1,076
2017	$95,630	$102,802	$110,518	$118,819	$427,768	$962	$879	$1,052
2018	$102,802	$110,518	$118,819	$127,751	$459,890	$937	$850	$1,031
2019	$110,518	$118,819	$127,751	$137,362	$494,450	$914	$823	$1,013
2020	$118,819	$127,751	$137,362	$147,703	$531,635	$894	$799	$997
2021	$127,751	$137,362	$147,703	$158,830	$571,645	$875	$777	$983
2022	$137,362	$147,703	$158,830	$170,803	$614,697	$858	$757	$971
2023	$147,703	$158,830	$170,803	$183,688	$661,024	$843	$738	$961

Source: College Money © 1997–2001. Version 2002 (Book).b.

Introducing The College Savings Calculator™

As easy as the tables are to use, they do not have the impact and the ease of use that interactive software can have. In the next chapter, we introduce The College Savings Calculator™ and show you how it can quickly answer questions that your client is likely to ask. Specifically, we demonstrate how to use the "Calculator" to help your client

1. Set reasonable college cost goals.

2. Understand the cost of procrastination in delaying the start of a college savings plan.

3. Explore the effects of risk and return on your client's college savings plan.

CHAPTER 2

Communicating with Your Client Using The College Savings Calculator™

I n Chapter 1, we developed a strategy for dealing with college costs and college inflation, culminating in a college cost forecast. In this chapter we introduce a tool, The College Savings Calculator,™ to help you communicate with your clients to help them develop realistic college savings goals.

The College Savings Calculator™ is useful in three specific situations:

- Helping clients set goals

- Helping clients quantify a risk/reward strategy to overcome college inflation

- Showing clients the cost of putting off the start of a savings plan

The data you gather by using this tool to explore college savings goals with your client will be invaluable later in designing a plan. The difference between simply letting the client tell you his or her plan and exploring options with your client using the College Savings Calculator™ is that the client will understand the numbers you agree on. This almost always results in better data and a deeper commitment to the college plan.

Please understand that this tool was not designed to generate a complete college savings plan. We introduce another tool, The College Funding Integrator,™ for this purpose in Chapter 6.

Working with The College Savings Calculator™

The College Savings Calculator™ is a spreadsheet template that is designed to work with Microsoft® Excel 2000. (See Appendix B for instructions on how to install the program on your computer.) The calculator has five separate pages:

- Main Page
- Introduction Page
- Savings Required Page
- Inflation Analysis Page
- College Cost Forecast Page

The *Main Page* is the only page that you will use with clients most of the time. It is the page where you will input data and show client results. Figure 2.1 is an illustration of the *Main Page* of The College Savings Calculator.™ Please note the six input areas:

- Client Name ❶
- Plan Start Year ❷
- College Start Year ❸
- College Type ❹
- College Geographic Region ❺
- Target Savings Growth Rate ❻

Plan Start Year is the year your client will begin to save for college (usually the current year). To simplify the calculations, the program assumes that savings begin in September of the *Plan Start Year* and continue through the end of college. The *College Start Year* is the year the student will start his or her freshman year of college. *College Type* coincides with the five college cost classifications we defined in Chapter 1. *College Geographic Region* also coincides with the four geographic regions, Northeast, Midwest, South, and West, we defined in Chapter 1. Finally, *Target Savings Growth Rate* is the expected design return on the money invested for college. All these input items represent variables that are going to allow you to help your client plan interactively.

The *Introduction Page* is reproduced in Table 2.1. It summarizes the assumptions in the model. Some of the data on this page, specifically the Benchmark Section, will change based on the geographic region you input on the *Main Page*. For example, when the West is chosen, the West benchmark

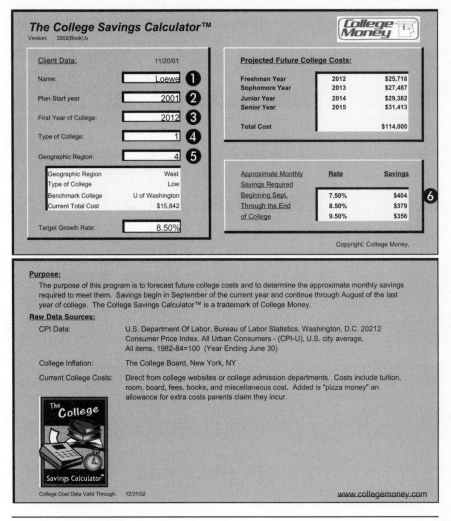

FIGURE 2.1 The College Savings Calculator™ Main Page

colleges appear at the bottom of the *Introduction Page.* Similarly, choosing the Northeast region produces Northeast benchmark colleges.

The *Savings Required Page,* Table 2.2, should be especially helpful to you. It coincides with the savings required tables that we introduced in Chapter 1. There are twenty of these tables, one for each benchmark college in Appendix A. Unfortunately, due to space limitations, we used only three sample growth rates in these tables. Using the software and printing new Savings Required Pages, you can expand the number of tables in Appendix A changing the *Savings Growth Rates* to any growth rate you desire.

TABLE 2.1 The College Savings Calculator™—Introduction Page

Last Update: July 01
Version: 2002.b

Purpose:

The purpose of this program is to create a series of worksheets designed to forecast future college costs and to determine the savings requirements to meet them.

Raw Data:

Raw Inflation data is updated annually to keep all worksheets current and valid.

Source—CPI Data: U.S. Department of Labor, Bureau of Labor Statistics,
Washington, DC 20212
Consumer Price Index, All Urban Consumers—(CPI-U),
U.S. city average. All items, 1982–84 = 100
July 1 to June 30

Source—College Inflation   The College Board, New York, NY

Inflation Analysis:

Inflation analysis section allows us to evaluate college and CPI data to establish a reasonable forecast of future college costs. It calculates 5-, 10-, 15-, 20-, 25-, and 30-year averages.

College Cost Forecast:

This section provides a 24-year forecast of college costs for five college cost categories. Base college costs are input annually. College costs forecasted are the sum of a tuition and fees component and an other component. Other includes room and board, books, and miscellaneous costs. Each is forecasted separately using a different inflation rate:

Tuition and fees are adjusted annually using college cost inflation data.
Other costs are adjusted based on CPI data.

Inflation for this study uses processed raw data from the "Infl Analysis" section:

years 1–5   average last five years
years 6–10   average last 10 years
years 11–25   average last 25 years

Benchmark College Costs Are for the School Year Ending: June-02
Geographic Region Selected Is: West

			Tuition and Fees	Room and Board	Other	Pizza	Total
41	1 U of Washington	Low	$3,983	$6,378	$3,381	$2,100	$15,842
42	2 U of Washington (NR)	Medium/Low	$13,258	$6,378	$3,381	$2,100	$25,117
43	3 University of Denver	Medium	$22,037	$3,748	$2,250	$2,100	$30,135
44	4 California Inst of Tech	High/Medium	$21,120	$6,543	$4,482	$2,100	$34,245
45	5 Stanford University	High— Ivy League	$25,917	$8,030	$2,400	$2,100	$38,447

Note: Pizza $ are average misc. costs reported by parents that are incurred above and beyond college estimated costs.

Source: College Money © 1997–2001.

TABLE 2.2 The College Savings Calculator™—Projected College Costs and Savings Required

Assumptions:

Planned Savings Starts in September	2001
Planned Withdrawals Begin in September	Freshman Year
Geographic Region (1 = Northeast, 2 = Midwest, 3 = South, 4 = West)	**4 West**
Cost Categories (1 = Low, 2 = Med/Low, 3 = Medium, 4 = Med/High, 5 = High)	**1 State College (Resident)**
Benchmark College:	**U of Washington**
Projected After-Tax Growth Rates on Savings Deposits	8.50% 9.50% 7.50%

Notes:

Assume Funding through August of the Last Year of College

College Costs are total costs based on college budget bill plus misc. costs reported by parents.

Cost Categories—1 Low for State schools (in-state resident), 5 High for Ivy League, 2–4 Medium range for Private

Projected Freshman Year	Projected Freshman Cost	Projected Sophomore Cost	Projected Junior Cost	Projected Senior Cost	Projected Four-Year Cost	Approx. Mo. Savings Req. 8.50%	Approx. Mo. Savings Req. 9.50%	Approx. Mo. Savings Req. 7.50%
2001						n/a	n/a	n/a
2002	$16,467	$17,118	$17,796	$18,503	$69,884	$1,111	$1,105	$1,117
2003	$17,118	$17,796	$18,503	$19,240	$72,658	$921	$911	$931
2004	$17,796	$18,503	$19,240	$20,116	$75,656	$786	$774	$799
2005	$18,503	$19,240	$20,116	$21,035	$78,895	$686	$671	$701
2006	$19,240	$20,116	$21,035	$21,998	$82,389	$608	$592	$625
2007	$20,116	$21,035	$21,998	$23,008	$86,157	$547	$529	$565
2008	$21,035	$21,998	$23,008	$24,067	$90,107	$496	$477	$516
2009	$21,998	$23,008	$24,067	$25,718	$94,791	$456	$436	$477
2010	$23,008	$24,067	$25,718	$27,487	$100,280	$424	$403	$447
2011	$24,067	$25,718	$27,487	$29,382	$106,654	$399	$377	$423
2012	$25,718	$27,487	$29,382	$31,413	$114,000	$379	$356	$404
2013	$27,487	$29,382	$31,413	$33,589	$121,870	$362	$337	$388
2014	$29,382	$31,413	$33,589	$35,921	$130,304	$347	$321	$374
2015	$31,413	$33,589	$35,921	$38,421	$139,343	$333	$306	$362
2016	$33,589	$35,921	$38,421	$41,101	$149,031	$321	$293	$351
2017	$35,921	$38,421	$41,101	$43,974	$159,416	$310	$281	$341
2018	$38,421	$41,101	$43,974	$47,055	$170,549	$299	$270	$332
2019	$41,101	$43,974	$47,055	$50,358	$182,487	$290	$259	$324
2020	$43,974	$47,055	$50,358	$53,901	$195,288	$282	$250	$317
2021	$47,055	$50,358	$53,901	$57,702	$209,016	$274	$242	$311
2022	$50,358	$53,901	$57,702	$61,778	$223,740	$267	$234	$305

Source: College Money © 1997–2001. Version: 2002 (Book).b.

The *Inflation Analysis Page,* Table 2.3, reproduces the inflation data used in our college forecast model. Although this may seem redundant, it is not. The College Savings Calculator™ program should be updated annually. Future updates to this program will give you updated inflation data to support a new updated college cost forecast. You will be able to examine the updated inflation data and note changes on this software-generated page.

Similarly, the *College Cost Forecast Page,* Table 2.4, is a reproduction of the regional college forecast data from Chapter 1. This page will change based on the region you choose to input on the *Main Page.* Again, this page may seem redundant, but upgrading your software annually will automatically update your college cost data and your college cost forecast. New data can be examined and studied on this page.

Helping Clients Set Realistic Goals

Remember, most clients have no idea what college really costs. They also have no idea what college inflation will do to future college costs. If your clients are exposed to the reality of college too quickly and without exploring options early in the game, clients may be overwhelmed and do nothing.

The following case study is an example of how you can discuss options with your client in a positive manner. By setting realistic goals, it is more likely your clients will actually implement their plans.

Jeff and Hillary Smith had a daughter, Chelsea. Chelsea, aged six, was very bright. Jeff and Hillary wanted to plan to send her to Stanford University. At the time we first met the Smiths, Jeff had an up-and-coming political career. Hillary was practicing as a part-time attorney. They did not have a lot of discretionary funds to invest for college, but they felt they could save $400 per month. They were also very conservative investors. They indicated they would be happiest if the money would be invested in Certificates of Deposit at their local bank.

Using the College Savings Calculator™ we were able to help Jeff and Hillary explore the cost of college. First, we showed them what they would need to do to send Chelsea to Stanford. The results are shown in Figure 2.2.

In order to save enough to meet the projected four-year cost of Stanford, $316,455, Jeff and Hillary would need to save $1,196 per month (Figure 2.2).

In fact, at 5 percent, Jeff's and Hillary's $400 per month would fall far short of pre-funding any of the major private colleges. It would, however, fully fund Chelsea's education at their state university, the University of North Carolina (Figure 2.3).

TABLE 2.3 The College Savings Calculator™—College Inflation versus CPI

Number of Years = 30
Last Year = 2000

Year	College Inflation	CPI	Difference
Average	**7.49%**	**5.14%**	**2.36%**
2000	4.77%	3.66%	1.11%
1999	4.24%	2.14%	2.10%
1998	4.77%	1.68%	3.09%
1997	4.62%	2.23%	2.39%
1996	5,05%	2.95%	2.10%
1995	5.32%	2.76%	2.56%
1994	5.44%	2.77%	2.67%
1993	5.99%	2.78%	3.21%
1992	5.79%	3.16%	2.63%
1991	7.61%	4.45%	3.16%
1990	7.83%	4.81%	3.02%
1989	8.61%	4.99%	3.62%
1988	7.89%	4.16%	3.73%
1987	7.39%	3.90%	3.49%
1986	8.02%	1.61%	6.41%
1985	8.15%	3.55%	4.60%
1984	8.03%	4.14%	3.89%
1983	9.78%	2.44%	7.34%
1982	14.35%	6.48%	7.87%
1981	13.95%	10.73%	3.22%
1980	12.00%	13.22%	−1.22%
1979	9.05%	11.27%	−2.22%
1978	7.37%	7.74%	−0.37%
1977	8.10%	6.72%	1.38%
1976	9.27%	5.43%	3.84%
1975	7.20%	9.65%	−2.45%
1974	5.93%	11.53%	−5.60%
1973	3.60%	5.73%	−2.13%
1972	6.07%	3.04%	003%
1971	8.60%	4.37%	4.23%
0	0.00%	0.00%	0.00%
0	0.00%	0.00%	0.00%
0	0.00%	0.00%	0.00%
0	0.00%	0.00%	0.00%
0	0.00%	0.00%	0.00%

Average	College Inflation	CPI	Difference
Last 5 Years	4.69%	2.53%	2.16%
Last 10 Years	5.36%	2.86%	2.50%
Last 15 Years	6.22%	3.20%	3.02%
Last 20 Years	7.38%	3.77%	3.61%
Last 25 Years	7.74%	4.79%	2.94%
Last 30 Years	7.49%	5.14%	2.36%

Source: College Money © 1997–2000. Version 2002.b.

TABLE 2.4 The College Savings Calculator™—College Cost Projections

Base Year: 2001					College Cost Region: West

		Base-Year Data				
College Type		1	2	3	4	5
College Description		Low	Low/Med	Medium	Med/High	High
Base-Year Tuition, Fees, Room, and Board		$10,361	$19,636	$25,785	$27,663	$33,947
Base-Year Other Costs		$5,481	$5,481	$4,350	$6,582	$4,500

			College Cost Projections			
			1	2	3	4	5
			Low	Low/Med	Medium	Med/High	High
Year	Inflation Rate Tuition	Inflation Rate Other	Total Costs	Total Costs	Total Costs	Total Costs	Total Costs
---	---	---	---	---	---	---	---
2001 Base-Year Data			$15,842	$25,117	$30,135	$34,245	$38,447
2002	4.69%	2.53%	$16,467	$26,177	$31,454	$35,709	$40,153
2003	4.69%	2.53%	$17,118	$27,283	$32,833	$37,238	$41,937
2004	4.69%	2.53%	$17,796	$28,438	$34,275	$38,835	$43,801
2005	4.69%	2.53%	$18,503	$29,645	$35,781	$40,504	$45,751
2006	4.69%	2.53%	$19,240	$30,904	$37,355	$42,246	$47,789
2007	5.36%	2.86%	$20,116	$32,405	$39,234	$44,324	$50,223
2008	5.36%	2.86%	$21,035	$33,982	$41,210	$46,508	$52,784
2009	5.36%	2.86%	$21,998	$35,639	$43,289	$48,803	$55,478
2010	5.36%	2.86%	$23,008	$37,381	$45,475	$51,216	$58,313
2011	5.36%	2.86%	$24,067	$39,210	$47,774	$53,752	$61,296
2012	7.74%	4.79%	$25,718	$42,033	$51,303	$57,657	$65,865
2013	7.74%	4.79%	$27,487	$45,064	$55,096	$61,853	$70,778
2014	7.74%	4.79%	$29,382	$48,318	$59,175	$66,360	$76,064
2015	7.74%	4.79%	$31,413	$51,814	$63,560	$71,202	$81,749
2016	7.74%	4.79%	$33,589	$55,568	$68,275	$76,405	$87,864
2017	7.74%	4.79%	$35,921	$59,600	$73,345	$81,996	$94,442
2018	7.74%	4.79%	$38,421	$63,932	$78,798	$88,004	$101,519
2019	7.74%	4.79%	$41,101	$68,585	$84,661	$94,461	$109,132
2020	7.74%	4.79%	$43,974	$73,585	$90,967	$101,400	$117,323
2021	7.74%	4.79%	$47,055	$78,956	$97,750	$108,859	$126,135
2022	7.74%	4.79%	$50,358	$84,728	$105,044	$116,876	$135,617
2023	7.74%	4.79%	$53,901	$90,929	$112,890	$125,494	$145,818
2024	7.74%	4.79%	$57,702	$97,594	$121,330	$134,758	$156,795
2025	7.74%	4.79%	$61,778	$104,757	$130,409	$144,718	$168,606
2026	7.74%	4.79%	$66,152	$112,455	$140,175	$155,425	$181,316
2027	7.74%	4.79%	$70,844	$120,729	$150,681	$166,938	$194,993
2028	7.74%	4.79%	$75,879	$129,623	$161,984	$179,317	$209,711
2029	7.74%	4.79%	$81,283	$139,183	$174,144	$192,628	$225,551
2030	7.74%	4.79%	$87,081	$149,461	$187,227	$206,942	$242,597
2031	7.74%	4.79%	$93,305	$160,511	$201,303	$222,335	$260,943
2032	7.74%	4.79%	$99,986	$172,390	$216,449	$238,889	$280,688
2033	7.74%	4.79%	$107,158	$185,163	$232,746	$256,693	$301,939
2034	7.74%	4.79%	$114,858	$198,897	$250,283	$275,842	$324,811
2035	7.74%	4.79%	$123,125	$213,665	$269,153	$296,438	$349,430
2036	7.74%	4.79%	$132,002	$229,546	$289,460	$318,592	$375,929
2037	7.74%	4.79%	$141,535	$246,624	$311,313	$342,423	$404,453
2038	7.74%	4.79%	$151,773	$264,991	$334,831	$368,057	$435,156
2039	7.74%	4.79%	$162,768	$284,745	$360,141	$395,634	$468,206
2040	7.74%	4.79%	$174,579	$305,991	$387,381	$425,301	$503,784
2041	7.74%	4.79%	$187,265	$328,843	$416,698	$457,219	$542,083
2042	7.74%	4.79%	$200,894	$353,424	$448,251	$491,558	$583,312
2043	7.74%	4.79%	$215,536	$379,865	$482,213	$528,504	$627,698
2044	7.74%	4.79%	$231,268	$408,309	$518,768	$568,257	$675,481
2045	7.74%	4.79%	$248,171	$438,907	$558,115	$611,030	$726,924
2046	7.74%	4,79%	$266,335	$471,826	$600,468	$657,056	$782,307

Source: College Money © 1997–2000. Version 2002-b.

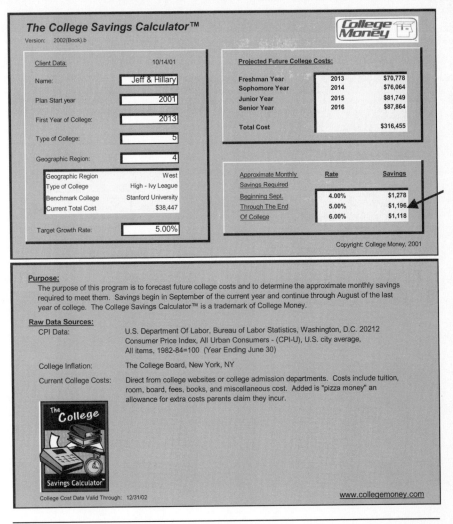

FIGURE 2.2 Smith Example 1—Savings for Stanford at 5 Percent Return

At this point in our meeting with Jeff and Hillary, the discussion could have gone in either of two directions. First, Jeff and Hillary could have gone into a state of depression at not being able to come close to meeting their goals. Or, second, the discussion could have turned into one of resolve. Fortunately, resolve won. The Smiths indicated that their plan would at least ensure that Chelsea would be financially able to attend college. In addition, they felt that they would be able to save more money later. They also asked if perhaps they could make their college savings grow faster. Clients often ask the right questions that lead us to where we want to go

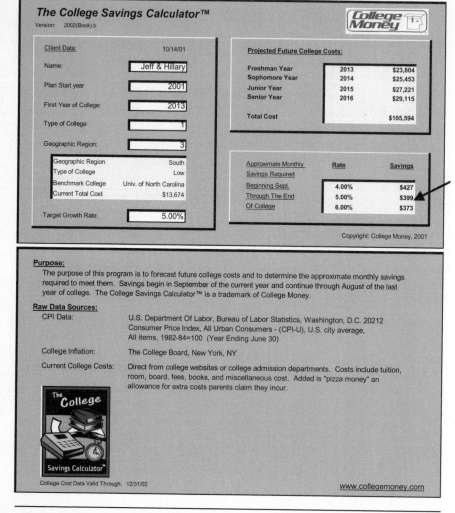

The College Savings Calculator™
Version: 2002(Book).b

College Money

Client Data: 10/14/01

Name: Jeff & Hillary

Plan Start year: 2001

First Year of College: 2013

Type of College: 1

Geographic Region: 3

Geographic Region	South
Type of College	Low
Benchmark College	Univ. of North Carolina
Current Total Cost	$13,674

Target Growth Rate: 5.00%

Projected Future College Costs:

Freshman Year	2013	$23,804
Sophomore Year	2014	$25,453
Junior Year	2015	$27,221
Senior Year	2016	$29,115
Total Cost		$105,594

Approximate Monthly Savings Required	Rate	Savings
Beginning Sept.	4.00%	$427
Through The End	5.00%	$399
Of College	6.00%	$373

Copyright: College Money, 2001

Purpose:
The purpose of this program is to forecast future college costs and to determine the approximate monthly savings required to meet them. Savings begin in September of the current year and continue through August of the last year of college. The College Savings Calculator™ is a trademark of College Money.

Raw Data Sources:

CPI Data: U.S. Department Of Labor, Bureau of Labor Statistics, Washington, D.C. 20212 Consumer Price Index, All Urban Consumers - (CPI-U), U.S. city average, All items, 1982-84=100 (Year Ending June 30)

College Inflation: The College Board, New York, NY

Current College Costs: Direct from college websites or college admission departments. Costs include tuition, room, board, fees, books, and miscellaneous cost. Added is "pizza money" an allowance for extra costs parents claim they incur.

The College Savings Calculator™

College Cost Data Valid Through: 12/31/02

www.collegemoney.com

FIGURE 2.3 Smith Example 2—State College (Resident) at 5 Percent Return

next, a discussion of how investment returns and risk will impact their college savings plans.

Helping Clients Quantify Risk and Reward to Overcome College Inflation

Too often clients are either too aggressive or too conservative when it comes to investing college savings dollars. The College Savings Calculator™ can show clients the relationship between the rate of investment growth and the amount they need to save to fund their college savings plan. Clients need to stay ahead of college inflation. Table 2.5, taken from the *Inflation Analysis*

Page of The College Savings Calculator,™ shows average college inflation rates over the last thirty years. Clients need to stay ahead of these rates yet not take undue risk in the process. This is why they need an advisor.

TABLE 2.5 College Inflation versus CPI Period Averages

Average	College Inflation	CPI	Difference
Last 5 years	4.69%	2.53%	2.16%
Last 10 years	5.36%	2.86%	2.50%
Last 15 years	6.22%	3.20%	3.02%
Last 20 years	7.38%	3.77%	3.61%
Last 25 years	7.74%	4.79%	2.94%
Last 30 years	7.49%	5.14%	2.36%

You will remember from our example of the Smith family that the Smiths asked us to calculate the savings required to fund Stanford at 5 percent. The result was $1,196 monthly. Using The College Savings Calculator™ (Figure 2.4), we can show Jeff and Hillary that the monthly savings requirement drops significantly by an increased return:

- $1,043 at 7 percent
- $973 at 8 percent
- $906 at 9 percent

As the plan designer, you need to make sure the returns the client seeks are reasonable.

Helping Clients Understand the Cost of Delayed Savings

Many clients offer an excuse to delay starting a savings plan. We gave a lot of those reasons in Chapter 1. Typically, clients feel they have time because college seems so far away and usually they have major bills to pay or expenditures on the horizon they want to clear up before starting a plan. The College Savings Calculator™ can show your clients the cost of delaying the start of a plan in terms of extra monthly savings they will need to make.

Figure 2.5 shows the increased monthly savings required by waiting one year. For convenience we have summarized them below.

Plan Start →	2001	2002
7%	$1043	$1158
8%	$973	$1087
9%	$906	$1019

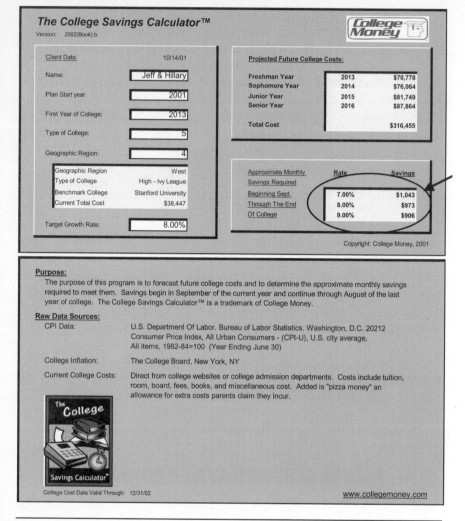

FIGURE 2.4 Smith Example—Stanford at 8 Percent Return

Summary

We've found that working with The College Savings Calculator™ brings insight into college savings planning to our clients and to us. We encourage you to play with this tool to gain a better sense of college costs and savings required and to explore them with your clients in a way that should help them to get going.

A problem with writing any book that gives hard data is that the data becomes obsolete. The concepts behind The College Savings Calculator™

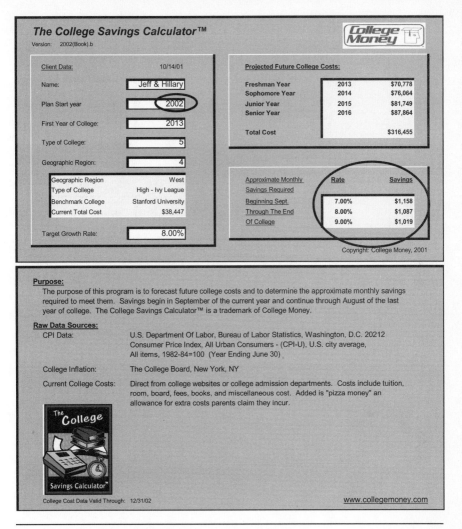

FIGURE 2.5 The Cost of Waiting

are valid. However the assumptions of inflation and college costs will change annually. This tool also gives us a unique way of updating important college planning data regularly after our book has become dated.

In Figure 2.6, you will note a message stating that the data is invalid. You may see this when using the software included with this book. Your software will still work, and you will still be able to re-create the illustrations in the book. However, the data needs to be updated if you plan to use the software in plan design.

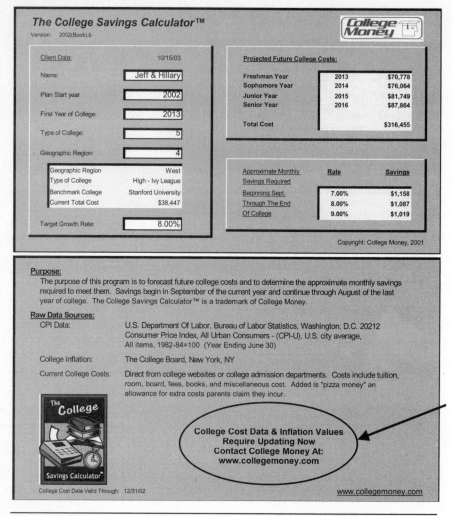

FIGURE 2.6 The College Savings Calculator™ Example of Warning Message

The Impact of Financial Aid

Whenever we do any college financial planning, we routinely do a financial aid test. We look at the financial aid test as a due diligence obligation to our client. We feel it is a critical piece because for some clients a financial aid award can dwarf tax savings. Even for those who do not get major aid awards, an extra $10,000 or $20,000 over a family's college-planning horizon can make a big difference. The key is to find out which clients are affected and to what degree. We can then help them plan accordingly.

Unfortunately, financial aid can be complex. Sometimes wealthier clients *do* qualify, especially if they have more than one child in college at a time and if their children attend higher-priced colleges. Sometimes the grand-children of a wealthy client are not wealthy. They may be precluded from qualifying for financial aid because a grandparent sets up a college plan the wrong way. If a grandparent fully funds college, this may not be a problem. But if a grandparent only partially funds college, the student's family may have difficulties coming up with the difference on their own and may be limited in their ability to access the financial aid system.

Parent income, student income, parent assets, and student assets can all have a direct effect on financial aid eligibility. Titling of assets and timing of liquidation of assets that will generate income can also be important. Even the choice of college and the number in college at one time can make a dif-ference. The point is that whether a client's student will qualify is not as obvious as it first seems and should not be taken for granted either way.

Do Not Skip This Step

Many planners make the mistake of skipping this step. Because financial aid is difficult to predict, they take the easy way out and ignore it. Instead they base their planning on tax savings only. Later, when parents find out that they received less financial aid because of the structure of their savings plan, they lose confidence in their planner. Do not let this happen to you. College is a great time to set up relationships with parents. Many planners do not make much money by handling college savings plans. They do, however, build strong relationships because they handle this important aspect of planning. These relationships are founded on the trust that leads clients to retain the planner to handle their retirement and estate planning needs. Jeopardizing these relationships after years of cultivation does not make sense.

Just as dealing with financial aid early can keep advisors from making a mistake, it can also help parents who are unable to qualify for aid get over a hurdle that impedes them from taking action. Many clients ignore planning because they are hoping for aid and do not understand the process. Sometimes they hang on so long that it becomes almost too late to start a good plan. For example:

> Mr. Bellamy, a self-employed consultant, frequently had to post a security bond as part of his normal business activities. He kept $500,000 liquid in U.S. Treasury bills for this purpose. In his mind, Mr. Smith did not consider this money available to pay for college. After all, it was necessary to keep these funds available as a condition of running his business. Because he did not have much in other assets, Mr. Bellamy felt he would surely qualify for financial aid.
>
> Unfortunately, most colleges tend to feel that business assets represent a source of financial strength. Although colleges may discount business assets' value somewhat, they are in fact a resource to help pay for college and will have a direct impact on financial aid eligibility. Mr. Bellamy simply needed to have his financial aid status clearly demonstrated to him. Only after he graphically understood how the financial aid system worked was he ready to embark on the college savings plan required to educate his children.

Many parents have seen neighbors sacrifice to save for college, while others who did not save received substantial financial aid. This situation is usually misleading. Most of the time, parents who save only to lose substantial aid lose it because they incorrectly planned where and how to save. In fact, it is critical to save as much as possible whether or not financial aid is in the picture. Having money gives families important options in choosing appropriate colleges. Not having money may mean settling for second best by being forced to choose colleges that give more free money.

> Two of my friends, Bob and Mary Jones, were planning for college for their son, Jim. Jim was a great student. He scored 1550 out of a possible 1600 on his college boards (SATs). He had lots of good colleges offer free tuition because of his test scores. Nevertheless, the best school for him was one that was extremely selective and offered no financial aid. Because his parents had saved, he was able to attend his first choice school.

Had Bob and Mary not saved, their son still would have gone to college, but in their opinion not the right college. If Jim had opted for free tuition, Bob and Mary would have had the dollars they saved for college for other things, such as a retirement supplement, a vacation, or maybe a new car. To Bob and Mary, however, the right college was more important than the money.

This scenario brings up an important point. Part of examining the impact that potential financial aid has on college savings is also to *consider the flexibility of how dollars can go back to the parent if the funds are not used for college.* The importance of exit strategies will be highlighted throughout this book.

Finally, most parents cannot physically save enough to pay for all college expenses. If we can help them save, but keep financial aid options open, we provide a real value-added service. Usually, financial aid and tax savings are at odds with one another. We need to help clients ferret out which will be most significant and, where possible, help them get the best of both.

What Is Financial Aid?

When we speak of financial aid in this book, we are usually referring to need-based financial aid. There are really four very different types of financial aid:

- Need-based

- Merit-based

- Discounted tuition

- Negotiated

While need-based financial aid is based on a combined balance sheet and income statement of the parent and the student, the last three forms of aid are based on the bargaining strength of the student relative to other students competing for seats at a particular college or university. These last three are not really affected by how much a parent saves or how the parent saves. On the other hand, need-based aid represents a large part of the financial aid pool and is significantly affected by how much a parent saves. Even more importantly, it is affected by a parent's choice of savings tools, account titling, and financial products.

The Financial Aid Package

Financial aid is given out in the form of a financial aid package. A financial aid package consists of three elements:

- Scholarships and grants
- Student loans
- Work-study stipends

Scholarships and grants represent free money. They never need to be repaid. Student loans represent cheap cash flow to parents and students. For some students, loans are forgiven if the students enter certain professions after graduation.

> One of the parents we recently worked with absolutely refused to have her daughter take on any student loans. She had the money and did not want her daughter starting life saddled with school debts. Much to her chagrin, one of the recruiting incentives for her daughter's first teaching job was an arrangement to pay off any student loans on her behalf. The mother in this case could have pocketed the $17,000 she paid out of savings to avoid student loans.

When forgiven, loans become equivalent to scholarships and grants. Many parents feel that student loans give students a vested interest in their education. In addition, loans can help students build credit after graduation. Student loans also represent a way that parents can cost share with their students.

The final component, work-study, gives students an opportunity to earn expense money through on-campus jobs.

A big misconception held by advisors and parents is that financial aid is mostly loans. At the more prestigious and usually more expensive colleges this is not true. *Peterson's College Money Handbook* and *www.college.board. com* are great reference sources to learn about how colleges and universities dole out their financial aid dollars. According to these two sources, the financial aid package at the University of Pennsylvania, an Ivy League school that gives only need-based financial aid, averaged over $22,000 for the academic year 2000–2001. Furthermore, the percentage of grants as opposed to loans and work-study was a whopping big 61 percent of their financial aid package.

These prestige colleges are often the schools of choice for the upper-middle-income and higher-income client of many financial advisors. For example, many of my clients are two-income families living in well-regarded communities. They typically have three children and want the best possible education for them. Often this means sending them to an esteemed, brand-name college. Having children in these schools can cost $120,000 per student over a four-year period at today's prices. That adds up to $360,000 for the family. When you factor in college inflation, these parents are often looking at a potential $500,000 bill. These parents feel so strongly about reaching their college education values that they will make a substantial commitment to college savings. But you had better believe they want their plan to consider any financial aid that can put a dent in their college bill. Often these parents cannot save enough to meet the entire college bill, and qualifying for financial aid can mean the difference in making their education goals come true.

How Is Need-Based Financial Aid Eligibility Determined?

Most colleges use one of two financial aid formulas to determine whether a student qualifies for need-based financial aid. The *federal methodology* (FM) is the formula for doling out federal and most state funds. The formula is developed by the Department of Education and approved by Congress. The federal methodology is the dominant financial aid formula for colleges that depend on government funds for financial aid. These are usually state colleges and universities and some smaller, less well-endowed private colleges.

The second formula is the *institutional methodology* (IM). The College Board, a trade association of colleges, developed this formula to help colleges administer financial aid. The institutional methodology is the dominant formula used by larger well-endowed private colleges and universities. Some colleges use their own formulas, but these are usually hybrids of the two major methodologies.

Both formulas are complex. Each one attempts to ascertain a family's ability to pay for college by evaluating their income, assets, family size, and the proximity of the parents to retirement. Both formulas calculate a value, the expected family contribution, or EFC, that represents what parents can afford to pay toward college expenses for the following year. Although both formulas are similar in structure, they evaluate assets, income, and the number of students in college at the same time differently.

Once the EFC is calculated, it is compared to the cost of college at the specific schools where the student applied. If the cost of college is higher than the EFC, the student is eligible for financial aid. The difference between the EFC and the cost of college represents financial need. Financial need is the maximum amount of need-based aid likely to be awarded.

Figure 3.1 shows this process.

If a college asks only for the Free Application for Federal Student Aid (FAFSA) form as part of its financial aid process, the college probably uses the federal methodology. If the college asks for both the FAFSA form and the PROFILE form, it most likely will base most of its financial aid decisions on the institutional methodology.

Understanding How Asset Titling Can Affect Financial Aid

Both financial aid formulas involve a complex array of deductibles, credits, and marginal brackets much like our federal income tax structure. For our purposes, several "rules of thumb" can help us understand how controlling income and assets can impact the amount of a financial aid award. Tables 3.1 and 3.2 contain these "rules of thumb" for the federal and institutional methodologies, respectively. These represent the maximum incremental percentages in each category.

TABLE 3.1 Financial Aid "Rules of Thumb"
The Federal Methodology

Parent assets	6%
Student assets	35%
Parent income	47%
Student income	50%

TABLE 3.2 Financial Aid "Rules of Thumb"
The Institutional Methodology

Parent assets	5%
Student assets	25%
Parent income	46%
Student income	50%

In Chapter 4, we introduce a tool, The Financial Aid Test,™ that will enable you to make financial aid calculations easily. Nevertheless, the "Rules of Thumb" listed in Tables 3.1 and 3.2 can help us understand the importance of proper savings plan design when financial aid considerations are important.

Suppose a family saves $50,000 for college. To simplify our example we will consider only the asset component and ignore the income component

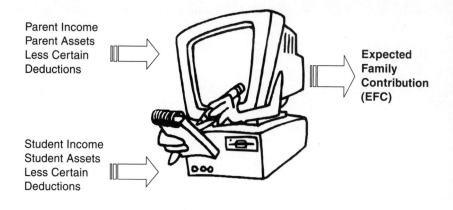

Parent Income
Parent Assets
Less Certain
Deductions

Expected
Family
Contribution
(EFC)

Student Income
Student Assets
Less Certain
Deductions

FIGURE 3.1 Financial Aid Process

in the form of investment gain. We will also look only at the federal methodology. Under current federal financial aid rules, this can affect a student's ability to qualify for need-based aid as follows:

- If the funds are titled in the name of the student, next year's financial aid eligibility will be reduced by $17,500 (35 percent of $50,000).

- If the funds are titled in the name of the parent, next year's financial aid eligibility will be reduced by $3,000 (6 percent of $50,000).

- Finally, if the funds are titled in the name of a third party such as a grandparent, next year's financial aid eligibility will be reduced by $0 (0 percent of $50,000).

Note that in each example, the family saved the same amount of money for college, but *how* they saved made a huge difference in financial aid eligibility. See Table 3.3.

TABLE 3.3 How Titling of Asset Affects Financial Aid

Amount Saved	Titling	Effect on Financial Aid Eligibility
$50,000	Student	$17,500 *less* aid
$50,000	Parent	$3,000 *less* aid
$50,000	Grandparent	No aid lost

Now let us suppose a family invests $10,000 in a college funding plan. The funds have doubled in value to $20,000 and are now to be liquidated to pay for college. In this example we will ignore the asset value and examine only the effect of the investment gain. Again, for simplicity we will consider only the federal methodology. Under current federal financial aid rules, this can affect a student's ability to qualify for need-based aid as follows:

■ If the funds were titled in the student's name and the student cashed in the investment the year before college, the student would incur a $10,000 capital gain, which is considered student income by the financial aid system. Financial aid eligibility for the following year would be reduced by $5,000 (50 percent of $10,000).

■ If the funds were titled in the parent's name and the parent liquidated the investment the year before college, the parent would incur a $10,000 gain, which is considered parent income by the financial aid system. Financial aid eligibility for the following year would be reduced by $4,700 (47 percent of $10,000).

■ If the funds were titled in a grandparent's name and the grandparent cashed in the investment the year before college, the grandparent would incur a $10,000 capital gain, which is considered grandparent income by the financial aid system. Financial aid eligibility for the following year would be reduced by $0 (0 percent of $10,000). Grandparent income is not relevant. However, if the grandparent made a payment directly to the school on behalf of the student, the funds are considered a reduction in college costs and financial aid is reduced by the full $10,000 payment.

■ If the funds were titled in the student's name and the student cashed in the investment two years before college, the student would incur a $10,000 capital gain, which is not considered student income by the financial aid system. Financial aid eligibility would be reduced by $0 (50 percent of $0). Student income is only relevant when it is generated in the year before the financial aid award is determined. The system currently does not look back more than one year.

■ Finally, if the funds were titled in the parent's name in a Section 529 Plan and the funds were used to pay for college expenses on behalf of the student, the student would incur $10,000 of non-taxable income, which is considered student income by the financial aid system. Financial aid eligibility would be reduced by $5,000 (50 percent of $10,000).

In all the above cases, we did not change the amount used to pay the student's college bill. How the plan was structured, however, had a huge impact on the student's financial aid eligibility. See Table 3.4.

TABLE 3.4 How Income from Assets Affects Financial Aid

Income from Asset	Income Attributed to	Effect on Financial Aid
$10,000	Account in student's name.	$5,000 *less* financial aid.
$10,000	Account in parents' name.	$4,700 *less* financial aid.
$10,000	■ Account in grandparents' name.	■ No loss of financial aid.
	■ Income paid directly to the college.	■ $10,000 dollar-for-dollar loss of financial aid.
$10,000	Account in student's name but income taken two years before college.	No loss of financial aid.
$10,000	Section 529 Plan in parent's name; income is attributed to student.	$5,000 *less* financial aid.

All the examples above dealt with the federal methodology. We could have used the institutional methodology table with similar results. A financial advisor has to learn to identify the types of assets and the methods of account titling that are financial aid friendly. We will be giving more examples as we go, and in Chapter 8 we provide a summary list that will be helpful.

There are also a number of life changes that can affect a student's financial aid eligibility. Most of these we cannot control in the planning process, but we need to build in flexibility to handle them. Developing an appropriate exit strategy from various funding tools and products that a planner recommends can be important as a hedge against these life events.

For example, the following changes in family circumstance will increase the chance to qualify for need-based aid:

- Parent income increases that do not keep pace with inflation

- Additional children being born or adopted into the family

- Parent income reductions due to layoffs or downsizing

- Private school tuition expense for younger children in the family

- Higher than normal family medical expenses

- Divorce or death of a parent

The following items are examples of changes that decrease the probability of financial aid:

- Promotions or increases in parent income that exceed college inflation

- Inheritances or other windfalls

- Significant increases in savings in non-retirement assets
- Non-need scholarships from academics or athletics
- Increased parent income due to a non-working spouse's going to work
- Death of a grandparent who is dependent on the parent for financial support

What Is a Financial Aid Test?

A financial aid test is a dry run of the process of filling out the real financial aid forms as if the student would attend college next year. It is important to note that a financial aid test deals only with need-based financial aid. Generally, if a family would be a financial aid candidate today, then the advisor should plan as though the family would qualify later. The financial aid test should be part of an annual update, and plans should be modified annually. Exit strategies to accommodate life changes are critical.

A good financial aid test applies a family's financial data to both financial aid formulas, the federal methodology, and the institutional methodology. By comparing today's EFC against today's college costs you can determine the probability of a family's financial aid eligibility for financial aid test purposes.

It is important to remember that not all colleges use just the federal methodology or the institutional methodology. When using a financial aid test in plan design, it is helpful to be sure which methodology to use. Table 3.5 shows the probable methodology for each of the twenty benchmark colleges. This may change over time as colleges change their philosophy on financial aid. Changes in the amount of endowment funds available can also restructure how a college determines financial need.

TABLE 3.5 Probable Methodology for Benchmark Colleges

College	Forms Required	Probable Methodology
Rutgers	FAFSA	Federal
Rutgers (Nonresident)	FAFSA	Federal
Lycoming College	FAFSA, Institution's own form	Hybrid*
American University	FAFSA, Institution's own form	Hybrid*
Univ. of Pennsylvania	FAFSA, CSS/PROFILE, Institution's own form	Institutional
Ohio State Univ.	FAFSA	Federal
Ohio State Univ. (NR)	FAFSA	Federal

TABLE 3.5 Probable Methodology for Benchmark Colleges *(Continued)*

College	Forms Required	Probable Methodology
Cornell College (IA)*	FAFSA, Institution's own form	Hybrid*
Kenyon College	FAFSA, CSS/PROFILE	Institutional
Northwestern University	FAFSA, CSS/PROFILE	Institutional
Univ. of North Carolina (main campus)	FAFSA, CSS/PROFILE	Institutional
U of N Carolina (NR)	FAFSA, CSS/PROFILE	Institutional
University of Richmond	FAFSA, Institution's own form	Hybrid*
Univ. of Miami	FAFSA	Federal
Duke University	FAFSA, CSS/PROFILE	Institutional
U of Washington	FAFSA	Federal
U of Washington (NR)	FAFSA	Federal
University of Denver	FAFSA	Federal
California Inst of Tech	FAFSA, CSS/PROFILE	Institutional
Stanford University	FAFSA, CSS/PROFILE	Institutional

Note: Items marked with an asterisk (*) will probably be slanted toward some version of the institutional methodology.

Table 3.6 is a fact-finder for a financial aid test. In Chapter 4, we introduce The Financial Aid Test™ software. It will be easier to show the mechanics of the financial aid test with the software than trying to do calculations manually.

TABLE 3.6 Fact-Finder for Financial Aid Test

Section 1—Parent Data	Parent #1	Parent #2
Last Name, First Name		
Home Address		
City, State, Zip Code		
Home Phone		
Work Phone		
Company, Occupation, Title		
Date of Birth		
Marital Status—Please indicate: Divorced– Widowed–Separated–Remarried		

(continues)

TABLE 3.6 Fact-Finder for Financial Aid Test *(Continued)*

Section 2—Family Financial Data		Value		
1	Age of older parent			
2	Number of parents in family			
3	Number of dependent children			
4	Number of children in college for plan year			
5	Total ages of all precollege children			
6	Father's wages			
7	Mother's wages			
8	Other taxable income			
9	Nontaxable income			
10	Untaxed benefits			
11	Losses from business, farm, capital losses			
12	Adjustments to income			
13	Child support paid			
14	Tuition tax credits			
15	Taxable student aid			
16	Medical and dental expense			
17	Federal income tax paid (line 52 on 1040, line 34 on 1040A, line 11 on 1040EZ)*			
18	Net home equity	Market value		Total of all mortgages
19	Net equity of other real estate	Market value		Total of all mortgages
20	Business/Farm value	Business (assets − liabilities)		Farm value − indebtedness
21	Parent cash (checking, savings, money market, etc.)			
22	Parent assets	Retirement plans		Other investments
23	Debts other than mortgages			

*Based on 2001 federal tax forms.

TABLE 3.6 Fact-Finder for Financial Aid Test *(Continued)*

Section 3—Student Data

A	B	C	D	E	F	G	H	I
Student First Name Date of Birth	High School Graduation Year	Undergrad School Plans	Graduate School Plans	Current School Costs	Student Savings and Investments	Income Last Year from Work	Income Last Year from Savings and Investments	Income Taxes Paid Last Year
Name: SAMPLE 6 / 27 / 83	2002	4 years High	None	None	$5,000	$2,700	$200	$75
Name: / /								
Name: / /								
Name: / /								
Name: / /								

Section 4—Design Data

1. Do any of your children have special skills or qualifications that may impact college funding such as athletic skills, high SAT scores, or grades, leadership skills, etc.?	
2. Please list any special scholarships or grants for which your student has or will apply.	
3. Are there any obligations to provide college funds to children from previous marriages?	
4. Will any student receive funds for college as part of a divorce or separation agreement?	
5. How much of your present monthly income could you use currently to pay or save for college?	
6. How much of parent cash and investments are allocated for college use?	
7. Do any of your students have any trust funds or other college resources not included above?	

Using the Financial Aid Test in Savings Plan Design

Many advisors try to use the financial aid test results in an inappropriate manner, one for which the financial aid test was not designed.

- The purpose of the financial aid test in savings plan design is to take a picture today and to use this picture to guide us in the *amount of flexibility* we need to design into the plan.

- It is *not designed to forecast* specific future financial aid awards.

- We can *plan to title assets* so they will not impede a family's ability to qualify for future financial aid.

- We *cannot forecast,* however, how much more or less financial aid a family will qualify for based on that re-titling.

- We *can redirect income* so that we will not hurt a family's ability to get future aid.

- We *cannot predict how much.*

- We *do not encourage a family to save less* because they may qualify for future aid.

- We *do encourage families to use appropriate products and vehicles* that keep financial aid options open.

- We *do build in exit strategies* to keep financial aid options open.

Financial aid is a complex issue, but dealing with it in an appropriate manner makes a difference. The next chapter gives us a tool, The Financial Aid Test,™ that enables us to easily explore financial aid and how to account for it in our planning.

Communicating with Your Client Using The Financial Aid Test™

I n Chapter 3, we introduce the importance of completing a financial aid test on every client you work with as part of a due diligence obligation to your client. This chapter introduces The Financial Aid Test™ software as an easy way to complete this test. (See Appendix D for instructions on how to install the program on your computer.) Completing a financial aid test using The Financial Aid Test™ software takes only a few minutes. It uses data you either already have or need to get anyway. Once you complete the test, you will be in a position to deal with financial aid appropriately, or conversely, to demonstrate to your client in a convincing manner why he or she is better off ignoring financial aid.

But The Financial Aid Test™ software allows you to do much more.

- If your software is kept up to date, it will allow you to do current financial aid planning for clients whose children are ready to attend college now. This type of planning is beyond the scope of this book, but the software is an excellent tool for this type of scenario.

- You will also be able to explore how the two financial aid formulas work by testing various scenarios until you understand how financial aid is actually calculated. Analytics will simply love this feature. We are going to let you explore this feature on your own.

- Finally, you will be able to test savings plan ideas and estimate their effect on financial aid. Although we do not recommend that you try to project financial aid into the future, you can back-test various forms of account titling and financial products and show the impact they would have had on today's financial aid formulas. We will give you several examples of how to do this.

Working with The Financial Aid Test™ Software

There are three sections to The Financial Aid Test™ software:

- Main Page
- Full Report
- Client Print Page

The *Main Page* (Figure 4.1) is the page you will use most with your clients. It contains three sections, each easily reachable with the [Page Down] key on your computer. The top section is the data input section. The second section is the "Quick Calc" or answer section. The third section gives you and your client data about the software. Section 3 also automatically gives you a warning message when you need to update your software because the financial aid formulas are outdated.

The *Full Report* section (Tables 4.1 through 4.6) gives you in-depth data on the financial aid calculations. This five-section, six-page report is usually too detailed to warrant giving to a client. It is ideal, however, for you to use to explore the financial aid system. It contains

- A data input summary
- A step-by-step calculation of the parent portion of the EFC (two pages)
- A step-by step calculation of the student portion of the EFC
- A summary of key counseling numbers
- An input data verification summary
- A copy of the client page discussed below.

Many planners print this section to have a comprehensive copy of client reports for their files.

The *Client Page* (Table 4.7) is an easy-to-print alternative to giving your client a copy of the *Main Page*. It summarizes all client input data and gives results.

Please note that it is important to always keep client input data with the output results. Occasionally, clients tell us that they received different financial aid results from other sources. In every case the reason is that input data was different. By keeping input and output together you will always be able to validate your reports. (See Appendix C for instructions for The Financial Aid Test™ Input Form.)

The Financial Aid Test™

Version: 2002-Book.f

19-Oct-01

Family Data:

Parent's Name (in report form)	Sample
Student's Name (in report form)	Mindy
Street Address	123 Main
City, State, ZIP	Voorhees, NJ 08053
Home Telephone:	856-596-1234
Business Telephone:	
State of Residence (All Caps, eg. NJ)	NJ
1 Age of Older Parent	46
2 Number of Parents in Family	1
3 Number of Dependent Children in Family	2
4 Number of students in college for plan year	1
5 Total ages of all pre college children	14

Student Financial Data:

23 Student Assets	$0
24 Student's Income	
a From Work	$4,000
b From Investments	$0
25 Student Income Tax Paid	$0
26 Assets in Siblings Names (IM only)	$0

Parent Financial Data:

6 Father's Wages	$0
7 Mother's Wages	$95,000
8 Other Taxable Income	$10,400
9 Non taxable income	$0
10 Untaxed Benefits	$0
11 Losses from Business, Farm, Capital Loss	$0
12 Adjustments to income	$0
13 Child Support Paid	$0
14 Tuition Tax Credits	$0
15 Taxable Student aid	$0
16 Medical & Dental Expense	$0
17 Federal Income Taxes Paid	$6,120
18 Net Home Equity (include farm - if you live on it)	
a Market Value	$90,000
b Sum of all Mortgages	$55,900
19 Net Equity of Other Real Estate	
a Market Value	$0
b Sum of all Mortgages	$0
20 Business/Farm Net Value (Your Share)	
a Business net value	$0
b Farm net value - if not used as residence	$0
21 Parent Cash	$1,500
22 Parent Investments	
a Qualified Retirement Plans	$400,000
b Other	$0
* Debts other than mortgages	$0

The Financial Aid Test™ - Quick Calc

Federal Methodology

Parent Expected Cont./Student	$26,904
Student Expected Contribution	$662
Expected Family Contribution/Student	$27,566

Key Counseling Numbers
Federal Methodology

	Assets	Income
% EPC From:	0.00%	100.00%
% ESC From:	0.00%	100.00%
Par. Marg.Cont.:	5.64%	47.00%
Stud. Marg. Cont.:	35.00%	50.00%

Institutional Methodology

Parent Expected Cont./Student	$23,554
Student Expected Contribution	$1,827
Expected Family Contribution/Student	$25,381

Key Counseling Numbers
Institutional Methodology

	Assets	Income
% EPC From:	0.00%	100.00%
% ESC From:	0.00%	100.00%
Par. Marg. Cont:	3.00%	46.00%
Stud. Marg. Cont:	25.00%	50.00%

This analysis provides estimated financial aid data for planning purposes only. Actual financial aid data are determined by each college at the time of admission. The validity of the input data can dramatically affect financial aid values. Which assets must be counted and how each asset is valued may be treated differently by the government and each individual college. Calculations are based on:

Federal Methodology 2001-02

Institutional Methodology 2001-02

Copyrights: College Money 1985–2001, all rights reserved.

Financial Aid Formulas Become Outdated After: 02/28/02

The College Financial Aid Test™ is a trademark of College Money.

www.collegemoney.com

FIGURE 4.1 Sample Client Main Page

TABLE 4.1 Data Input Summary

Counselor Worksheet	Version: 2002-Book.f
The Financial Aid Test™—Data Verification	19-Oct-01

Parents' name	Sample
Student's name	Mindy
Address	123 Main
City, state, zip	Voorhees, NJ 08053
Home telephone	856-596-1234
Business telephone	0

1	Age of Older Parent	46
2	Number of Parents in Family	1
3	Number of Dependent Children in Family	2
4	Number of Children in College for Plan Year	1
5	Total Ages of All Pre-College Children	14
6	Father's Wages	$0
7	Mother's Wages	$95,000
8	Other Taxable Income	$10,400
9	Untaxed Benefits	$0
10	Losses from Business, Farm, Capital Losses	$0
11	Nontaxable Income	$0
12	Child Support Paid	$0
13	Tuition Tax Credits	$0
14	Taxable Student Aid	$0
15	Medical and Dental Expense	$0
16	Adjustments to Income	$0
17	Federal Income Tax Paid	$6,120
18	Net Home Equity	
	a Market Value	$90,000
	b Sum of All Mortgages	$55,900
19	Net Equity of Other Real Estate	
	a Market Value	$0
	b Sum of All Mortgages	$0
20	Business/Farm Net Value (Your Share)	$0
21	Parent Cash	$1,500
22	Parent Investments	
	a Qualified Retirement Plans	$400,000
	b Other	$0
23	Student Assets	$0
24	Student Income	
	a From Work	$4,000
	b From Investments	$0
25	Student Income Tax Paid	$0
26	Assets in Siblings' Names (IM only)	$0
	State Code New Jersey	NJ

TABLE 4.2 Step-by-Step Calculation of Parent Portion of EFC

Counselor Worksheet	Page 2
The Financial Aid Test™	Version: 2002-Book.f
(2000–2001 Federal and Institutional Methodologies)	

Parents' name	Sample
Student's name	Mindy
Prepared on:	19-Oct-01

Parent Expected Contribution—Calculations		Federal	Institutional
Parents' Income			
Father's Income from Work		$0	$0
Mother's Income from Work		$95,000	$95,000
Other Taxable Income		$10,400	$10,400
Nontaxable Income		$0	$0
Untaxed Benefits		$0	$0
Losses from Business, Farm, Capital Losses (Add Back)		n/a	$0
Total Income		$105,400	$105,400
Income Exclusions			
Child Support Paid		$0	$0
Tuition Tax Credits		$0	n/a
Taxable Student Aid		$0	n/a
Total Income Exclusions		$0	$0
Total Income Less Exclusions		$105,400	$105,400
Deductions:			
FICA Tax—Father		$0	$0
FICA Tax—Mother		$6,102	$6,102
Total FICA Tax		$6,102	$6,102
Adjustments to Income		$0	$0
U.S. Income Tax Paid		$6,120	$6,120
State and Other Taxes		$7,378	$9,486
Employment Allowance		$2,900	$2,940
Medical and Dental Allowance		n/a	$0
Annual Education Savings Allowance	$1,602	n/a	$1,602
Income Protection Allowance		$15,890	$15,730
Total Deductions		$38,390	$41,980
Available income (AI)		$67,010	$63,420
Total Parent Contribution from Income (IM only)	46.00%	n/a	$23,554

TABLE **4.3** Step-by-Step Calculation of Parent Portion of EFC

Counselor Worksheet				Page 3
The Financial Aid Test™				Version: 2002-Book.f
(2000–2001 Federal and Institutional Methodologies)				

Parents' name	Sample			
Student's name	Mindy			
Prepared on:	19-Oct-01			

Parents' Assets				
Parent Cash			$1,500	$1,500
Home Equity (IM only)			n/a	$34,100
Market Value	$90,000			
Mortgage Value	$55,900			
Other Real Estate Equity			$0	$0
Market Value	$0			
Mortgage Value	$0			
Parent Investments (Excl Ret Plans)			$0	$0
Business/Farm Net Worth	$0		$0	$0
Assets in Siblings' Names (IM Only)			n/a	$0
Net Worth			$1,500	$35,600
Asset Protection Allowance (FM Only)			$24,900	n/a
Emergency Reserve Allowance (IM Only)		n/a		$14,520
Cumulative Educ Savings Allowance (IM Only)		n/a		$40,453
Low Income Allowance (IM Only)		n/a		$0
Total Asset Allowances				$54,973
Discretionary Net Worth (DNW)			−$23,400	$0
Asset Conversion Rate			$0	$0
Income Supplement (FM Only)			$0	n/a
Total Parent Contribution from Assets (IM Only)		n/a		$0
Adjusted Available Income (AAI)			$67,010	n/a
AAI Taxation Rates			$0	n/a
Total Contribution from Income (IM Only)			n/a	$23,554
Total Parents' Contribution		$26,904	$26,904	$23,554
Number of Students in College			1	1
Number in College Adjustment				1
Parents' Contribution per Student			$26,904	$23,554

TABLE 4.4 Step-by-Step Calculation of Student Portion of EFC

Counselor Worksheet	Page 4
The Financial Aid Test™	Version: 2002-Book.f
(2000–2001 Federal and Institutional Methodologies)	

Parents' name	Sample
Student's name	Mindy
Prepared on:	19-Oct-01

Dependent Student Contribution:	Federal	Institutional
Student Income		
Student's Earned Income	$4,000	$4,000
Student's Other Income	$0	$0
Student's Total Income	$4,000	$4,000
Student's Deductions		
U.S. Income Tax Paid	$0	$0
FICA Tax Paid	$306	$306
State and Other Taxes	$120	$40
Income Protection Allowance	$2,250	n/a
Parent Negative AI Offset	$0	n/a
Total Deductions	$2,676	$346
Net Student Income	$1,324	$3,654
Income Assessment Rate	$1	$1
Available Income	$662	$1,827
Student's Assets	$0	$0
Conversion Rate	$0	$0
Income Supplement	$0	$0
Student Contribution	**$662**	**$1,827**
TOTAL FAMILY CONTRIBUTION	**$27,566**	**$25,381**

TABLE 4.5 Summary of Key Counseling Numbers

Counselor Worksheet | Page 5
The Financial Aid Test™ | Version: 2002-Book.f
(2000–2001 Federal and Institutional Methodologies)

KEY COUNSELING NUMBERS Federal Methodology	Totals	% From Assets	% From Income
Total Parent Expected Cont.	$26,904		
Parent Expected Cont./Student	$26,904	0.00%	100.00%
Student Expected Contribution	$662	0.00%	100.00%
Family Expected Cont.This Student	$27,566		
Parent Asset Gap	$23,400		
Student Income Gap	$0		

FINANCIAL AID PLANNING RULES OF THUMB Federal Methodology	% From Assets	% From Income
Parents' Marginal Contribution Percentage	5.64%	47.00%
Student's Marginal Contribution Percentage	35.00%	50.00%

KEY COUNSELING NUMBERS Institutional Methodology		Totals	% From Assets	% From Income
Total Parent Expected Cont. (Formula)		$23,554	0.00%	100.00%
Parent Expected Cont. This Student	1	$23,554		
Student Expected Contribution		$1,827	0.00%	100.00%
Family Expected Cont.This Student		$25,381		
Parent Asset Gap		$19,373		
Student Income Gap		$0		

FINANCIAL AID PLANNING RULES OF THUMB Institutional Methodology	% From Assets	% From Income
Parents' Marginal Contribution Percentage	3.00%	46.00%
Student's Marginal Contribution Percentage	25.00%	50.00%

TABLE 4.6 Input Data Verification Summary—*Planner Copy*

The Financial Aid Test™	Version: 2002-Book.f

Prepared for:	Sample
And Student:	Mindy

INPUT DATA VERIFICATION SUMMARY AS OF:	19-Oct-01
1 Age of Older Parent	46
2 Number of Parents in Family	1
3 Number of Dependent Children in Family	2
4 Number of Children in College for Plan Year	1
5 Total Ages of All Pre-College Children	14
6 Father's Wages	$0
7 Mother's Wages	$95,000
8 Other Taxable Income	$10,400
9 Untaxed Benefits	$0
10 Losses from Business, Farm, Capital Losses	$0
11 Nontaxable Income	$0
12 Child Support Paid	$0
13 Tuition Tax Credits	$0
14 Taxable Student Aid	$0
15 Medical and Dental Expense	$0
16 Adjustments to Income	$0
17 Federal Income Tax Paid	$6,120
18 Net Home Equity (Not Used in Federal Methodology)	$34,100
19 Net Equity of Other Real Estate	$0
20 Business Net Value (Your Share)	$0
21 Parent Cash	$1,500
22 Parent Investments (Nonretirement)	$0
23 Student Assets	$0
24 Student Income	
a From Work	$4,000
b From Investments	$0
25 Student Income Tax Paid	$0
26 Assets in Siblings' Names (Not Used in Federal Methodology)	$0
State Code	NJ

FAMILY EXPECTED CONTRIBUTION SUMMARY:	Federal	Institutional
Parent Contribution per Student	$26,904	$23,554
Student Contribution	$662	$1,827
FAMILY CONTRIBUTION THIS STUDENT:	$27,566	$25,381

This analysis provides estimated financial aid data for planning purposes only. Actual financial aid awards are determined by each college at the time of admission. The validity of the input data can dramatically affect financial aid values. Which assets must be counted and how each asset is valued may be treated differently by the government and each individual college. Calculations are based on:
 Federal Methodology 2001–02
 Institutional Methodology 2001–02

Source: College Money © 1985–2001, all rights reserved.

TABLE 4.7 Input Data Verification Summary—*Parent Copy*

The Financial Aid Test™	Version: 2002-Book.f

Prepared for:	Sample
And Student:	Mindy

INPUT DATA VERIFICATION SUMMARY AS OF:	10/19/01
1 Age of Older Parent	46
2 Number of Parents in Family	1
3 Number of Dependent Children in Family	2
4 Number of Children in College (planned)	1
5 Total Ages of All Pre-College Children	14
6 Father's Wages	$0
7 Mother's Wages	$95,000
8 Other Taxable Income	$10,400
9 Untaxed Benefits	$0
10 Losses from Business, Farm, Capital Losses	$0
11 Nontaxable Income	$0
12 Child Support Paid	$0
13 Tuition Tax Credits	$0
14 Taxable Student Aid	$0
15 Medical and Dental Expense	$0
16 Adjustments to Income	$0
17 Federal Income Tax Paid	$6,120
18 Net Home Equity (Not Used in Federal Methodology)	$34,100
19 Net Equity of Other Real Estate	$0
20 Business Net Value (Your Share)	$0
21 Parent Cash	$1,500
22 Parent Investments (Nonretirement)	$0
23 Student Assets	$0
24 Student Income	
a From Work	$4,000
b From Investments	$0
25 Student Income Tax Paid	$0
26 Assets in Siblings' Names (Not Used in Federal Methodology)	$0
State Code	NJ

FAMILY EXPECTED CONTRIBUTION SUMMARY:	Federal	Institutional
Parent Contribution per Student	$26,904	$23,554
Student Contribution	$662	$1,827
FAMILY CONTRIBUTION THIS STUDENT:	$27,566	$25,381

This analysis provides estimated financial aid data for planning purposes only. Actual financial aid awards are determined by each college at the time of admission. The validity of the input data can dramatically affect financial aid values. Which assets must be counted and how each asset is valued may be treated differently by the government and each individual college. Calculations are based on:
  Federal Methodology 2001–02
  Institutional Methodology 2001–02

Source: College Money © 1985–2001, all rights reserved.

Doing a Financial Aid Test

Doing a financial aid test is an easy four-step process.

Step 1: Simply complete the data sheet that we introduced in Chapter 3 with your client.

Step 2: Enter the data in the top section of the **Main Page** of The Financial Aid Test™ software. When complete, [Page Down] to the Quick Calc section. The EFC for both methodologies is clearly denoted.

Step 3: Decide which methodology is appropriate for your client's choice of colleges.

Step 4: Subtract your client's EFC from today's cost of college. If the result is positive, your client is eligible for need-based financial aid and you should plan appropriately.

The following example should clarify the process:

> The Crosby family has twins: a daughter, Christine, and a son, Kyle, aged three. They also have an older son, Bob, aged five. Mr. and Mrs. Crosby have a combined adjusted gross income of better than $160,000. They supplied you with additional financial data that you input into The Financial Aid Test™ software. When you do a financial aid test, you always do it for a particular student as though that student would be attending college next year. In this case the results for Bob appear in Figure 4.2. Please note that the year that Bob starts college, the Crosby family will have only one student, Bob, in college.

Based on the input data and the results, you need to determine whether this client is a financial aid candidate. To do this, you need to know the college cost category that the family is planning for Bob and the cost in today's dollars of the benchmark college for that category. You also need to know which methodology to use.

Let us first assume that Mr. and Mrs. Crosby wish to have Bob attend a northeast region, high-cost, prestige school. By going back to Table 1.1 in Chapter 1, we can determine that the benchmark college in the northeast region representing high-cost, prestige colleges is the University of Pennsylvania, with a total cost for 2001–2002 of $39,310. Table 3.5 in Chapter 3 shows that the dominant financial aid methodology for this benchmark school will most likely be the institutional methodology.

Table 4.8 shows that under this scenario, Bob Crosby would be a marginal aid candidate. His financial need representing the gross magnitude

The Financial Aid Test™

Version: 2002-Book.f
19-Oct-01

Family Data:

Parent's Name (in report form)	Crosby
Student's Name (in report form)	Bob
Street Address	123 Main
City, State, ZIP	Voorhees, NJ 08053
Home Telephone:	856-596-1234
Business Telephone:	
State of Residence (All Caps, eg. NJ)	NJ
1 Age of Older Parent	46
2 Number of Parents in Family	2
3 Number of Dependent Children in Family	3
4 Number of students in college for plan year	1
5 Total ages of all pre college children	32

Student Financial Data:

23 Student Assets	$0
24 Student's Income	
a From Work	$0
b From Investments	$0
25 Student Income Tax Paid	$0
26 Assets in Siblings Names (IM only)	$0

Parent Financial Data:

6	Father's Wages	$55,000
7	Mother's Wages	$95,000
8	Other Taxable Income	$10,400
9	Non taxable income	$0
10	Untaxed Benefits	$0
11	Losses from Business, Farm, Capital Loss	$0
12	Adjustments to income	$0
13	Child Support Paid	$0
14	Tuition Tax Credits	$0
15	Taxable Student aid	$0
16	Medical & Dental Expense	$0
17	Federal Income Taxes Paid	$28,000
18	Net Home Equity (include farm - if you live on it)	
	a Market Value	$250,000
	b Sum of all Mortgages	$200,000
19	Net Equity of Other Real Estate	
	a Market Value	$0
	b Sum of all Mortgages	$0
20	Business/Farm Net Value (Your Share)	
	a Business net value	$0
	b Farm net value - if not used as residence	$0
21	Parent Cash	$50,000
22	Parent Investments	
	a Qualified Retirement Plans	$400,000
	b Other	$0
*	Debts other than mortgages	$0

The Financial Aid Test™ - Quick Calc

Federal Methodology

Parent Expected Cont./Student	$35,633
Student Expected Contribution	$0
Expected Family Contribution/Student	$35,633

Key Counseling Numbers
Federal Methodology

	Assets	Income
% EPC From:	0.91%	99.09%
% ESC From:	0.00%	0.00%
Par. Marg.Cont.:	5.64%	47.00%
Stud. Marg. Cont:	35.00%	50.00%

Institutional Methodology

Parent Expected Cont./Student	$30,164
Student Expected Contribution	$1,150
Expected Family Contribution/Student	$31,314

Key Counseling Numbers
Institutional Methodology

	Assets	Income
% EPC From:	0.25%	99.75%
% ESC From:	0.00%	100.00%
Par. Marg. Cont:	3.00%	46.00%
Stud. Marg. Cont:	25.00%	50.00%

This analysis provides estimated financial aid data for planning purposes only. Actual financial aid awards are determined by each college at the time of admission. The validity of the input data can dramatically affect financial aid values. Which assets must be counted and how each asset is valued may be treated differently by the government and each individual college. Calculations are based on:

Federal Methodology   2001-02
Institutional Methodology 2001-02

Financial Aid Formulas Become Outdated After: 02/28/02
The College Financial Aid Test™ is a trademark of College Money.

www.collegemoney.com

FIGURE 4.2 Crosby Family Financial Aid Test: One Student in College

of his most likely financial aid award is $7,996. Although $7,996 may not seem like a large number, four times $7,996 or $31,984 over four years of college does.

TABLE 4.8 Determining Financial Need:
One Student at High-Cost College

College Cost Category	High	
Benchmark college	University of Pennsylvania	$39,310
EFC methodology	Institutional	$31,314
Financial need		$7,996

Suppose, however, that the goal was to send Bob to a northeast region state college. Again from the same tables as above, we can determine the benchmark college is Rutgers University, with a 2001–2002 cost of $18,497. The appropriate methodology in this case is the federal methodology. In this case, the Crosby family is not an aid candidate because the financial need is negative. (See Table 4.9.)

TABLE 4.9 Determining Financial Need:
One Student at Low-Cost College

College Cost Category	Low	
Benchmark college	Rutgers University	$18,497
EFC methodology	Federal	$35,633
Financial need		Not eligible

It is important not to stop here. The Crosby family has other children. There will be two years when three children are in college at the same time. This is the year that Christine, one of the twins, will start college. Doing a financial aid test as though Christine were to start college next year gives us very different results. Figure 4.3 shows the results of Christine's financial aid test.

Assuming the same set of goals as above, we have summarized the results for Christine in Tables 4.10 and 4.11 below.

TABLE 4.10 Determining Financial Need:
Three Students at High-Cost Colleges

Benchmark college	University of Pennsylvania	$39,310
EFC methodology/student	Institutional	$16,058
Financial need/student		$23,252

TABLE 4.11 Determining Financial Need:
Three Students at Low-Cost Colleges

Benchmark college	Rutgers University	$18,497
EFC methodology	Federal	$12,561
Financial need		$5,936

If the Crosby family's children all attended high-cost colleges, there would be a period of two years when each of the three children would be eligible for $23,252 of need-based financial aid per year or $69,756 on a family basis or $139,512 for the two-year period. We did not even count the aid for two years with two in college or the two years when only Bob was in school. This is not an extreme example. Many families with good incomes will have two or three in college at one time and will be eligible for substantial amounts of aid.

As a planner you need to take all this data into consideration. If Bob were the only student to consider, there would only be marginal financial aid to be concerned with and tax issues might still dominate the planning. When taking into account the whole family, financial aid becomes very significant.

Exploring the Effect of Plan Design on Financial Aid

Another effective use of The Financial Aid Test™ software is to test concepts you are thinking about implementing. You need to test them in the past, however—not in the future. For example, suppose the Crosbys' goal is to accumulate about $50,000 per child toward the college bill. The balance will come from current income during the college years, some financial aid if possible, and parent and student loans if necessary. You can use the software to decide how to position the money. To do this, take the strategy you are considering:

- Assume the family had implemented such a strategy in the past.

- Plug the achieved results into the software as though the student were going to college next year.

- Observe the effect on financial aid.

- Use the results to help you plan a future strategy.

Let us examine three different ways the Crosby family could have saved for college and see what effect they would have had on financial aid eligibility.

- Option 1: Use a UGMA account.

- Option 2: Save in the parents' name.
- Option 3: Use a Section 529 Plan.

Because our purpose here is to examine the effects on financial aid, we need to make some simplifying assumptions. We are going to ignore taxes. Obviously, taxes will affect the amount of accumulated savings per dollar saved. Chapter 7 discusses the relationship between taxes, financial aid, and control over investments. In this case, however, we are going to assume only that $50,000 was accumulated for each student, no matter which option was chosen.

For the example, assume we are dealing with Christine, one of the twins. At the time Christine enters her freshman year, the Crosby family will have all three students in college. Under the original example, the EFC for Christine, $16,058, can be taken from Figure 4.3.

In Option 1, the Crosbys would have saved for Christine using a UGMA account. The Financial Aid Test™ results are summarized in Figure 4.4. Please note the following:

- Christine shows an increased student asset of $50,000. ❶
- Bob's and Kyle's money does not show up in this scenario as sibling assets because that category is only for pre-college children and they are in college. ❷
- The parents show no additional assets. ❸
- Christine's EFC jumps to $28,558, a loss of $12,500 of financial aid eligibility. ❹

In Option 2, the parents would have saved in their own names. The Financial Aid Test™ results are summarized in Figure 4.5.

- Christine shows no student assets. ❺
- Bob and Chris show no sibling assets. ❻
- The parents show an increase of $125,000 in their assets: $50,000 each for Christine and Kyle, and $25,000 for Bob because they spent $12,500 on his freshman and sophomore years. ❼
- Christine's EFC would be $18,705, a loss of $2,647. ❽

In Option 3, the parents would have saved in a Section 529 Plan. The Financial Aid Test™ results are summarized in Figures 4.6 and 4.7:

- Bob used one-half of his $50,000 account in the years before Christine and Kyle entered school. Therefore, in Christine's freshman year, the parents' assets were already reduced by $25,000. ❾

The Financial Aid Test™

Version: 2002-Book.f

19-Oct-01

Family Data:

Parent's Name (in report form)	Crosby
Student's Name (in report form)	Christine
Street Address	123 Main
City, State, ZIP	Voorhees, NJ 08053
Home Telephone:	856-596-1234
Business Telephone:	
State of Residence (All Caps, eg. NJ)	NJ
1 Age of Older Parent	46
2 Number of Parents in Family	2
3 Number of Dependent Children in Family	3
4 Number of students in college for plan year	3
5 Total ages of all pre college children	0

Student Financial Data:

23 Student Assets	$0
24 Student's Income	
a From Work	$0
b From Investments	$0
25 Student Income Tax Paid	$0
26 Assets in Siblings Names (IM only)	$0

Parent Financial Data:

6 Father's Wages	$55,000
7 Mother's Wages	$95,000
8 Other Taxable Income	$10,400
9 Non taxable income	$0
10 Untaxed Benefits	$0
11 Losses from Business, Farm, Capital Loss	$0
12 Adjustments to income	$0
13 Child Support Paid	$0
14 Tuition Tax Credits	$0
15 Taxable Student aid	$0
16 Medical & Dental Expense	$0
17 Federal Income Taxes Paid	$28,000
18 Net Home Equity (include farm - if you live on it)	
a Market Value	$250,000
b Sum of all Mortgages	$200,000
19 Net Equity of Other Real Estate	
a Market Value	$0
b Sum of all Mortgages	$0
20 Business/Farm Net Value (Your Share)	
a Business net value	$0
b Farm net value - if not used as residence	$0
21 Parent Cash	$50,000
22 Parent Investments	
a Qualified Retirement Plans	$400,000
b Other	$0
* Debts other than mortgages	$0

The Financial Aid Test™ - Quick Calc

Federal Methodology

Parent Expected Cont./Student	$12,561
Student Expected Contribution	$0
Expected Family Contribution/Student	$12,561

Key Counseling Numbers
Federal Methodology

	Assets	Income
% EPC From:	0.87%	99.13%
% ESC From:	0.00%	0.00%
Par. Marg.Cont.:	5.64%	47.00%
Stud. Marg. Cont:	35.00%	50.00%

Institutional Methodology

Parent Expected Cont./Student	$14,908
Student Expected Contribution	$1,150
Expected Family Contribution/Student	$16,058

Key Counseling Numbers
Institutional Methodology

	Assets	Income
% EPC From:	1.74%	98.26%
% ESC From:	0.00%	100.00%
Par. Marg. Cont:	3.00%	46.00%
Stud. Marg. Cont:	25.00%	50.00%

This analysis provides estimated financial aid data for planning purposes only. Actual financial aid awards are determined by each college at the time of admission. The validity of the input data can dramatically affect financial aid values. Which assets must be counted and how each asset is valued may be treated differently by the government and each individual college. Calculations are based on:

Federal Methodology 2001-02

Institutional Methodology 2001-02

Copyrights: College Money 1985–2001, all rights reserved.

Financial Aid Formulas Become Outdated After: 02/28/02

The College Financial Aid Test™ is a trademark of College Money.

The College

Financial Aid Test™

www.collegemoney.com

FIGURE 4.3 Crosby Family Financial Aid Test: Three Students in College

The Financial Aid Test™

Version: 2002-Book.f

19-Oct-01

Family Data:

Parent's Name (in report form)	Crosby
Student's Name (in report form)	Christine
Street Address	123 Main
City, State, ZIP	Voorhees, NJ 08053
Home Telephone:	856-596-1234
Business Telephone:	
State of Residence (All Caps, eg. NJ)	NJ
1 Age of Older Parent	46
2 Number of Parents in Family	2
3 Number of Dependent Children in Family	3
4 Number of students in college for plan year	3
5 Total ages of all pre college children	0

Student Financial Data:

23 Student Assets	❶	$50,000
24 Student's Income		
a From Work		$0
b From Investments		$0
25 Student Income Tax Paid		$0
26 Assets in Siblings Names (IM only)	❷	$0

Parent Financial Data:

6 Father's Wages		$55,000
7 Mother's Wages		$95,000
8 Other Taxable Income		$10,400
9 Non taxable income		$0
10 Untaxed Benefits		$0
11 Losses from Business, Farm, Capital Loss		$0
12 Adjustments to income		$0
13 Child Support Paid		$0
14 Tuition Tax Credits		$0
15 Taxable Student aid		$0
16 Medical & Dental Expense		$0
17 Federal Income Taxes Paid		$28,000
18 Net Home Equity (include farm - if you live on it)		❸
a Market Value		$250,000
b Sum of all Mortgages		$200,000
19 Net Equity of Other Real Estate		
a Market Value		$0
b Sum of all Mortgages		$0
20 Business/Farm Net Value (Your Share)		
a Business net value		$0
b Farm net value - if not used as residence		$0
21 Parent Cash		$50,000
22 Parent Investments		
a Qualified Retirement Plans		$400,000
b Other		$0
* Debts other than mortgages		$0

The Financial Aid Test™ - Quick Calc

Federal Methodology

Parent Expected Cont./Student	$12,561
Student Expected Contribution	$17,500
Expected Family Contribution/Student	$30,061

Key Counseling Numbers
Federal Methodology

	Assets	Income
% EPC From:	0.87%	99.13%
% ESC From:	100.00%	0.00%
Par. Marg.Cont.:	5.64%	47.00%
Stud. Marg. Cont:	35.00%	50.00%

Institutional Methodology

Parent Expected Cont./Student	$14,908
Student Expected Contribution	$13,650
Expected Family Contribution/Student	$28,558 ❹

Key Counseling Numbers
Institutional Methodology

	Assets	Income
% EPC From:	1.74%	98.26%
% ESC From:	91.58%	8.42%
Par. Marg. Cont:	3.00%	46.00%
Stud. Marg. Cont:	25.00%	50.00%

This analysis provides estimated financial aid data for planning purposes only. Actual financial aid awards are determined by each college at the time of admission. The validity of the input data can dramatically affect financial aid values. Which assets must be counted and how each asset is valued may be treated differently by the government and each individual college. Calculations are based on:

Federal Methodology   2001-02

Institutional Methodology 2001-02

Financial Aid Formulas Become Outdated After: 02/28/02

The College Financial Aid Test™ is a trademark of College Money.

www.collegemoney.com

FIGURE 4.4 Option 1: Parents Saved in UGMA Account

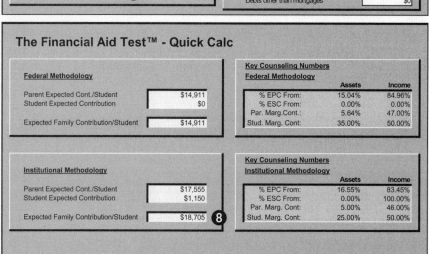

The Financial Aid Test™

Version: 2002-Book.f
21-Oct-01

Family Data:

Parent's Name (in report form)	Crosby	
Student's Name (in report form)	Christine	
Street Address	123 Main	
City, State, ZIP	Voorhees, NJ 08053	
Home Telephone:	856-596-1234	
Business Telephone:		
State of Residence (All Caps, eg. NJ)	NJ	
1 Age of Older Parent		46
2 Number of Parents in Family		2
3 Number of Dependent Children in Family		3
4 Number of students in college for plan year		3
5 Total ages of all pre college children		0

Student Financial Data:

23 Student Assets		$0
24 Student's Income		
a From Work		$0
b From Investments		$0
25 Student Income Tax Paid		$0
26 Assets in Siblings Names (IM only)	6	$0

Parent Financial Data:

6 Father's Wages		$55,000
7 Mother's Wages		$95,000
8 Other Taxable Income		$10,400
9 Non taxable income		$0
10 Untaxed Benefits		$0
11 Losses from Business, Farm, Capital Loss		$0
12 Adjustments to income		$0
13 Child Support Paid		$0
14 Tuition Tax Credits		$0
15 Taxable Student aid		$0
16 Medical & Dental Expense		$0
17 Federal Income Taxes Paid		$28,000
18 Net Home Equity (include farm - if you live on it)		
a Market Value		$250,000
b Sum of all Mortgages		$200,000
19 Net Equity of Other Real Estate		
a Market Value		$0
b Sum of all Mortgages		$0
20 Business/Farm Net Value (Your Share)		
a Business net value		$0
b Farm net value - if not used as residence		$0
21 Parent Cash	7	$175,000
22 Parent Investments		
a Qualified Retirement Plans		$400,000
b Other		$0
* Debts other than mortgages		$0

The Financial Aid Test™ - Quick Calc

Federal Methodology

Parent Expected Cont./Student	$14,911
Student Expected Contribution	$0
Expected Family Contribution/Student	$14,911

Key Counseling Numbers
Federal Methodology

	Assets	Income
% EPC From:	15.04%	84.96%
% ESC From:	0.00%	0.00%
Par. Marg.Cont.:	5.64%	47.00%
Stud. Marg. Cont:	35.00%	50.00%

Institutional Methodology

Parent Expected Cont./Student	$17,555
Student Expected Contribution	$1,150
Expected Family Contribution/Student	$18,705 8

Key Counseling Numbers
Institutional Methodology

	Assets	Income
% EPC From:	16.55%	83.45%
% ESC From:	0.00%	100.00%
Par. Marg. Cont:	5.00%	46.00%
Stud. Marg. Cont:	25.00%	50.00%

This analysis provides estimated financial aid data for planning purposes only. Actual financial aid awards are determined by each college at the time of admission. The validity of the input data can dramatically affect financial aid values. Which assets must be counted and how each asset is valued may be treated differently by the government and each individual college. Calculations are based on:

Federal Methodology   2001-02

Institutional Methodology 2001-02

FIGURE 4.5 Option 2: Parents Saved in Their Own Names

- Christine's parents own the Section 529 Plan account; therefore, they show a parent asset on behalf of Christine of $50,000. They also show an asset of $75,000 for Bob and Kyle. They still have their original $50,000 of parent assets for a total of $175,000. ❿

- Christine's EFC for her freshman year would be $18,705. ⓫

- Assuming that $30,000 was actually invested in the Section 529 Plan, there was a 40 percent gain on investments resulting in a total account value of $50,000.

- Christine used one-fourth of her $50,000 account to pay for college in her first year. Note the number on Figure 4.7 reflects the reduction of three sets of $12,500. ⓬

- In Figure 4.7, you will see that Christine's EFC would increase to $19,187 in the next year because Christine would need to show nontaxable income of 40 percent of $12,500 or $5,000. ⓭

Table 4.12 compares the effects on financial aid for the three options we investigated:

TABLE 4.12 Financial Aid Comparisons

	Original EFC	New EFC	Change
Option 1: UGMA	$16,058	$28,558	$12,500
Option 2: Parent owned	$16,058	$18,705	$2,647
Option 3: 529 Plan first year	$16,058	$18,705	$2,647
Option 3: 529 Plan second year	$16,058	$19,187	$3,129

It is critical not to generalize conclusions from these examples. From the table above, a Section 529 Plan would certainly be the most promising choice to investigate. The results, however, could be radically different in different situations, including the following:

- Only one student in the family
- Different pattern of students in college
- Higher percentage growth on the Section 529 Plan account
- Unequal withdrawals from a Section 529 Plan

In fact, with the examples of the Crosby family, we did not take into consideration the financial aid picture of the entire family. It is possible that factoring in the entire college experience for all three children might make one option significantly better. We must remember, however, that we are not trying to project financial aid, only to explore the need for plan flexibility.

The Financial Aid Test™

Version: 2002-Book.f
19-Oct-01

Family Data:

Parent's Name (in report form)	Crosby
Student's Name (in report form)	Christine
Street Address	123 Main
City, State, ZIP	Voorhees, NJ 08053
Home Telephone:	856-596-1234
Business Telephone:	
State of Residence (All Caps, eg. NJ)	NJ
1 Age of Older Parent	46
2 Number of Parents in Family	2
3 Number of Dependent Children in Family	3
4 Number of students in college for plan year	3
5 Total ages of all pre college children	0

Student Financial Data:

23 Student Assets	$0
24 Student's Income	
a From Work	$0
b From Investments	$0
25 Student Income Tax Paid	$0
26 Assets in Siblings Names (IM only)	$0

Parent Financial Data:

6	Father's Wages	$55,000
7	Mother's Wages	$95,000
8	Other Taxable Income	$10,400
9	Non taxable income	$0
10	Untaxed Benefits	$0
11	Losses from Business, Farm, Capital Loss	$0
12	Adjustments to income	$0
13	Child Support Paid	$0
14	Tuition Tax Credits	$0
15	Taxable Student aid	$0
16	Medical & Dental Expense	$0
17	Federal Income Taxes Paid	$28,000
18	Net Home Equity (include farm - if you live on it)	
	a Market Value	$250,000
	b Sum of all Mortgages	$200,000
19	Net Equity of Other Real Estate	
	a Market Value	$0
	b Sum of all Mortgages	$0
20	Business/Farm Net Value (Your Share)	
	a Business net value	$0
	b Farm net value - if not used as residence	$0
21	Parent Cash	$175,000
22	Parent Investments **9,10**	
	a Qualified Retirement Plans	$400,000
	b Other	$0
*	Debts other than mortgages	$0

The Financial Aid Test™ - Quick Calc

Federal Methodology

Parent Expected Cont./Student	$14,911
Student Expected Contribution	$0
Expected Family Contribution/Student	$14,911

Key Counseling Numbers
Federal Methodology

	Assets	Income
% EPC From:	15.04%	84.96%
% ESC From:	0.00%	0.00%
Par. Marg.Cont.:	5.64%	47.00%
Stud. Marg. Cont:	35.00%	50.00%

Institutional Methodology

Parent Expected Cont./Student	$17,555
Student Expected Contribution	$1,150
Expected Family Contribution/Student	$18,705 **11**

Key Counseling Numbers
Institutional Methodology

	Assets	Income
% EPC From:	16.55%	83.45%
% ESC From:	0.00%	100.00%
Par. Marg. Cont:	5.00%	46.00%
Stud. Marg. Cont:	25.00%	50.00%

This analysis provides estimated financial aid data for planning purposes only. Actual financial aid awards are determined by each college at the time of admission. The validity of the input data can dramatically affect financial aid values. Which assets must be counted and how each asset is valued may be treated differently by the government and each individual college. Calculations are based on:

Federal Methodology 2001-02
Institutional Methodology 2001-02

The College
Financial Aid Test™

www.collegemoney.com

FIGURE 4.6 Year One of Option 3: $50,000 Each in Section 529 Plan in Parents' Name

The Financial Aid Test™

Version: 2002-Book.f
19-Oct-01

Family Data:

Parent's Name (in report form)	Crosby
Student's Name (in report form)	Christine
Street Address	123 Main
City, State, ZIP	Voorhees, NJ 08053
Home Telephone:	856-596-1234
Business Telephone:	
State of Residence (All Caps, eg. NJ)	NJ
1 Age of Older Parent	46
2 Number of Parents in Family	2
3 Number of Dependent Children in Family	3
4 Number of students in college for plan year	3
5 Total ages of all pre college children	0

Student Financial Data:

23 Student Assets	$0
24 Student's Income	
a From Work	$0
b From Investments ⑬	$5,000
25 Student Income Tax Paid	$0
26 Assets in Siblings Names (IM only)	$0

Parent Financial Data:

6	Father's Wages	$55,000
7	Mother's Wages	$95,000
8	Other Taxable Income	$10,400
9	Non taxable income	$0
10	Untaxed Benefits	$0
11	Losses from Business, Farm, Capital Loss	$0
12	Adjustments to income	$0
13	Child Support Paid	$0
14	Tuition Tax Credits	$0
15	Taxable Student aid	$0
16	Medical & Dental Expense	$0
17	Federal Income Taxes Paid	$28,000
18	Net Home Equity (include farm - if you live on it)	
	a Market Value	$250,000
	b Sum of all Mortgages	$200,000
19	Net Equity of Other Real Estate	
	a Market Value	$0
	b Sum of all Mortgages	$0
20	Business/Farm Net Value (Your Share)	
	a Business net value	$0
	b Farm net value - if not used as residence	$0
21	Parent Cash ⑫	$137,500
22	Parent Investments	
	a Qualified Retirement Plans	$400,000
	b Other	$0
*	Debts other than mortgages	$0

The Financial Aid Test™ - Quick Calc

Federal Methodology

Parent Expected Cont./Student	$14,206
Student Expected Contribution	$1,300
Expected Family Contribution/Student	$15,506

Key Counseling Numbers
Federal Methodology

	Assets	Income
% EPC From:	11.23%	88.77%
% ESC From:	0.00%	100.00%
Par. Marg.Cont.:	5.64%	47.00%
Stud. Marg. Cont:	35.00%	50.00%

Institutional Methodology

Parent Expected Cont./Student	$16,712
Student Expected Contribution	$2,475
Expected Family Contribution/Student	$19,187 ⑬

Key Counseling Numbers
Institutional Methodology

	Assets	Income
% EPC From:	12.34%	87.66%
% ESC From:	0.00%	100.00%
Par. Marg. Cont:	5.00%	46.00%
Stud. Marg. Cont:	25.00%	50.00%

This analysis provides estimated financial aid data for planning purposes only. Actual financial aid awards are determined by each college at the time of admission. The validity of the input data can dramatically affect financial aid values. Which assets must be counted and how each asset is valued may be treated differently by the government and each individual college. Calculations are based on:

Federal Methodology 2001-02

Institutional Methodology 2001-02

Financial Aid Formulas Become Outdated After: 02/28/02

The College Financial Aid Test™ is a trademark of College Money.

www.collegemoney.com

FIGURE 4.7 Year Two of Option 3: Each Student Withdrew $12,500 from His or Her Section 529 Plan and Shows $5,000 of Reportable Income

Summary

The Financial Aid Test™ software is a tool you should use to examine whether financial aid can be an important planning factor for each of your clients and, if so, to help you determine which tools are best suited for your client. Financial aid is only one factor to consider. Chapter 7 examines the interaction between financial aid and taxes and control of money.

Please be sure to use The Financial Aid Test™ software properly:

- Do use it to examine financial aid eligibility.

- Do use it to backtest strategies you are thinking about using.

- Do not use it to forecast financial aid into the future.

Chapters 5 and 6 examine college planning time horizons and give you another tool, The College Funding Integrator,™ to quantify the numeric portion of a college funding plan.

5

The College Funding Time Horizon

he length of the time horizon over which we choose to fund college has
a dramatic effect not only on the amount we save monthly but also on
the investment vehicles that are appropriate. Usually the longer we
spread the college planning period, the easier it becomes for parents to handle
the problem. But making the time horizon too lengthy may make college
merge into the retirement years. In order to understand the college planning
horizon, we need to first understand the four ways to pay for college.

The Four Ways to Pay for College

Saving or Prefunding

Over the last twenty-three plus years we have worked with tens of thousands of parents. Our experience has shown that parents really have only
four ways to pay for college. The first is to *save or prefund* the college
bill. Most parents do not save enough. We learned in Chapter 1 that college
costs are extremely high. The sheer amount of monthly savings required to
fund college can be overwhelming. In addition, it costs a considerable
amount of money to raise children, especially if parents want to give them
the well-rounded experience required to make children college-competitive.
A very small percentage of families actually save enough to pay for the
first year, let alone the entire college bill. We can do a better job of moti-
vating parents to save for college by helping them set better goals. Even
then, however, most parents need a longer time period to get the job done.

"Paying-as-You-Go"

The second way to pay for college is the *"pay-as-you-go"* method. "Paying-as-you-go" involves taking money out of current income during the college years to pay college bills. Unfortunately, many parents feel that if they do not save enough, they still have time to solve the college problem because they can use the "pay-as-you-go" system. The seeming extra time allows parents to procrastinate. It allows them to delay their sense of strategic urgency.

There are several problems with relying on the "pay-as-you-go" method. Fluctuations in income or expenses could preclude a child from going to college. Sometimes things go wrong.

- A parent loses his or her job just before or during the college period.

- High expenses—for example, medical bills—can have an impact. Families may need to cut other expenses to make up the difference.

In this situation, families may become financial aid eligible, and although financial aid may help, it may not be enough or it may force a student to attend a less desirable college.

Many parents plan to contribute to college costs by having a non-working spouse go back to work. Federal income taxes can impose a negative barrier to this strategy. Table 5.1 shows how much additional gross income is required to fund a $10,000 net college payment at various tax brackets. This table considers only federal income taxes.

TABLE 5.1 The Effect of Taxes on College Funding Using the "Pay-as-You-Go" Method

Net College Payment	Federal Tax Bracket				
	15.00%	28.00%	31.00%	36.00%	39.50%
$10,000	$11,765	$13,889	$14,493	$15,625	$16,529
$15,000	$17,647	$20,833	$21,739	$23,438	$24,793
$20,000	$23,529	$27,778	$28,986	$31,250	$33,058
$25,000	$29,412	$34,722	$36,232	$39,063	$41,322
$30,000	$35,294	$41,667	$43,478	$46,875	$49,587
$35,000	$41,176	$48,611	$50,725	$54,688	$57,851
$40,000	$47,059	$55,556	$57,971	$62,500	$66,116

Our federal income tax system is not the only impediment to paying for college out of current income. There are other barriers to the "pay-as-you-go" strategy. State income taxes, social security and medicare taxes, lost financial aid, and additional family expense related to work all have a negative effect. For example:

Joe and Barbara Johnson did not save enough for college. Their contingency plan was to have Barbara, a previously non-working spouse, go back to work. Since Barbara had not worked outside the home over the past eighteen years, she found her work options somewhat limited. She was able to find a job earning $30,000 annually. The family felt this would contribute significantly toward the $25,000 college bill for their daughter Samantha.

Joe and Barbara received several big and not-so-pleasant surprises summarized in Table 5.2. The first surprise came when Barbara received her first paycheck. The reduction in size from gross to net income caused by federal and state income taxes and social security and medicare taxes surprised them. They began to wonder if they could meet their college payment plan.

But the next surprise was even greater. Their financial aid package came in substantially lower because of Barbara's income. Finally, it cost Barbara money to go to work. Some of the extra expenses that the family incurred were

- Barbara's car needed to be replaced because of all the extra mileage of going back and forth to work everyday.

- Barbara needed a new wardrobe to meet the office dress code.

- Barbara needed to buy lunch.

- Because Barbara got home late from the office, the family ate out more.

The list could have been longer. Because the children were older, the Johnson family did not incur the child care costs that many families do. All the other expenses, however, added up to a substantial amount, reducing significantly the net available to pay for college.

TABLE 5.2 Barriers to Using the "Pay-as-You-Go" System

Barbara's gross income		**$30,000**
Federal income taxes @ 28%	$8,400	
Social Security and Medicare taxes @ 7.65%	$2,295	
State Income Taxes @ 3%	$900	
Lost financial aid @ 47% of net income after taxes	$8,650	
Extra costs including:	$5,000	
Clothing		
Transportation		
Meals out		
Total costs		**$25,245**
Net contribution to college costs		**$4,755**

Relying on the "pay-as-you-go" system alone usually gives parents a rude awakening. However, when used carefully in combination with the other ways to pay for college, it can help. In some cases it may be the only alternative. Parents and advisors need to understand the implications that taxes and financial aid will have on the net available income, after all the expenses, left to pay college bills. Thinking ahead can shortcut many of the potential problems. For example, if financial aid is an issue, borrowing during the college years and having a non-working spouse go back to work beginning in the senior year of college to help pay off college debt may solve the financial aid problem. But the other problems, including taxes and expenses, are not as easy to solve.

Borrowing

The third way to pay for college involves *borrowing* and repaying college debt prior to retirement or in some cases, even amortizing college debt into the retirement years. This is how the college problem can become a retirement problem. There are a number of great college loan programs that can reduce pressure on the college funding problem, but serious thought needs to be given to the impact of college borrowing on retirement. Remember, there are lots of loans available for college, but no one is going to lend you money for retirement.

- Stafford loans make up the bulk of student loans currently available. These are usually low-interest loans and are sometimes subsidized by the federal government. Stafford loans give parents the opportunity to cost-share with their children. The responsibility to repay the loan belongs to the student not the parent. Using Stafford loans can give parents extra flexibility. They can, if they wish, gift money to their children to repay these loans, or they can leave the loan repayment responsibility to the student. Student loans can also be consolidated, lengthening the term of the loan to as long as 30 years and converting the loan from a variable to a fixed interest rate to help in the planning process.

- Federal PLUS loans are another easy option currently available. These low-interest loans currently capped at 9 percent are signature loans that are easy for most parents to get. Usually a ten-year, variable interest rate loan, they can be consolidated, lengthening the term to as long as 30 years and locking in a fixed interest rate to help with planning.

- Although student and parent loan interest is tax deductible to debtors with incomes below certain thresholds, interest on home equity loans is almost always tax-deductible. Home equity loans come as fixed-interest, fixed-term loans or as credit lines giving parents and advisors numerous planning options. Usually, home equity arrangements carry relatively low interest rates because they are backed by collateral.

It is not our intention to itemize all the loan options available to pay for college. Specific loan options will change over time. It is important, however, to consider the impact that borrowing can have on the college plan. If you utilize borrowing in your plan, be sure to consider life and disability insurance to cover large loans. The unexpected death or disability of a parent can destroy college opportunities for younger children and destroy retirement for a surviving spouse. Also, be sure to consider the impact of loan repayment on retirement.

Letting Someone Else Pay

Finally we have my favorite, the fourth way to pay for college: *"Let someone else pay for it."* There are two ways to let someone else pay for college.

- Grandparents and other relatives can help.

- Maybe the student will qualify for financial aid.

We have already discussed that trying to predict the magnitude of a financial aid package and incorporating it into our plan is not a good practice. You cannot rely on future financial aid. The rules and family circumstances can change too much over a long planning horizon. When we know that financial aid is a possibility (because we did a financial aid test), *we should build flexibility but not build projections into the plan.*

Grandparents and other relatives can help significantly, but their help should be incorporated into the plan so that they do not do damage. We have seen some parents announce to relatives, especially grandparents, that there is a college plan and that it might be an ideal place for holiday and birthday gifts. This helps avert problems that arise when well-meaning relatives open savings plans without consulting with the parents.

Defining the Three College Funding Periods

When designing college savings plans there are three distinct periods that define a college planning horizon:

- The savings or prefunding period

- The spending period

- The recovery period

These planning periods are consistent with the four ways to pay for college listed above.

The *savings or prefunding period* is the period between the onset of the college savings plan and the first year that the family has a student in college. This represents a period of accumulation. Dollars deposited into the plan during this period are leveraged by interest and growth. The earlier this period begins, the more aggressive investments can be. This can help savings and investment keep pace with college inflation. This is important. We learned earlier that college inflation rates tend to be higher than CPI.

The *spending period* is the period beginning with the start of the first college year for the family. It continues through the end of the last year a family member is a student. This is a period of depletion. Savings and investments are used up to pay college expenses. Additionally, college funds are usually supplemented with dollars taken from current income and borrowing. Negative leverage usually occurs during this period because interest expense begins to accumulate and debt begins to rise.

The *recovery period* begins upon the payment of the last college bill (not loan payments). It continues through the date set by the parents as their goal date to be out of college debt. This date is usually no later than the parents' retirement date. It can be earlier and sometimes it must be extended. See Figure 5.1.

Using any one period by itself to fund college usually is not very effective. It concentrates the financial pressure of college into too short a time period. Combining all three together can help to significantly reduce this financial pressure on family finances.

Although the process begins by forecasting college costs for the entire family, the family does not have to save the entire amount prior to the

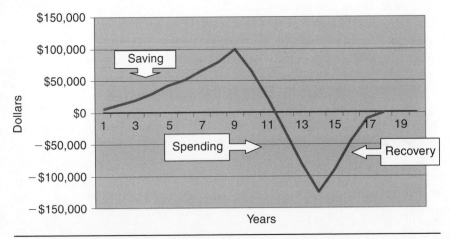

FIGURE 5.1 The College Funding Time Horizon

beginning of college. Parents can elect to stretch the college funding period by saving what they can during the prefunding period and paying the difference out of current income during the college years. If that is not enough, they can borrow any extra money that is needed and try to amortize any loans prior to retirement. If that is still not enough, a parent can postpone retirement or carry debt into retirement. There are lots of options with which to work. The best plan for a family will depend on their resources, their desires, and the shrewdness of their plan and their planner.

Strategies to Make the College Funding Plan Work

Once you have a picture of the college funding time horizon, there are lots of strategies that families can mix and match to make their plan work. The following represent a few of them:

- Change the college cost category goal
- Commit more or fewer existing assets to college
- Adjust the start of the college planning period
- Save more or less each year during the savings period
- Use an increasing annual savings commitment
- Use a "pay-yourself-first" strategy
- Adjust portfolio returns with a more aggressive or less aggressive asset allocation
- Increase returns by investing long (apply financial leverage)
- Adjust the family commitment to the "pay-as-you-go" plan
- Delay or accelerate the start of retirement

Changing the college cost categories means, in effect, changing college goals. As you work through all the options, you may find that you need to adjust college goals downward to make the numbers work. Sometimes parents simply cannot afford high-priced schools for all their children. For example, by planning early to fund for state colleges for in-state residents, parents can guarantee that at least each of their children will go to college. Later, if finances improve, goals can be changed to allow for higher-priced colleges. Planning college costs can also make parents think through the special needs of each child. Some children may fit well at large public schools, while others may require small teaching colleges that are usually more expensive. You may need to vary college cost categories for each student in the family during the planning process.

Sometimes parents have resources in the form of savings or investments that can be diverted to the college plan from other things, such as a planned trip. Showing how diverting these resources affect the college plan can motivate parents to make changes. Seeding the college plan with a lump sum makes a big difference, because interest earnings or investment growth can compound significantly. Other sources of lump-sum resources include contributions from other relatives or inheritances.

Conversely, parents who have the ability to save substantial dollars or who find they have overfunded the college plan may be able to use resources from the college plan for other things. Parents often put themselves under extreme pressure to save for college. If this pressure becomes too great, the plan can fall apart. Moving resources around can help overall family finances function better.

When to start the college plan is another factor to consider. There is a cost of waiting to start a plan. Putting off the start of a plan increases the amount of savings required in each of the remaining years, or more resources or borrowing during the college years will be required. Sometimes parents can be motivated to start earlier. Sometimes there are reasons to delay the start of the plan. In either case, parents and advisors need to explore and understand the consequences.

The amount of savings required is dependent on the length of the savings period as well as the resources that parents will expend during the other periods. Two considerations can help here:

■ Consider using an increasing savings commitment. As college gets closer parents who have not saved enough will need to ante up more money anyway. Increasing the savings commitment by a fixed percentage amount can help a parent get used to the increased commitment more gradually.

■ A "pay-yourself-first" system built into a plan can help parents stay on track. It is easy for parents to stop saving as the unpredictable costs of raising children wreak havoc with their finances. Using payroll deduction or an automatic withdrawal from a checking account can make it more difficult for a parent to stop saving, keeping a plan on target.

Adjusting college savings portfolio returns can make a difference. Sometimes parents are too conservative in their investment choices. College inflation historically almost always runs higher than CPI. This can call for a more aggressive asset allocation. Advisor prudence is critical here. Too aggressive an asset allocation may expose a portfolio to severe market volatility, causing a parent to stop the plan due to adverse investment results. The plan needs to fit the client just right. Expected returns directly affect the resources the plan will require the parent to commit.

One of the ways planners can increase returns may be to lengthen the period before investments need to be liquidated. Standard planning practice is to reduce investment risk as the need to pay expenses from the investment nears. If a family starts late or has a short savings period, investing usually must be conservative. This usually means lower returns. Because college loan terms are extremely attractive, borrowing may offer a form of financial leverage allowing parents to stay more aggressively invested, longer. Planners need to help clients assess this risk before going ahead.

Still another option is to save less and use the "pay-as-you-go" system more. We discussed previously some of the traps in doing this. Sometimes, however, "pay-as-you-go" is the right option.

Finally, postponing retirement can lengthen the college planning period. Not only does this option allow us more time to pay off college debt, but also it shortens the retirement period, reducing the need for retirement funds. Unfortunately, many families do not have this option. They have jobs that require retirement at specific ages. More and more, however, we are finding parents who are ready and willing to postpone retirement in order to make their college plans come true.

Consider the family we counseled a few years ago. Dad was a college professor, and Mom was an executive for a nonprofit corporation. They had two daughters, four years apart. It was the parents' dream that their daughters attend Ivy League–type schools.

When we analyzed their planning situation, it was clear that their lofty goals were going to be very difficult to meet. The age difference between the girls of four years resulted in an eight-year college horizon. The family would not be able to capitalize on having two students in college at the same time. Financial aid was not going to be an option for them. Furthermore, although the parents lived a modest lifestyle, it was going to be virtually impossible to save enough to meet the projected college costs.

One option we presented to the parents was to consider deferring their retirement. Neither employer had a mandatory retirement age policy, so it was possible to factor this in to their plan. Delaying retirement not only meant that they would have more time to pay off the inevitable college loans, but they would be retired for fewer years and thus need less in the way of retirement assets. In Chapter 6, we illustrate the plan for this family.

Chapter 6 introduces a tool, The College Funding Integrator,™ which allows us to explore just how mixing and matching the options above can be woven into a successful plan.

Communicating with Your Client Using The College Funding Integrator™

Introduction

The College Funding Integrator™ is a tool to help you explore how you are going to balance college funding over the three periods in the college planning time horizon. Those three periods include

- The savings period
- The spending period
- The recovery period

As a tool, the Integrator's graphics can have significant impact when used in a client presentation. Many advisors use The College Funding Integrator™ to finalize the numeric portion of a college funding plan, leaving only the choice of funding tools and funding products to finalize the plan.

Working with The College Funding Integrator™

The College Funding Integrator™ is an Excel spreadsheet template with four sections:

- The Main Page
- The Client Report

- The College Cost Forecast
- Benchmark Colleges

The *Main Page* (Figure 6.1) is the interactive page you will use for most client presentations. It is the page where you input data and where you show clients their results. The Main Page has three sections that can be reached easily with the [Page Down] key. The top section allows you to input data about the parents and the students you are working with. The top section also contains a bar graph depicting projected family college costs as well as a summary section giving total family college costs and the annual savings required to meet these costs. Holding your cursor over any bar on the graph will also give you the family expenditure for college in that year.

The second section [Page Down] allows you to input plan design data. There is also a line graph that denotes the three planning periods in the college planning horizon along with a summary section giving the annual loan payment required to amortize college debt during the recovery period and the total loan payments required. Changing the planning data causes an immediate change in the graph.

Section 3 [Page Down] gives data about the program. A warning message will also appear here when your program requires updating because college cost data is obsolete.

The *Client Report* is a multi-page report that expands data from the *Main Page.* It includes

- A disclaimer page (Table 6.1a)
- A page summarizing the input data (Table 6.1b)
- A family college cost forecast page (Table 6.1c)
- A composite planning page (Table 6.1d)
- A planning recommendation page (Table 6.1e)

These pages give more depth to the data underlying the graphs on the *Main Page* and are suitable for an advisor's file or to give to a client.

The *College Cost Forecast Page* (Table 6.2) gives the advisor the backup data underlying the college cost forecast. It is included here for easy reference. This data coincides with the forecast data in The College Savings Calculator.™

Finally, the *Benchmark College Page* (Table 6.3) is reproduced to make easy reference during a parent meeting.

Appendix E provides instructions on how to install this program on your computer.

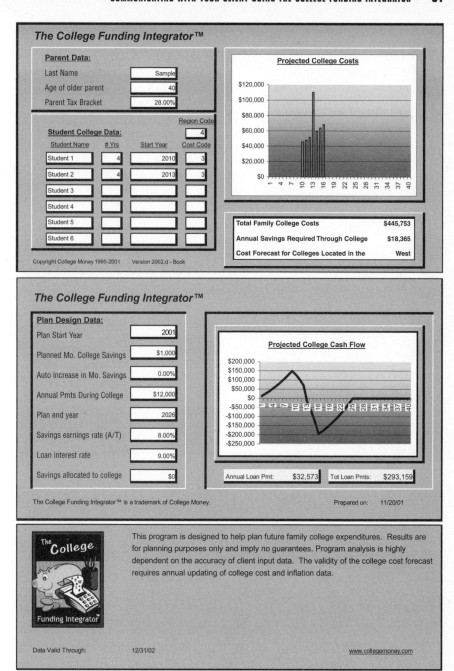

FIGURE 6.1 The College Funding Integrator™ Main Page Example

TABLE 6.1a Disclaimer

Prepared for: **Sample**

Subject: **College Funding Analysis**

The analysis that follows has been prepared especially for your family. The purpose of this analysis is to help you design a plan to handle anticipated future college costs in a reasonable and effective manner. You should understand that any analysis of this type is for planning purposes only. The projections imply no guarantees. Projections are based on future college cost data, interest and inflation assumptions, and personal data you supplied, all of which can change over time. If used properly, however, this analysis can help you be better prepared to handle college for your family. For best results this analysis should be updated annually.

The college cost forecast underlying this program is based on a dynamic model which requires annually updating college cost and inflation data. Data for this program is valid through December 31, 2002.

> The College Funding Integrator™ was developed by College Money, Marlton, NJ. Copyright College Money 1995–2001. Version 2002.c - Book.

TABLE 6.1b Summary of Input Data

College Planning Model Data Verification as of:					Page 2 of 5 28-Oct-01

Parent Data:

* Client name	Sample
* Age of older parent	40
* Plan end (year of older parent retirement or sooner)	2026
* Year oldest student starts college	2010
* Year youngest student finishes college	2017
* After-tax savings earnings rate	8.00%
* Loan interest rate	9.00%
* Parent tax bracket	28.00%
* Savings already set aside for college	$0

Plan Design Data:

Planned monthly college savings	$1,000.00
Planned annual increase in monthly savings (percentage)	0.00%
Planned annual payments during college	$12,000

College Cost Database Used: West

Student Data:

Student #	1	2	3	4	5	6
Student Name	Student 1	Student 2	Student 3	Student 4	Student 5	Student 6
Undergrad Start Year:	2010	2013				
School Cost Code*	3	3	0	0	0	0
# Undergrad Years	4	4	0	0	0	0
Last Year Undergrad	2014	2017				
Grad Start Year	0	0	0	0	0	0
School Cost Code*	5	5	0	0	0	0
# Grad School Years	0	0	0	0	0	0
Last Year Grad	0	0	0	0	0	0

*School Cost Codes
  1 Low Cost (e.g., State college for in-state resident)
  2 Low Medium (e.g., lower-cost private college)
  3 Medium Cost (e.g., average private college)
  4 High Medium (e.g., higher-cost private college)
  5 Highest Cost (e.g., Ivy League)

TABLE 6.1c Family College Cost Forecast

COLLEGE COST FORECAST   **Page 3 of 5**

The first step in developing a good college plan is to forecast what college is likely to cost for your family. The following table projects future college costs for each member of your family based on the types of colleges you selected for each student and our college cost model for the geographic West.

Age Older Parent	Year	COLLEGE COSTS FOR STUDENT #1	#2	#3	#4	#5	#6	TOTAL COSTS
40	2001	$0	$0	$0	$0	$0	$0	$0
41	2002	$0	$0	$0	$0	$0	$0	$0
42	2003	$0	$0	$0	$0	$0	$0	$0
43	2004	$0	$0	$0	$0	$0	$0	$0
44	2005	$0	$0	$0	$0	$0	$0	$0
45	2006	$0	$0	$0	$0	$0	$0	$0
46	2007	$0	$0	$0	$0	$0	$0	$0
47	2008	$0	$0	$0	$0	$0	$0	$0
48	2009	$0	$0	$0	$0	$0	$0	$0
49	2010	$45,475	$0	$0	$0	$0	$0	$45,475
50	2011	$47,774	$0	$0	$0	$0	$0	$47,774
51	2012	$51,303	$0	$0	$0	$0	$0	$51,303
52	2013	$55,096	$55,096	$0	$0	$0	$0	$110,192
53	2014	$0	$59,175	$0	$0	$0	$0	$59,175
54	2015	$0	$63,560	$0	$0	$0	$0	$63,560
55	2016	$0	$68,275	$0	$0	$0	$0	$68,275
56	2017	$0	$0	$0	$0	$0	$0	$0
57	2018	$0	$0	$0	$0	$0	$0	$0
58	2019	$0	$0	$0	$0	$0	$0	$0
59	2020	$0	$0	$0	$0	$0	$0	$0
60	2021	$0	$0	$0	$0	$0	$0	$0
61	2022	$0	$0	$0	$0	$0	$0	$0
62	2023	$0	$0	$0	$0	$0	$0	$0
63	2024	$0	$0	$0	$0	$0	$0	$0
64	2025	$0	$0	$0	$0	$0	$0	$0
65	2026	$0	$0	$0	$0	$0	$0	$0
66	2027	$0	$0	$0	$0	$0	$0	$0
67	2028	$0	$0	$0	$0	$0	$0	$0
68	2029	$0	$0	$0	$0	$0	$0	$0
69	2030	$0	$0	$0	$0	$0	$0	$0
70	2031	$0	$0	$0	$0	$0	$0	$0
71	2032	$0	$0	$0	$0	$0	$0	$0
72	2033	$0	$0	$0	$0	$0	$0	$0
73	2034	$0	$0	$0	$0	$0	$0	$0
74	2035	$0	$0	$0	$0	$0	$0	$0
75	2036	$0	$0	$0	$0	$0	$0	$0
76	2037	$0	$0	$0	$0	$0	$0	$0
77	2038	$0	$0	$0	$0	$0	$0	$0
78	2039	$0	$0	$0	$0	$0	$0	$0
79	2040	$0	$0	$0	$0	$0	$0	$0
TOTALS		**$199,648**	**$246,105**	**$0**	**$0**	**$0**	**$0**	**$445,753**

TABLE 6.1d Composite College Funding Plan

A Composite College Funding Plan for: Sample   20-Nov-01

1. Add new savings to your college funding account this year in the amount of		$12,000
2. Increase college savings each year until college starts at the rate of		0.00%
3. Once college starts make transfers from current income each year of		$12,000
4. Borrow the balance and repay loans prior to retirement @ interest of	9.00%	$32,573
5. Invest net proceeds @ an interest rate of	8.00%	

Age of Older Parent	Year	Total College Cost West	Save	Transfer	Loan Pmts	Net Interest	Acct Bal
40	2001	$0	$12,000	$0	$0	$0	$12,000
41	2002	$0	$12,000	$0	$0	$960	$24,960
42	2003	$0	$12,000	$0	$0	$1,997	$38,957
43	2004	$0	$12,000	$0	$0	$3,117	$54,073
44	2005	$0	$12,000	$0	$0	$4,326	$70,399
45	2006	$0	$12,000	$0	$0	$5,632	$88,031
46	2007	$0	$12,000	$0	$0	$7,042	$107,074
47	2008	$0	$12,000	$0	$0	$8,566	$127,640
48	2009	$0	$12,000	$0	$0	$10,211	$149,851
49	2010	$45,475	$0	$12,000	$0	$11,988	$128,364
50	2011	$47,774	$0	$12,000	$0	$10,269	$102,859
51	2012	$51,303	$0	$12,000	$0	$8,229	$71,785
52	2013	$110,192	$0	$12,000	$0	$5,743	−$20,664
53	2014	$59,175	$0	$12,000	$0	−$1,860	−$69,699
54	2015	$63,560	$0	$12,000	$0	−$6,273	−$127,531
55	2016	$68,275	$0	$12,000	$0	−$11,478	−$195,284
56	2017	$0	$0	$0	$32,573	−$17,576	−$180,287
57	2018	$0	$0	$0	$32,573	−$16,226	−$163,939
58	2019	$0	$0	$0	$32,573	−$14,755	−$146,121
59	2020	$0	$0	$0	$32,573	−$13,151	−$126,698
60	2021	$0	$0	$0	$32,573	−$11,403	−$105,528
61	2022	$0	$0	$0	$32,573	−$9,498	−$82,452
62	2023	$0	$0	$0	$32,573	−$7,421	−$57,300
63	2024	$0	$0	$0	$32,573	−$5,157	−$29,884
64	2025	$0	$0	$0	$32,573	−$2,690	$0
65	2026	$0	$0	$0	$0	$0	$0
66	2027	$0	$0	$0	$0	$0	$0
67	2028	$0	$0	$0	$0	$0	$0
68	2029	$0	$0	$0	$0	$0	$0
69	2030	$0	$0	$0	$0	$0	$0
70	2031	$0	$0	$0	$0	$0	$0
71	2032	$0	$0	$0	$0	$0	$0
72	2033	$0	$0	$0	$0	$0	$0
73	2034	$0	$0	$0	$0	$0	$0
74	2035	$0	$0	$0	$0	$0	$0
75	2036	$0	$0	$0	$0	$0	$0
76	2037	$0	$0	$0	$0	$0	$0
77	2038	$0	$0	$0	$0	$0	$0
78	2039	$0	$0	$0	$0	$0	$0
79	2040	$0	$0	$0	$0	$0	$0
TOTALS		**$445,753**	**$108,000**	**$84,000**	**$293,159**	**−$39,405**	**n/a**

TABLE 6.1e Planning Recommendations

Prepared for: **Sample**	**Page 5 of 5**
Prepared on: **28-Oct-01**	
Subject: **Planning Recommendations:**	

1. **Begin a savings plan as quickly as possible.**

   You don't have to save everything right now. Saving even small amounts is more important than not saving. Early savings enjoy the benefit of compound growth. This means that every dollar you save now will result in more than a dollar that won't have to be borrowed later.

2. **Make sure that your savings plan considers the following key features:**

   a. Your plan should avoid the "Kiddie Tax".

   b. Your plan should allow for controlled taxation of savings growth.

   c. Your plan should allow for controlled taxation during the withdrawal phase.

   d. Your plan should provide flexibility to deal with future financial aid eligibility.

   e. Your plan should allow multiple investment options that consider:

      1. Staying ahead of college inflation rates.

      2. Diversifying your risk.

      3. Making changes at reasonable cost both as markets change and as your needs change, particularly as you get close to the withdrawal phase.

   f. Your plan should consider self-completion in the event of the death or disability of all breadwinners.

   g. Your plan should consider a "pay yourself first" option that allows automatic, systematic plan deposits.

3. **Complete a Financial Aid Test™ now.**

   The Financial Aid Test™ can help you to assess your potential future eligibility for financial aid. Knowing your likelihood of qualifying for future financial aid will help you judge the desirability of implementing "pay as you go" or other strategies during the college years.

4. **Review your retirement plans, now.**

   College is part of the retirement problem. Without proper thought, you are likely to invade retirement funds to pay for college or are likely to over-borrow for college and be caught repaying college loans at a time you should be saving for your own retirement.

5. **Review your plan at least annually.**

TABLE 6.2 The College Savings Calculator™—College Cost Projections

Base Year: 2001					College Cost Region: West
	<— Base-Year Data —>				
College Type	1	2	3	4	5
College Description	Low	Low/Med	Medium	Med/High	High
Base-Year Tuition, Fees,					
Room, and Board	$10,361	$19,636	$25,785	$27,663	$33,947
Base-Year Other Costs	$5,481	$5,481	$4,350	$6,582	$4,500

			<— College Cost Projections —>				
			1	2	3	4	5
			Low	Low/Med	Medium	Med/High	High
	Inflation	Inflation					
	Rate	Rate	Total	Total	Total	Total	Total
Year	Tuition	Other	Costs	Costs	Costs	Costs	Costs
2001	Base-Year Data		$15,842	$25,117	$30,135	$34,245	$38,447
2002	4.69%	2.53%	$16,467	$26,177	$31,454	$35,709	$40,153
2003	4.69%	2.53%	$17,118	$27,283	$32,833	$37,238	$41,937
2004	4.69%	2.53%	$17,796	$28,438	$34,275	$38,835	$43,801
2005	4.69%	2.53%	$18,503	$29,645	$35,781	$40,504	$45,751
2006	4.69%	2.53%	$19,240	$30,904	$37,355	$42,246	$47,789
2007	5.36%	2.86%	$20,116	$32,405	$39,234	$44,324	$50,223
2008	5.36%	2.86%	$21,035	$33,982	$41,210	$46,508	$52,784
2009	5.36%	2.86%	$21,998	$35,639	$43,289	$48,803	$55,478
2010	5.36%	2.86%	$23,008	$37,381	$45,475	$51,216	$58,313
2011	5.36%	2.86%	$24,067	$39,210	$47,774	$53,752	$61,296
2012	7.74%	4.79%	$25,718	$42,033	$51,303	$57,657	$65,865
2013	7.74%	4.79%	$27,487	$45,064	$55,096	$61,853	$70,778
2014	7.74%	4.79%	$29,382	$48,318	$59,175	$66,360	$76,064
2015	7.74%	4.79%	$31,413	$51,814	$63,560	$71,202	$81,749
2016	7.74%	4.79%	$33,589	$55,568	$68,275	$76,405	$87,864
2017	7.74%	4.79%	$35,921	$59,600	$73,345	$81,996	$94,442
2018	7.74%	4.79%	$38,421	$63,932	$78,798	$88,004	$101,519
2019	7.74%	4.79%	$41,101	$68,585	$84,661	$94,461	$109,132
2020	7.74%	4.79%	$43,974	$73,585	$90,967	$101,400	$117,323
2021	7.74%	4.79%	$47,055	$78,956	$97,750	$108,859	$126,135
2022	7.74%	4.79%	$50,358	$84,728	$105,044	$116,876	$135,617
2023	7.74%	4.79%	$53,901	$90,929	$112,890	$125,494	$145,818
2024	7.74%	4.79%	$57,702	$97,594	$121,330	$134,758	$156,795
2025	7.74%	4.79%	$61,778	$104,757	$130,409	$144,718	$168,606
2026	7.74%	4.79%	$66,152	$112,455	$140,175	$155,425	$181,316
2027	7.74%	4.79%	$70,844	$120,729	$150,681	$166,938	$194,993
2028	7.74%	4.79%	$75,879	$129,623	$161,984	$179,317	$209,711
2029	7.74%	4.79%	$81,283	$139,183	$174,144	$192,628	$225,551
2030	7.74%	4.79%	$87,081	$149,461	$187,227	$206,942	$242,597
2031	7.74%	4.79%	$93,305	$160,511	$201,303	$222,335	$260,943
2032	7.74%	4.79%	$99,986	$172,390	$216,449	$238,889	$280,688
2033	7.74%	4.79%	$107,158	$185,163	$232,746	$256,693	$301,939
2034	7.74%	4.79%	$114,858	$198,897	$250,283	$275,842	$324,811
2035	7.74%	4.79%	$123,125	$213,665	$269,153	$296,438	$349,430
2036	7.74%	4.79%	$132,002	$229,546	$289,460	$318,592	$375,929
2037	7.74%	4.79%	$141,535	$246,624	$311,313	$342,423	$404,453
2038	7.74%	4.79%	$151,773	$264,991	$334,831	$368,057	$435,156
2039	7.74%	4.79%	$162,768	$284,745	$360,141	$395,634	$468,206
2040	7.74%	4.79%	$174,579	$305,991	$387,381	$425,301	$503,784
2041	7.74%	4.79%	$187,265	$328,843	$416,698	$457,219	$542,083
2042	7.74%	4.79%	$200,894	$353,424	$448,251	$491,558	$583,312
2043	7.74%	4.79%	$215,536	$379,865	$482,213	$528,504	$627,698
2044	7.74%	4.79%	$231,268	$408,309	$518,768	$568,257	$675,481
2045	7.74%	4.79%	$248,171	$438,907	$558,115	$611,030	$726,924
2046	7.74%	4.79%	$266,335	$471,826	$600,468	$657,056	$782,307

Source: College Money © 1997–2000. Version 2002.d-Book.

TABLE 6.3 Benchmark College Costs

Benchmark College Costs
For the School Year Ending June-02

Code	College	Type	Tuition and Fees	Room and Board	Other	Pizza	Total	Region
11	Rutgers	Low	$6,652	$6,852	$2,893	$2,100	$18.497	Northeast
12	Rutgers (Non-Res)	Medium/Low	$10,688	$6,852	$2,893	$2,100	$22,533	Northeast
13	Lycoming College	Medium	$19,404	$5,376	$2.200	$2,100	$29,080	Northeast
14	American Univ.	High/Medium	$22,478	$8.829	$1,900	$2,100	$35,307	Northeast
15	Univ. of Pennsylvania	High—Ivy League	$26,630	$8,244	$2,336	$2,100	$39,310	Northeast
21	Ohio State Univ	Low	$4,788	$5,807	$3,129	$2,100	$15,824	Midwest
22	Ohio State Univ (NR)	Medium/Low	$13,554	$5,807	$3,129	$2,100	$24,590	Midwest
23	Cornell College (IA)*	Medium	$20,250	$5,600	$2,000	$2,100	$29,950	Midwest
24	Kenyon College	High/Medium	$27,550	$4,580	$1,600	$2,100	$35,830	Midwest
25	Northwestern University	High—Ivy League	$25,839	$7,752	$2,655	$2,100	$38,346	Midwest
31	Univ. of North Carolina	Low	$3,184	$5,930	$2,460	$2,100	$13,674	South
32	U of N Carolina (NR)	Medium/Low	$12,350	$5,930	$2,960	$2,100	$23,340	South
33	University of Richmond	Medium	$22,570	$4,730	$2,100	$2,100	$31,500	South
34	Univ of Miami	High/Medium	$23,462	$7,940	$3,050	$2,100	$36,552	South
35	Duke University	High—Ivy League	$26,810	$7,648	$2,332	$2,100	$38,890	South
41	U of Washington	Low	$3,983	$6,378	$3,381	$2,100	$15,842	West
42	U of Washington (NIR)	Medium/Low	$13,258	$6,378	$3,381	$2,100	$25,117	West
43	University of Denver	Medium	$22,037	$3,748	$2,250	$2,100	$30,135	West
44	California Inst of Tech	High/Medium	$21,120	$6,543	$4,482	$2,100	$34,245	West
45	Stanford University	High—Ivy League	$25,917	$8,030	$2,400	$2,100	$38,447	West

Region Definition Table

1 Northeast
2 Midwest
3 South
4 West

Exploring Time Horizons in Developing the College Plan

There are several scenarios we can explore with The College Funding Integrator.™ Making adjustments to some or all of them will allow you to customize a plan for your client.

- Change the college cost category goal.
- Commit more or fewer existing assets to college.
- Adjust the start of the college planning period.
- Save more or less each year during the savings period.
- Use an increasing annual savings commitment.

- Adjust portfolio returns with a more aggressive or less aggressive asset allocation.

- Adjust the family commitment during college to the "pay-as-you-go" plan.

- Delay or accelerate the start of retirement.

Let us examine some of them to see how they help us develop a college funding plan.

In Chapter 2, we discussed the case of Jeff and Hillary Smith, who wanted to send their six-year-old daughter Chelsea to Stanford. Unfortunately, the Smiths were only able to save $400 per month. This allowed them to prefund a state college but not Stanford. The College Funding Integrator™ allows us to explore more options with the Smiths. Figure 6.2 reflects the Smiths' current commitment to college of $400 monthly through the end of college. ❶

The Smiths had not considered using the recovery period to help make Stanford affordable. The recovery period, again, is the period between the end of college and the beginning of retirement. This is a fairly long period for the Smiths because they are young parents. In this case the Smiths could send Chelsea to Stanford, but it would mean taking on college debt with college loan payments of slightly more than $1,868 per month or $22,418 annually. ❷ This may or may not be wise for the Smiths, but it does give them the extra time to make their goal possible, and they will be making loan payments with future dollars at a time that they felt they should be financially better off.

Another option we could offer the Smiths would be to use an increasing savings plan and increase their out-of-pocket expenditures during the college years. In Figure 6.3, we increased their savings commitment by 10 percent annually. ❸ We also increased their out-of-pocket commitment during the college years from $4,800 to $12,000 annually. ❹ This is a logical progression for most parents because career growth would increase their incomes, and it also increases the financial commitment as the college bills come closer. By the way, the Smiths' increasing savings at 10 percent annually would place their savings the year before college at $12,450, so there would not be a material change in their out-of-pocket expenses during college. By increasing their commitment during the savings and spending periods, the Smiths reduced their obligation during the recovery period by almost half, $11,777 versus $22,418 annually. ❺

College is an emotional issue. Parents tend to stretch for their children. The College Funding Integrator™ can help you explore with them how to make their college and retirement goals come true. By helping them define their commitments, you can also help them evaluate the wisdom of their plan.

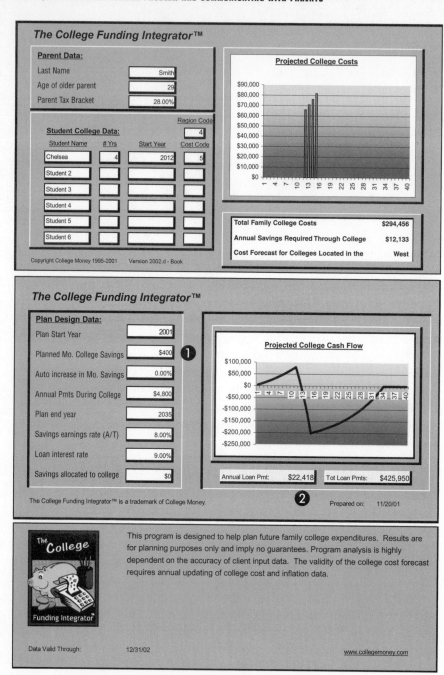

FIGURE 6.2 Original Savings Plan for the Smith Family

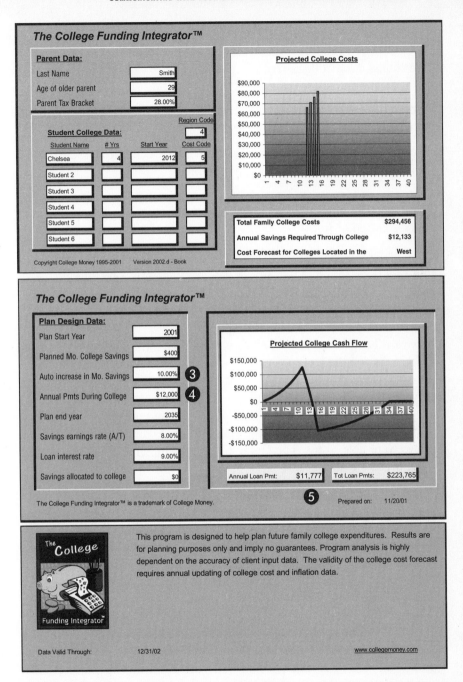

FIGURE 6.3 Plan Using 10 Percent Annual Increase in Savings Amount

In the above example, we explored three modifications to the Smiths' college plan:

- We changed the college cost category to a more expensive college cost classification to show the Smiths that they could achieve their dreams.

- We used an increasing annual savings amount to allow the Smiths to gradually adapt to their college commitment.

- We increased the planned out-of-pocket family commitment during the college years (the "pay-as-you-go" plan).

- We took advantage of the recovery period using loans and repaying them prior to retirement in order to spread the college obligation over a longer period of time.

There is still more that we can do. Let us suppose that the Smiths communicated their plan to Chelsea's grandparents and that each grandparent was willing to contribute $10,000 to the college plan. ❻ Figure 6.4 shows that adding a lump sum to the plan reduced loan payments during the recovery period to $5,177 annually. ❼

Conversely, we could have reduced the length of the recovery period. Suppose that the Smiths feel they can handle a $12,000 annual loan payment. Figure 6.5 shows that the Smiths could reduce the recovery period by fourteen years from 2035 to 2021 by increasing loan payments to $11,912. ❽

In Chapter 5, we talk about a family that actually postponed retirement in order to meet some rather lofty college goals. Figures 6.6 and 6.7 show how we were able to use The College Funding Integrator™ to make their college dreams come true.

The Wending family had two children, aged ten and fourteen. Both were very bright. Their parents, Bob and Sarah Wending, were graduates of Northwestern University and wanted both children to have the opportunity to attend their alma mater. Education at a prestige college was extremely important to the Wendings, and they were willing to go on the hook to pay for it. Unfortunately, both Mr. and Mrs. Wending were fifty years old ❾ when they started their plan. The day their youngest child, Kathleen, graduates from college, they will both be sixty-two.

The Wendings need a level payment plan for college of no more than $2,000 per month. ❿ They are limited to this amount because of commitments to their retirement plans and other family expenditures. Because of their professions, they do not expect significant pay raises. They can begin saving now and are willing to continue payments through the beginning of retirement. Normal retirement would begin when the Wendings reach age sixty-five.

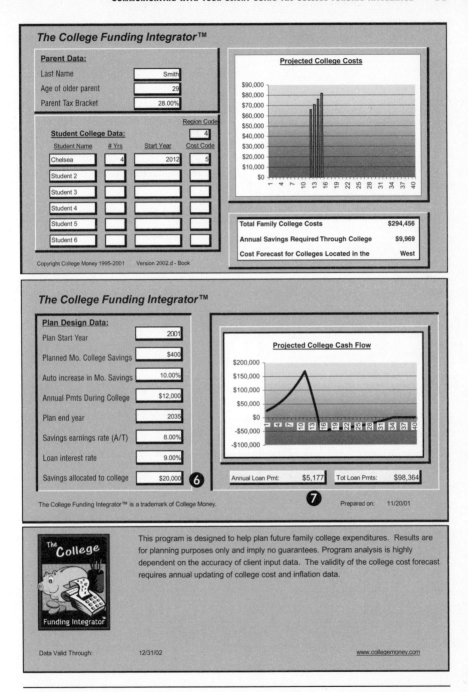

FIGURE 6.4 Plan Showing Lump-Sum Contribution from Grandparents

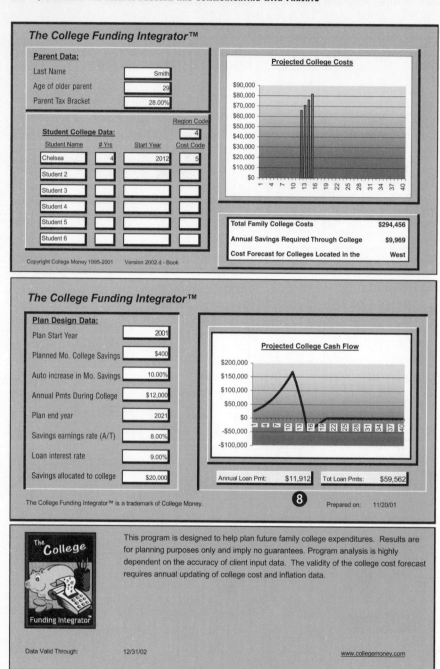

FIGURE 6.5 Plan Illustrating Increased Loan Payments,
Reduced Repayment Period

As Figure 6.6 indicates, the Wendings will not have enough time to pre-fund much of the college bill for their children. They will acquire substantial college loans. Amortizing college debt to their normal retirement age of sixty-five will require annual loan payments of $45,566, substantially more than their budget allows. ⓫

Fortunately, both of the Wendings love their jobs and neither will be forced to retire at age sixty-five. This gives them a planning advantage. If the Wendings can extend their retirement date to 2023, age seventy-two ⓬, they can reduce their annual college loan payments to $17,972 (see Figure 6.7), a number within their budget range. ⓭

The financial wisdom of extending college into retirement is always questionable. Sometimes, however, it is the only way parents who plan late can make the numbers work. The Wending family's circumstances are becoming less and less unusual. Families are having children later in life, and many are considering retiring later both to have more time to accumulate retirement funds and because of increased longevity. Because most families would prefer to be free of college debts long before retirement, extending the recovery period can help parents meet their dreams of college for their children.

There are two other factors that can have a major impact on the college plan. They are

- The loan interest rate

- The portfolio growth rate

Because the design of a long-term college savings plan usually projects years into the future, loan rates are hard to predict. Most of our plans use 9 percent as a loan interest rate because it is the highest rate that can be charged under the federal PLUS loan program, a major college loan. Parents need to shop for loans as college gets close. Table 6.4 shows how much the loan payment varies per $10,000 over a ten-year period at various interest rates.

TABLE 6.4 College Loan Payments
$10,000 Amortized over Ten Years

Interest Rate	Monthly Payment	Annual Payment	Total Loan Payments
7%	$116.11	$1,393.32	$13,933.20
8%	$121.33	$1,455.96	$14,559.60
9%	$126.68	$1,520.16	$15,201.60
10%	$132.16	$1,585.92	$15,859.20
11%	$137.76	$1,652.40	$16,524.00

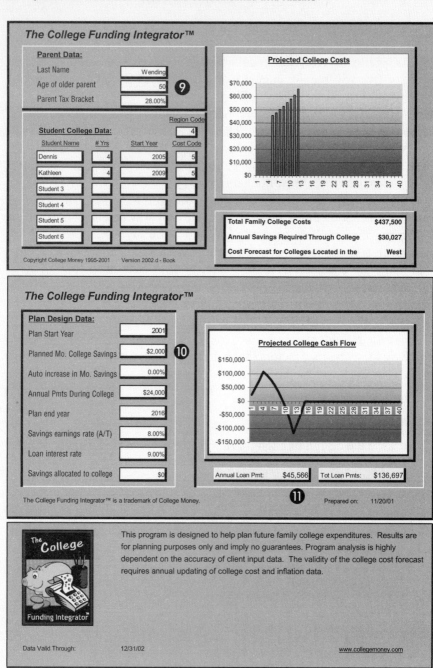

FIGURE 6.6 Wending Family—First Illustration
Shows Enormous Loan Payments

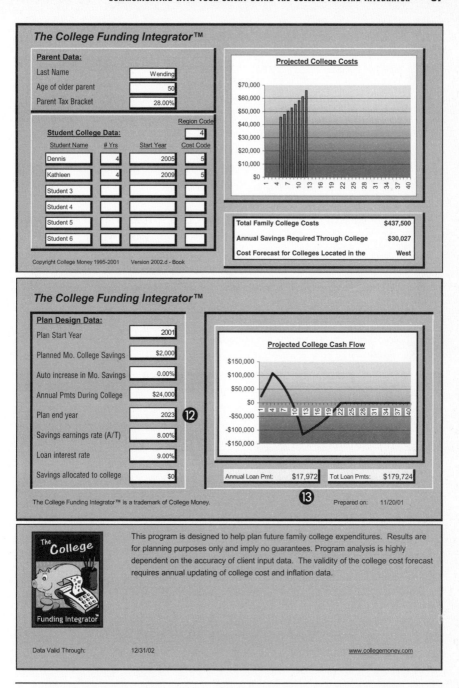

FIGURE 6.7 Wending Family—Second Illustration Shows Delaying
Retirement Makes Loan Payments More Reasonable

Loan rates are especially important in plans that use a long recovery period. You can also use The College Funding Integrator™ to show how different loan interest rates will affect the college plan. Let us go back to the Wending case above and look at two loan rates. Remember, the Wendings extended retirement to age seventy-two to make their college plans work. In Figure 6.8, we changed only the loan interest rate from 9 percent to 7.5 percent. ⑭ Annual payments during the recovery period will decrease from $17,972 to $16,591. ⑮ More importantly to the Wendings, they could use the lower interest rates to shorten the recovery period. Please note in Figure 6.9 that we reduced the recovery period by a year and still reduced annual payments slightly to $17,853. ⑯

Adjustments to the portfolio growth rate can also have a significant impact on a plan. The impact of the growth rate is accentuated when

- The savings period is long.

- The plan is seeded with a lump sum, the larger the better.

- The monthly savings rate is constant and high.

Before increasing the growth rate to make the plan look better you should discuss investment risk with your client. Traditionally, college savings plans have been designed to be aggressive when children are young and gradually made more conservative as money was needed to pay college bills. This causes overall returns to be lower. One tool that planners may wish to utilize is the federal PLUS loan. Federal PLUS loans can provide liquidity to pay college bills. Most parents find them easy to qualify for, and parents can borrow the entire college bill each year if necessary. PLUS loans are signature loans and require only good credit, not collateral.

The Cohlers are good savers but are very conservative. They have two children, Max, aged six, and Adam, aged three. They currently have $50,000 set aside for college in CDs yielding 4.5 percent. They are saving $400 monthly so that they can pre-fund college for each of their sons at an eastern state college. They do not feel that they can save more money for college. They are also concerned about avoiding college debt.

Figure 6.10 shows how their current plan will work. Their current investment plan comes up short and will cause the Cohlers to take on substantial total loan payments of $197,743, or $17,977 annually. ⑰

Figure 6.11 shows how the Cohlers' plan will work if their investment return increases to 7.5 percent. ⑱ Total college loan payments are reduced significantly to $4,005. ⑲

Of course it is the advisor's job to make sure that investment risks are appropriate. Often, however, college savings plans have long planning

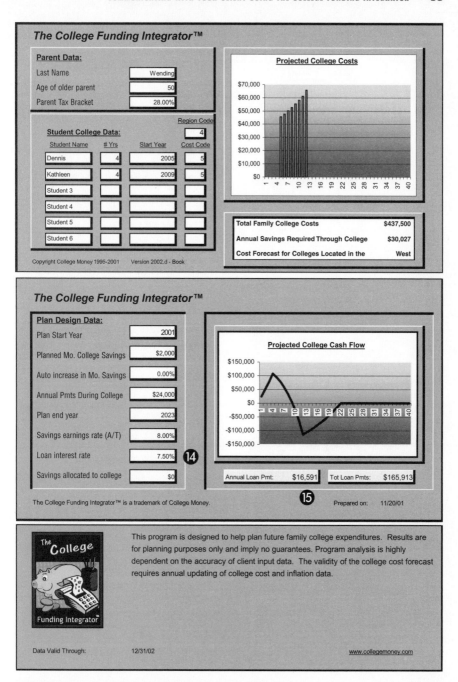

FIGURE 6.8 Wending Family—Reduced Loan Interest Rate to 7.5 Percent, Providing Savings of $18,279

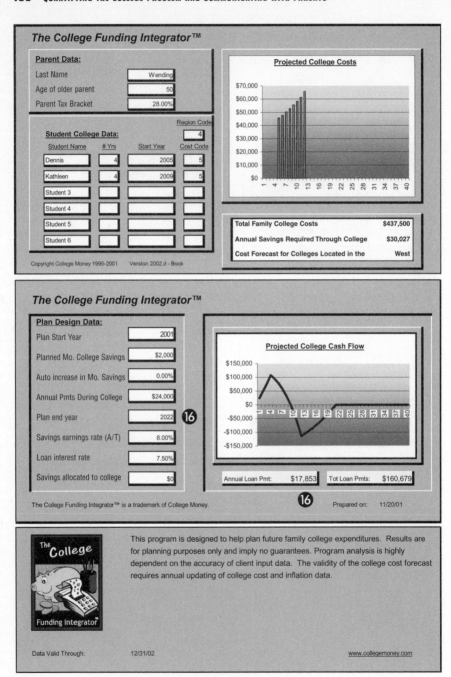

FIGURE 6.9 Wending Family—Reduced Recovery Period by One Year

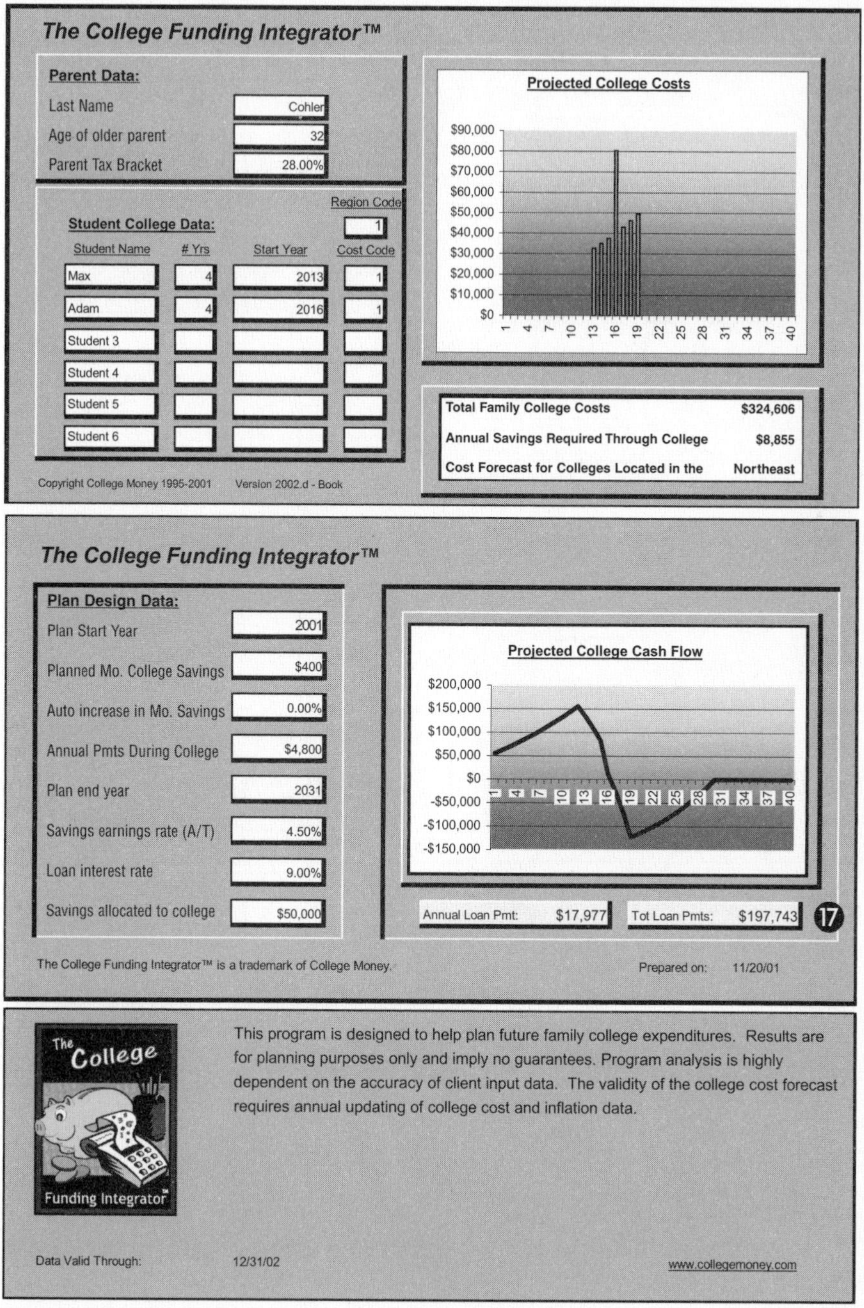

The College Funding Integrator™

Parent Data:

Last Name	Cohler
Age of older parent	32
Parent Tax Bracket	28.00%

Student College Data:

Region Code: 1

Student Name	# Yrs	Start Year	Cost Code
Max	4	2013	1
Adam	4	2016	1
Student 3			
Student 4			
Student 5			
Student 6			

Copyright College Money 1995-2001   Version 2002.d - Book

Projected College Costs

Total Family College Costs	$324,606
Annual Savings Required Through College	$8,855
Cost Forecast for Colleges Located in the	Northeast

The College Funding Integrator™

Plan Design Data:

Plan Start Year	2001
Planned Mo. College Savings	$400
Auto increase in Mo. Savings	0.00%
Annual Pmts During College	$4,800
Plan end year	2031
Savings earnings rate (A/T)	4.50%
Loan interest rate	9.00%
Savings allocated to college	$50,000

Projected College Cash Flow

Annual Loan Pmt:	$17,977	Tot Loan Pmts:	$197,743

The College Funding Integrator™ is a trademark of College Money.   Prepared on: 11/20/01

This program is designed to help plan future family college expenditures. Results are for planning purposes only and imply no guarantees. Program analysis is highly dependent on the accuracy of client input data. The validity of the college cost forecast requires annual updating of college cost and inflation data.

The College Funding Integrator™

Data Valid Through: 12/31/02   www.collegemoney.com

FIGURE 6.10 Cohlers' Original Plan

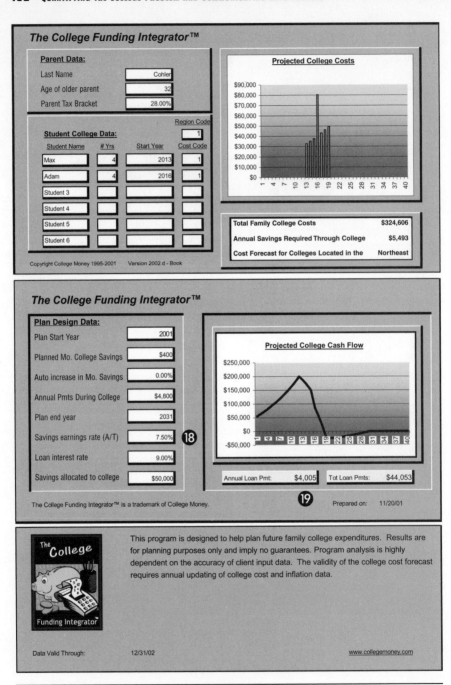

FIGURE 6.11 Cohler Plan Using Increased Rate of Return

horizons. Remember college savings plan returns need to stay ahead of college inflation because college inflation has almost always been higher than CPI. All of these factors need to be considered in the college savings plan design.

One final note is that savings in the early years compound faster than savings later on. Once a plan is developed, it is important for parents to consistently contribute to the plan. Many parents interrupt college savings plans when money gets tight. They tend not to interrupt retirement plans because the dollars are taken right out of their paycheck. These withdrawals are difficult to stop; therefore, they do not stop. Setting college savings plans on a "pay yourself first" basis also works to keep savings constant and consistent. Using automatic checking account withdrawals to fund college works well in achieving that consistency.

There are several other changes you as advisors can test using The College Funding Integrator.™ They include

- Committing more or fewer existing assets to the college plan

- Delaying the start of college

- Saving more or less each year during the savings period

Exploring some or all of these options will allow the advisor to fine-tune the plan. Using The College Funding Integrator™ coupled with the advisors' knowledge and creativity should help finalize the numeric part of the plan. Next will be to add the tools and products that the advisor finds suitable for each particular client.

Chapter 7 explores the integration and balancing of tax savings, financial aid, control of money issues, return on investment, and creditor protection as a prelude to choosing the appropriate college funding tools and products.

PART

II

Exploring College Planning Tools and Products

Beginning Plan Design Using The Attribute Evaluation Worksheet™

n the last six chapters, we explored a number of tools and concepts that we can use to help a client quantify the college funding problem. Using these tools, clients will have a pretty good idea of how much money they will need to

- Save before college

- Take out of income during the college years

- Borrow during the college years

- Repay during the recovery period

In the next few chapters, we are going to examine a number of tools, products, and strategies to fund the college savings plan.

This chapter introduces a new tool, The Attribute Evaluation Worksheet.™ The Attribute Evaluation Worksheet™ helps us create a framework of analysis to evaluate tools, products, and strategies that we may consider using to help us understand their appropriateness to the client's plan. There are a number of attributes or potential benefits that we might want to build into a college funding plan. Not every tool can supply all the benefits we might want. Some tools will be more efficient in supplying these benefits than others. No one tool will be appropriate for all situations. Before we can choose the appropriate tool to solve the college problem, we need to know which attributes are important to the client and which tools will give us the best attribute mix for that client's situation.

The attributes that we are referring to fit into four distinct classifications:

- Taxes

- Financial aid

- Control

- Creditor protection

Every client wants to save *taxes*. We also know that if money grows on a tax-deferred, or better yet a tax-free basis, our plan dollars will grow faster. Whenever possible we want to keep dollars in the plan and not give them to the taxman. There are four types of taxes that usually affect a college funding plan. They include

- Federal income taxes

- State income taxes

- Estate taxes

- Gift taxes

Not all these taxes are significant all the time, but in the world of college planning, all of them crop up at one time or another.

In Chapters 2 and 3, we discuss the implications of *financial aid* on college funding plans. Financial aid is not a factor for all clients or even for some clients all the time. Clients may not benefit from financial aid every year but may get significant benefits when two or three students are in college at the same time. These "pockets of aid" can be significant. Sometimes financial aid benefits can dwarf tax savings. When we evaluate a college funding tool or product, we need to be sensitive to what effect they will have on both financial aid methodologies:

- The federal methodology

- The institutional methodology

Control issues are sometimes given less scrutiny than they should be by advisors. There are two major concerns here:

- When do parents effectively transfer control of dollars to their student?

- When do parents transfer control of the investment decisions to someone else, and how might this transfer impact the rate of return or the risk incurred with the college savings portfolio?

Creditor protection also needs to be given more attention by advisors than it often is. Sometimes parents work in professions in which there is an ongoing potential of a major lawsuit. Sometimes parents are concerned over their students' spending habits. It may be valuable to be able to creditor-proof a college savings account.

Table 7.1, The Attribute Evaluation Worksheet,™ can be used as a tool to tabulate what you know about your client with regard to the college planning attributes listed above. It allows you to highlight which attributes are most important to the client with whom you are currently working. In the balance of this chapter and in Chapters 8 and 9, we list tools, products, titling techniques, and strategies that you can evaluate for each client. We tabulate potential attributes of each tool in a format that is similar to the worksheet. This should make it easier for you to choose the right tool.

TABLE 7.1 The Attribute Evaluation Worksheet™

Prepared for _____

Prepared on _____

Attribute	Why Important?	Attribute Ranking
Taxes		
Federal income tax		
State income tax		
Federal estate tax		
Federal gift tax		
Financial Aid		
Federal methodology		
Institutional methodology		
Control Issues		
Investment control		
Ownership rights		
Flexibility		
Creditor Protection		

Using the Attribute Evaluation Worksheet™

Suppose that you have a client, Jonathan Miller, a grandparent, who wants to set up a college plan for his son Robert's two children. In completing an interview with the client, we uncover the following facts:

- Jonathan has been doing some estate planning. One of his primary goals is to reduce the size of his estate.

- Jonathan makes a lot of money and complains vociferously about how much he has to pay in taxes each year.

- Robert is in business for himself. He has a moderate income. He is concerned about all the recent lawsuits that seem to be occurring in his industry.

- You complete a Financial Aid Test™ for Robert. He is not likely to qualify for any type of aid.

- Jonathan tells you that once a plan is set up, he does not want to worry about investments. He wants reasonable growth and is willing to take reasonable risks.

- Jonathan has some concerns about his "flakey" grandchildren. He wants to make sure that the money is used for education.

Table 7.1a shows how you can use The Attribute Evaluation Worksheet™ to record your thoughts. Attribute rankings are usually arbitrary, but they can help you weight the importance of each attribute based on feelings and soft data you gather from an interview. There is no right or wrong way to use the worksheet, but it is a helpful guide during the interview and the design process.

TABLE 7.1a The Attribute Evaluation Worksheet™

Prepared for *Jonathan Miller* Prepared on _____		
Attribute	Why Important?	Attribute Ranking
Taxes		
Federal income tax	■ *Jonathan does not want to incur additional income tax liability.* ■ *Robert is also in a relatively high bracket.*	2

TABLE 7.1a The Attribute Evaluation Worksheet™ *(Continued)*

Attribute		Why Important?	Attribute Ranking
	State income tax	■ *Jonathan lives in NY with a high state income tax.* ■ *Robert has no state income tax.*	2
	Federal estate tax	*Jonathan's primary goal is to reduce estate taxes.*	1
	Federal gift tax		
Financial Aid			
	Federal methodology	*Financial aid is not a factor.*	
	Institutional methodology	*Financial aid is not a factor.*	
Control Issues			
	Investment control	*Not of major concern.*	
	Ownership rights	*Jonathan wants to ensure funds are not misused.*	4
	Flexibility		
Creditor Protection			
		Robert is concerned about lawsuits.	3

The Importance of Account Titling

In addition to the key attributes we discussed above, we need to also consider how account titling can change the attributes of a planning tool. For example, sometimes whether a financial product or a planning tool is titled in the name of a parent, a trust, a grandparent, or a student can change how the tool or product will affect taxes or financial aid. Because this can be so critical, it is important to discuss ownership issues and how they affect each of our key attributes. There are a large number of options available for titling assets. In choosing the ownership options reviewed below, we selected those that are among the most popular, some that are frequently abused, and a few that are underutilized in the college planning process. They include

■ Direct parent ownership

■ Joint accounts (parent and student)

■ Direct student ownership

- UGMA (Uniform Gifts to Minors Act) or UTMA (Uniform Transfers to Minors Act) accounts

- Ownership by a grandparent or other relative

- Ownership by a trust

- Ownership by a business

  — Sole proprietorship

  — C Corporation

- Ownership by an FLP (Family Limited Partnership) or LLC (Limited Liability Company)

Please understand that this is not meant to be a complete resource on account titling. If you are not familiar with some of the account titling terms, you may need to supplement your knowledge from another source. It is important that advisors focus equally on tools used and the titling of those tools. A saving account for college may seem to be a simple tool, but ownership changes on that account can change the attributes of the account radically.

In the next two chapters, we apply our analysis framework and our knowledge of college planning account titling to a series of college planning tools and products to help advisors and clients make good choices.

It is important to understand that no matter which planning tool is used or which way accounts are titled, there will always be tradeoffs among tax, financial aid, and control issues. Usually choosing a tax attribute costs a financial aid benefit or a control benefit. Conversely, choosing a control attribute often causes loss of financial aid and tax benefits. The job of the advisor is to understand where your client can benefit most and choose the appropriate vehicles to complete the plan. The treatment below assumes that the advisor has a basic knowledge of account titling. The summary below is designed only to review some account titling options and focus in on the college planning aspects of those options.

Direct Parent Ownership

One way of setting up college accounts is to make a parent the owner. Two examples of direct parent ownership include the following types of account titling:

- John J. Smith

- John J. Smith, In Trust for Mary C. Smith

In each of these cases John J. Smith has his social security number listed on the account. As long as John is alive, he controls the account and he pays taxes on any taxable income or gains. Some advisors like to use the "In Trust for" designation, not so much for beneficiary designation but because it allows easy identification of the person that the funds are put aside for, in this case the student. Sometimes this type of account can backfire. At the death of the owner the ownership changes to that of the beneficiary. This changes the attributes of the account to those of a student-owned account discussed in a later section and summarized in Table 7.5. Table 7.2 summarizes how direct parent ownership affects each of the key college planning attributes listed earlier.

TABLE 7.2 Summary—Direct Parent Ownership

Taxes	
Federal income tax	Taxes paid by parent at his or her normal tax bracket.
State income tax	Taxes paid by parent at his or her normal tax bracket.
Federal estate tax	If owned at death, taxable at parent's estate tax bracket, if any.
Federal gift tax	Not usually a factor; no gifts have been made because the parent is keeping ownership.
Financial Aid	
Federal methodology	■ 6 percent rule applies to asset value.
	■ 47 percent rule applies to investment income.
Institutional methodology	■ 5 percent rule applies to asset value.
	■ 46 percent rule applies to investment income.
Control Issues	
Investment control	Parent has complete investment choice—no restrictions.
Ownership rights	Parent can use account proceeds as he or she chooses— parent can shift between college, retirement, or whatever.
Flexibility	Maximum flexibility.
Creditor Protection	As an asset of the parent, the account assets are subject to creditor claims of the parent.

Parent-owned accounts are usually most beneficial in college planning when

■ Parent's tax bracket is low.

■ Student's financial aid probability is high.

■ There is a need for parent control of money.

Beware of the "In Trust for" account. The easy ID feature is convenient, but the death of the original owner can destroy a plan.

Joint Accounts

A number of joint titling options are available. Generally, joint ownership between spouses affects the college plan in a manner similar to direct parent ownership. Joint ownership between parent and student, however, can sometimes be useful in a college funding plan situation. Tables 7.3 and 7.4 and the summaries that follow demonstrate how.

TABLE 7.3 Summary—Joint Ownership between Parent and Student
(Parent Social Security Number on Account)

Taxes

Federal income tax	At parent's tax bracket.
State income tax	At parent's tax bracket.
Federal estate tax	At parent's tax bracket.
Federal gift tax	Usually none—if amounts deposited by student are large and parent withdraws them, gift taxes may come into play.

Financial Aid

Federal methodology	▪ 6 percent rule applies to asset value.
	▪ 50 percent rule applies to investment income.
Institutional methodology	▪ 5 percent rule applies to asset value.
	▪ 50 percent rule applies to investment income.

Control Issues

Investment control	Both have equal rights, but parent can usually exercise practical control.
Ownership rights	Both.
Flexibility	Flexible.

Creditor Protection   Could be subject to the creditors of both parent and student.

Joint ownership between parent and student using the parent's social security number is useful to handle student earnings in a situation where financial aid is probable and total taxes will not be too high. The student can draw from the account, making the student feel he or she has control over dollars the student has earned; yet for financial aid purposes, the money belongs to the parent.

The second joint ownership option we need to investigate has the student's social security number on the account. Table 7.4 highlights how each key factor works in this situation.

TABLE 7.4 Summary—Joint Ownership between Parent and Student (Student Social Security Number on Account)

Taxes

Federal income tax	At student's tax bracket.
State income tax	At student's tax bracket.
Federal estate tax	At student's tax bracket.
Federal gift tax	Usually none. If the student deposits large dollar amounts and the parent makes a withdrawal, there may be gift tax consequences.

Financial Aid

Federal methodology	■ 35 percent rule applies to asset value.
	■ 50 percent rule applies to investment income.
Institutional methodology	■ 25 percent rule applies to asset value.
	■ 50 percent rule applies to investment income.

Control Issues

Investment control	Both have equal rights, but parent can usually exercise control.
Ownership rights	Both.
Flexibility	Flexible.

Creditor Protection	Could be subject to the creditors of both parent and student.

This is often a choice used for student accounts because the consequences are not thought out properly. Parents want to be on the account for emergency purposes. If financial aid is not a factor, this type of titling works well because the student is usually in a lower tax bracket.

Generally most parents and advisors do not think about these accounts because they are usually small and they think only of the convenience. Lost financial aid can be significant when the student's social security number is used.

Please note that the death of the parent can change the ownership attributes of a joint account. The student becomes the owner, and the tax and financial aid attributes change. Because attributes change, it is usually desirable to keep balances in these accounts small.

Direct Student Ownership

Direct ownership by the student occurs rarely in college planning, and it often causes a problem when it does. Usually a student sets up a savings or checking account to deposit money from high school job earnings or for convenience at college. If financial aid is probable, these accounts can hurt. Often the better option is the joint account with the parent, using the parent's social security number. Please note that the ownership effect on key attributes in Table 7.5 is substantially similar to those in Table 7.4 above.

TABLE 7.5 Summary—Direct Student Ownership

Taxes

Federal income tax	At student's tax bracket.
State income tax	At student's tax bracket.
Federal estate tax	At student's estate tax bracket.
Federal gift tax	Not applicable—no gift is made.

Financial Aid

Federal methodology	■ 35 percent rule applies to asset value.
	■ 50 percent rule applies to investment income.
Institutional methodology	■ 25 percent rule applies to asset value.
	■ 50 percent rule applies to investment income.

Control Issues

Investment control	Student
Ownership rights	Student
Flexibility	Parent cannot easily use the money. Student would need to make a gift, and in some situations the student may not have the legal capacity to do so.

Creditor Protection	Dollars are subject to the student's creditors.

UGMA or UTMA Accounts

UGMA and UTMA accounts used to be a mainstay in college planning. Today they have diminished in value largely due to the "Kiddie Tax." Furthermore, the creation of alternative tax vehicles such as the Education Savings Account (formerly Education IRA) and the Qualified Tuition Plan (Section 529 Plan) have served to make UGMA and UTMA accounts less attractive. Finally, the Institutional Methodology has begun including accounts titled in the college student's younger siblings' names as a parent asset. This means that parents can no longer reduce assets for financial aid purposes by putting money in a UGMA account in a younger sibling's name. This strategy double backfires because when the younger student goes to college later on, this asset counts as a student asset at the 25 percent rate.

UTMA accounts are newer and slightly more liberal than the UGMA account. You cannot arbitrarily use a UTMA over a UGMA or a UGMA over a UTMA. State law determines which account titling is available. Every state has adopted a law authorizing either a UGMA or UTMA account to make it easy to transfer assets to a minor and for parents or custodians to manage those transferred assets on behalf of a minor until the minor becomes an adult. There are two basic differences between the two accounts:

- Assets that can be placed into these accounts vary slightly:

  — UGMA authorizes cash, bank accounts, stocks, bonds, mutual funds, and so forth.

  — UTMA broadens the holdings to include real estate, limited partnership interests, and so forth.

- Age of majority is more flexible under the UTMA structure:

  — UGMA sets the age of majority at either 18 or 21 depending on state law.

  — UTMA gives the custodian some leeway to set the age of majority.

Gifts made to either UGMA or UTMA accounts are considered gifts of present interest and therefore eligible for the $11,000 annual gift exclusion.

Interest income from a custodial account is taxed to the minor, who is usually in a lower tax bracket than his or her parents. But if the minor is under the age of fourteen, the "Kiddie Tax" comes into play.

From a financial aid standpoint, assets are considered student assets.

Table 7.6 summarizes how UGMA or UTMA accounts affect each of the key college planning attributes.

TABLE 7.6 Summary—UGMA or UTMA Accounts

Taxes

Federal income tax	At student's tax bracket—"Kiddie Tax" may apply.
State income tax	At student's tax bracket.
Federal estate tax	Donor funds transferred to accounts are removed from donor's estate.
Federal gift tax	Transfers are gifts of present interest and qualify for the annual gift tax exclusion.

Financial Aid—Accounts are considered student assets.

Federal methodology	■ 35 percent rule applies to asset value.
	■ 50 percent rule applies to investment income.
Institutional methodology	■ 25 percent rule applies to asset value.
	■ 50 percent rule applies to investment income.

Control Issues

Investment control	Custodian controls until majority.
Ownership rights	Custodian makes ownership decisions until majority.
Flexibility	Dollars must be for the benefit of the student because a completed gift is made at the time of transfer. The custodian can spend money on behalf of the student until majority.

Creditor Protection	Most states protect account assets from creditors until majority. Income distributions are not protected.

UGMA and UTMA accounts are probably overused for college planning. Although they give a parent some control while the student is young, that control is lost at majority. There are a number of major disadvantages to these accounts:

- Sometimes students do not go on to college. Because dollars usually transfer to the student at the time of normal entrance to college, the parent can no longer exert control. This money then is often not used for its intended purpose, college. There are many stories of children going to the bank on their eighteenth birthday, withdrawing funds from their UGMA account, and spending the funds against parent wishes on a new car, or worse yet, on a drug habit.

- Sometimes another student in the family needs the funds more. Once put in a UGMA, money is usually difficult to transfer back. Many times a parent would rather direct funds to a different student because of special needs.

- Although there are small tax advantages by utilizing the students' tax bracket, these are limited to the first $1,500 of taxable income in 2001. If the student is under the age of fourteen, the "Kiddie Tax" comes into play, limiting further tax advantages.

Ownership by a Grandparent or Other Relative

Sometimes grandparents and other relatives will want to help with the college savings plan. Their first impulse is to make gifts to a child or a parent. Often they set up UGMA or UTMA accounts. If estate planning motives are present, outright gifts to UGMA accounts or gifts in trust may be beneficial. If not, however, it may be best for the grandparent (or other relative) to retain ownership and make the gift later. The best option depends on maximizing benefits for everyone concerned.

When an external party (grandparent or other relative) maintains ownership, that individual maintains investment control and ownership control. There are no negative financial aid implications because third-party assets are not calculated into the financial aid formulas. Timing of gifts and the manner in which a gift is made can be important to avoid losing financial aid. For example:

- If a grandparent makes a direct tuition payment on behalf of the student, it is treated as though the student received an outside scholarship, and financial aid is reduced on a dollar-for-dollar basis.

- If a grandparent makes a gift prior to the award of financial aid in a given year and the asset is deposited in a savings, investment, or checking account, the asset may count as a student asset and reduce aid by as much as 35 percent of the value of the gift.

■ If the gift is made after a financial aid award is made and the gift is spent for college expenses, the gift will probably have no effect on financial aid.

Table 7.7 summarizes key attributes for external third-party ownership.

TABLE 7.7 Summary—Third-Party Ownership
(Grandparent or Other Relative)

Taxes

Federal income tax	Paid at the third party's tax bracket.
State income tax	Paid at the third party's tax bracket.
Federal estate tax	Asset is in the estate of the third party.
Federal gift tax	Later gifts at larger amount due to asset growth may exceed annual exclusion and may be subject to gift taxes.

Financial Aid

Federal methodology	No implications—If transfers are handled carefully, third-party assets and income are not considered.
Institutional methodology	No implications—If transfers are handled carefully, third-party assets and income are not considered.

Control Issues

Investment control	Third party can invest as desired.
Ownership rights	Third party has full right and can redirect assets as desired.
Flexibility	Maximum.

Creditor Protection	Assets are subject to creditors of the third party—including Medicaid.

Ownership by a Trust

Given the advent of new planning tools and the current taxation of trusts, we will probably see trusts used less and less in college planning. There are two trusts that have been traditionally used that advisors need to know about. They are Section 2503(b) and Section 2503(c) trusts. These trusts, known as minors' trusts, were used primarily because they gave more control to a parent or trustee than did UGMA/UTMA accounts.

Generally, a gift in trust can reduce the estate of the donor. Gift taxes can come into play unless the gift is a gift of present interest. The trust tax bracket can be onerous on undistributed trust income. Trusts can keep investment control in the hands of a trustee, and the distribution of trust proceeds and income can be controlled by the trust document or by the discretion of a trustee.

Disadvantages of trusts include setup and ongoing administrative expenses, high taxes, and, sometimes, inflexible trust rules that make handling the needs of a beneficiary difficult.

Table 7.8 summarizes key college planning attributes for trust ownership.

TABLE 7.8 Summary—Trust Ownership

Taxes	
Federal income tax	If income is not distributed, it is taxed at the trust tax bracket (usually higher than individual tax brackets). If distributed to a beneficiary, the income is taxed at the beneficiary's tax bracket.
State income tax	State income tax rules apply.
Federal estate tax	Usually removed from the estate of the donor.
Federal gift tax	Gift taxes are sometimes incurred in transferring funds to a trust.
Financial Aid	
Federal methodology	■ Usually not an asset for financial aid purposes.
	■ 50 percent rule applies to investment income distributed to the student.
	■ Undistributed income is not counted.
Institutional methodology	■ 25 percent rule applies to asset value (usually imputed to student—financial aid administrators often ask for copies of trust documents.
	■ 50 percent rule applies to investment income distributed to the student.
Control Issues	
Investment control	Trustee is usually limited to the terms of the trust.
Ownership rights	Trustee maintains control but may be forced to distribute trust assets at times specified by the trust document.
Creditor Protection	Trusts offer good creditor protection, but distributions usually are available to creditors.

Ownership by a Business

The main advantage of keeping assets in a business account as opposed to a personal account is a financial aid benefit. The main disadvantage is more exposure to creditor risk.

The financial aid system understands that business assets need to be used by the business. The system also feels that business assets make the owner's balance sheet stronger and, therefore, also strengthen the owner's ability to pay for college. The system thus counts the value of business assets, but discounts their value for financial aid purposes as shown in Table 7.9. For example, your client owns a business with $50,000 of business assets.

The financial aid formulas will reduce this asset to $20,000 before totaling all parent assets as part of either methodology.

TABLE 7.9 Business Asset Discounts for Financial Aid Calculations

Asset Range	Discount Percentage
$0 to $90,000	40%
$90,000 to $275,000	50%
$275,000 to $445,000	60%
Over $445,000	100%

Table 7.10 summarizes key attributes for ownership by a sole proprietorship.

TABLE 7.10 Summary—Business Ownership: Sole Proprietor

Taxes

Federal income tax	Taxed at the business owner's personal tax bracket.
State income tax	Taxed at the business owner's personal tax bracket. May also be subject to state business taxes in some states.
Federal estate tax	Evaluated as part of the business for estate tax purposes.
Federal gift tax	N/A—no gifts are being made.

Financial Aid

Federal methodology	■ Considered a parent asset—6 percent rule discounted as much as 40 percent to 2.4 percent (40 percent × 6 percent) depending on total value of business assets.
	■ 47 percent rule applies to investment income.
Institutional Methodology	■ Considered a parent asset—6 percent rule discounted as much as 40 percent to 2.4 percent depending on total value of business assets.
	■ 46 percent rule applies to investment income.

Control Issues

Investment control	Parent as business owner controls.
Ownership rights	Parent as business owner controls.
Flexibility	Flexible.

Creditor Protection — May have more exposure.

A sole proprietor may gain a significant financial aid advantage by characterizing college savings as a business asset because business assets are treated at reduced value. If the business has any significant creditor risks, however, this strategy may not be prudent.

If the business in question is a C corporation, there may be an income tax benefit. Because a C corporation has its own tax bracket, investment income is not automatically passed through to the parent. This means no negative financial aid impact from investment earnings. If the corporate bracket is lower than the parent's personal tax bracket, some financial leverage may come into play. Sometimes dollars for college can actually be stored in a qualified retirement plan or a nonqualified deferred compensation plan that can give both financial aid and tax leverage.

Table 7.11 gives the key college planning attributes for business ownership by a C corporation.

TABLE 7.11 Summary—Business Ownership: C Corporation

Taxes

Federal income tax	At corporate bracket.
State income tax	At corporate bracket.
Federal estate tax	Estate of the parent—sometimes discounted for lack of business liquidity.
Federal gift tax	No gifts are being made.

Financial Aid—Considered parent assets.

Federal methodology	■ 6 percent rule applies to asset value after discounting as a business asset. ■ Corporate income—none.
Institutional methodology	■ 3 to 5 percent rule applies to asset value after business discount. ■ Income—none.

Control Issues

Investment control	Parent has discretion over corporate assets.
Ownership rights	Parent has discretion over corporate assets.
Flexibility	High.

Creditor Protection | Subject to business creditors.

Ownership by an FLP or LLC

Family limited partnerships (FLPs) or limited liability companies (LLCs) offer some ownership opportunities that need to be examined. They are particularly interesting for wealthy clients and especially for wealthy grandparents who want to exert control. From a financial aid perspective they create assets that may be heavily discounted and an income stream that can be closely controlled. This makes them interesting when grandchildren are not so wealthy. From a creditor protection viewpoint, they offer heavy potential protection. The biggest disadvantage is setup cost and the ongoing cost of administration.

Table 7.12 summarizes key planning attributes for ownership by an FLP.

TABLE 7.12 Summary—Family Limited Partnership and LLC

Taxes

Federal income tax	Income is apportioned among partners by the managing partner. Each partner pays tax on that partner's proportionate share.
State income tax	Income is apportioned among partners by the managing partner. Each partner pays tax on his or her proportionate share.
Federal estate tax	In each partner's estate to the extent of ownership. Share values are often discounted for lack of liquidity.
Federal gift tax	Gift taxes can be significant. Careful planning is required.

Financial Aid

Federal methodology	■ Asset values will be based on share values. ■ Income distribution can be controlled by the managing partner.
Institutional methodology	■ Asset values will be based on share values. ■ Income distribution can be controlled by the managing partner.

Control Issues

Investment control	Managing partner.
Ownership rights	Each partner owns his or her own shares.
Flexibility	Moderate.

Creditor Protection

	Most creditors do not want involvement with FLP or LLC shares because they may have tax liability and an unfriendly managing partner not willing to distribute cash to pay the tax bill.

Summary Checklist

As a final checklist, some account titling and ownership options help advisors build desirable benefits or attributes into a plan. The following list is a partial summary of some of these attributes and some of the account titling options that should be investigated when those assets are desired:

■ Parent tax brackets are high.

— UGMA/UTMA accounts

— FLPs or LLCs

■ Financial aid is probable.

— Direct parent ownership

— Joint ownership (parent/student with parent's social security number)

- — C corporation ownership
- — Grandparent/other relative ownership
- Parent wants control.
  - — Direct parent ownership
  - — FLPs or LLCs
- Creditor protection is important.
  - — FLPs or LLCs
  - — Trusts
  - — UGMA/UTMA accounts
- Estate taxes are an issue.
  - — UGMA/UTMA accounts
  - — FLPs or LLCs
  - — Trust ownership

In the next two chapters, we look at some specific college planning tools.

Exploring the
College Funding Tools

I n Chapter 7, we develop the framework of analysis that is used to begin
the process of choosing the appropriate tools for the college plan. So we
need to ask to what extent the tool will provide financial aid benefits,
tax benefits, control of money, and creditor proofing. Account titling is
an integral part of the framework because it can change the attributes and
benefits of a particular tool.

Now we need to begin the task of choosing the best college funding
tool. This chapter examines the myriad options available to families. Some
have been very specifically designed as college savings tools through state
and federal legislation. Others are more generic, but at the same time they
can fit the needs of the plan like a glove. The tools we will analyze include

- U.S. Savings Bond College Savings Plan

- Coverdell Education Savings Account College Funding Plan

- IRA College Savings Plan and Roth IRA College Savings Plan

- The Simple Plan™

- Life Insurance College Savings Plan

- Retirement Plan College Savings Plan

- Direct tuition payments to the college by grandparents

- Qualified Tuition Plans, both Prepaid Plans and Savings Plans (these are
  discussed in Chapter 9).

Using the information learned in earlier chapters, we look at each tool through the four filters that impact the success of any college savings plan: the effect on financial aid, the effect of taxes, control of money issues, and creditor proofing. In addition, we specifically discuss the account titling that is appropriate for each tool when used in a college savings plan. Naturally, the impact of inflation and return on investment are fundamental parts of any savings accumulation program, so each planner should examine the underlying investments of each tool.

U.S. Savings Bond College Savings Plan

Savings bonds have a unique feature that people have capitalized on for years—payroll deduction. Successful savers know that money taken out of their paychecks is rarely missed. Uncle Sam has collected millions of dollars through savings bonds over the past century by making it easy to do.

In the late 1980s the federal government made it even more attractive to use savings bonds to save for college by making the interest tax-free under certain circumstances. Table 8.1 details the limitations on using savings bonds to save for college. The income phaseout precludes many parents from taking advantage of the tax-free growth of the bonds.

TABLE 8.1 The Rules for Series EE and Series I Savings Bonds

All or part of the interest on EE bonds and I bonds is tax-free if the bonds are used for college tuition and fees under certain circumstances:

- The bond must have been purchased after December 31, 1989.

- The owner must be at least twenty-four years old *before* the bond issue date.

- The funds must be used for tuition and fees for a dependent, spouse, or the bond owner at a qualifying educational institution.

- Room and board and books are not qualified expenses.

- Qualified expenses do include contributions to a state tuition program or an Education Savings Account.

- If the amount redeemed exceeds the actual education expenses in the year of redemption, the amount that can be excluded from income taxes is based on the ratio of expenses to the redemption amount.

- Married taxpayers filing separately may not use the bond exclusion.

- Modified AGI phaseout effective January 1, 2002:

  1. Married filing jointly—$81,100 to $111,100.

  2. Single or head of household—$54,100 to $69,100.

  3. Married filing separately—Not Eligible.

Account Titling

It is important to note that in order to take advantage of the tax-free interest feature of U.S. Savings Bonds, the *owner* of the bond had to have been at least twenty-four years old at the time of purchase. So bonds in the traditional aged student's name do not qualify for the exemption. Conversely, a parent who decides to go to college or graduate school could use the bonds for him- or herself and get the exemption on the interest if they can meet the income phaseout.

Financial Aid

The ownership of savings bonds determines the financial aid treatment. Therefore, bonds owned by a parent are assessed at the 5 to 6 percent rate, and those owned by the student figure into the calculation at 25 to 35 percent. Although when the parent bonds are cashed the interest is tax-free when used for qualified education expenses, the financial aid forms do add the interest to the parents' income. So income is attributed to the parent.

Note that if the parent is the student, then the asset and the income are assessed at the student rates. For purposes of Table 8.2, we assumed a typical scenario of parent-owned bonds being used for a traditional aged student.

Tax Savings

Interest is tax-free when used for tuition and fees, when the bond owner's modified AGI is below the limits set by the Treasury Department. U.S. Savings Bonds are always state-income-tax-free. There is no special treatment for federal estate taxes or federal gift taxes. The usual rules would apply in these cases. Please note, to arrive at the modified AGI, bond interest must be included even though it may not ultimately be taxed. This often will push parents above the phaseout limits.

U.S. Savings Bonds can be rolled into a Coverdell Education Savings Account or a Qualified Tuition Account without creating a taxable event. Here is the way it works:

- The bonds must be cashed in, but if the cash is then deposited in an Education Savings Account or a Qualified Tuition Account within sixty days, there is no tax due.

- The process is very similar to the old IRA rollover. The taxpayer should be careful to maintain the paper trail.

- This is a tax-savings strategy for families that begin as financial aid candidates but over time move into the group of families that will not qualify for need-based financial aid.

■ It also broadens the possible use of the funds. For example, when rolled into an Education Savings Account the money can now be used for K–12 expenses. If rolled into a QTP, the funds can then be used for room and board, books, and so forth, as well.

Control of Money

Parents exert considerable control over the U.S. Savings Bond College Plan. They can decide whether to cash them in, when to cash them in, and how to use the money. There is no requirement that the bonds be used for education even if that was the original intention. If retirement appears to be more important, the parents can hold the bonds until later and pay the tax due on the interest.

From a perspective of return on investment, by choosing U.S. Savings Bonds, the parents are pretty much making the decision how aggressive they want to be with their investment. It should be noted that the rate of return on Series EE U.S. Savings Bonds is not likely to keep pace with college inflation, making them not very effective when it comes to saving for those exorbitant college bills.

However, in 1998 the Treasury Department began offering Series I bonds that are indexed for inflation. They do offer a slightly better potential rate of return. These relatively new bonds offer a fixed rate of 3 percent. Then on a semiannual basis, each May and November, the semiannual inflation rate is added to the fixed rate. Bear in mind, however, that deflation causes the rate to be lower than the fixed rate. The Treasury Department will not let the bond decrease from its most recent redemption value.

Creditor Protection

U.S. Savings Bonds are available to the creditors of the owner. Therefore, if this is a major issue with clients, you may wish to explore some of the other tools we have that offer more creditor protection.

When to Use U.S. Savings Bonds

In spite of the drawbacks of U.S. Savings Bonds, if a planner has a client who is a conservative investor and who has a very difficult time saving on a regular basis, payroll deduction savings bonds might provide some sort of a buffer for them.

If they meet the income phaseout limits, it is possible they might qualify for some need-based financial aid. Therefore, it is important to consider carefully when to cash in the bonds. As we noted previously, the interest income must be reported on the financial aid forms. This increases the expected family contribution, resulting in a loss of some need-based financial aid.

One of the anomalies of savings bonds as a college planning tool is that they give a tax benefit to lower-income taxpayers, who get only marginal benefits from the tax savings. These taxpayers normally would qualify for financial aid. Cashing in the bonds lumps years of income together, causing a larger, more concentrated loss of aid. For this reason, bonds are probably best used in the senior year of college, or to cover part-time school costs of a parent when financial aid is not a factor. Table 8.2 summarizes key planning attributes for using parent-owned U.S. Savings Bonds as a college funding tool for a traditional age student.

TABLE 8.2 Summary—U.S. Savings Bond College Plan, Parent-Owned/Traditional Age Student

---

Taxes

Federal income tax	Taxed at parent bracket when cashed unless used for qualified education expense.
State income tax	None. U.S. Savings Bonds are tax-exempt at the state level.
Federal estate tax	If parent(s) die, income tax will be due and the asset is included in the estate.
Federal gift tax	If parents are the owner, then no gift has been made.

Financial Aid

Federal methodology	■ Asset—6 percent reduction in financial aid. ■ Income—47 percent reduction in financial aid.
Institutional methodology	■ Asset—3 percent to 5 percent reduction in financial aid. ■ Income—46 percent reduction in financial aid.

Control Issues

Investment control	Only control the parent has is the decision to buy U.S. savings bonds; the underlying investment is predetermined.
Ownership rights	Parent controls transfer of funds—timing and to whom.
Flexibility	Some flexibility is offered in that the owner can decide to transfer to Education Savings Account or Qualified Tuition Plan, keep it for another use, etc.

Creditor Protection | Subject to the creditors of the owner.

Education IRA (Coverdell Education Savings Account) College Funding Plan

Congress enacted the Education IRA as a college savings tool in the mid-1990s. While the elected officials in Washington, DC, were hyping this new tool to encourage college savings, financial advisors quickly recognized its shortcomings. Many mutual fund companies were reluctant to create

Education IRAs because of the danger of how easy it would be to have excess contributions. With the limited contribution amount, it was very possible that two sets of grandparents could create a tracking nightmare by setting up Education IRAs without informing the parents.

June of 2001 brought some modifications to the Education IRAs that are intended to enhance and encourage college savings. This tool was also renamed to the Coverdell Education Savings Account. Table 8.3 details the rules governing use of Education Savings Accounts. Those marked with an asterisk (*) are recent changes enacted in 2001 and became effective after December 31, 2001.

TABLE 8.3 The Rules for Education Savings Accounts

- Contributions are not deductible.
- Maximum annual contribution for each beneficiary is $2,000.*
- Contributions are not allowed after the beneficiary has reached age eighteen.
- Contributions for a taxable year may be made anytime up until the due date for filing the tax return. Extensions are not permitted.*
- Excess contributions must be distributed before June 1 of the taxable year following the contribution year.*
- Income phaseouts for donor contribution are as follows:
  1. Married filing jointly—$190,000 to $220,000.*
  2. All others—$95,000 to $110,000.
- Qualified education expenses include
  1. elementary and secondary education expenses, including tuition, fees, books, supplies, room and board, academic tutoring, special needs services, uniforms, transportation, and supplementary items and services (including extended day care required or provided by the school), computer technology or certain equipment, or internet access if such items are to be used by the beneficiary while the beneficiary is in school.*
  2. For "qualified higher education expenses," room and board are now included if the housing is owned and operated by the school.*
- Age limitations for *special needs beneficiaries* are eliminated with respect to contributions after the beneficiary is age eighteen. Furthermore, the balance in the Education Savings Account need not be distributed after the beneficiary attains age thirty.*
- Contributions can be made to both the Education Savings Account and a qualified tuition program in the same year without penalty.*
- Taxpayers may claim a Hope Scholarship Credit or Lifetime Learning Credit in the same year that amounts are distributed from an Education Savings Account on behalf of the beneficiary as long as there are sufficient qualified education expenses to cover both.*

TABLE **8.3** The Rules for Education Savings Accounts *(Continued)*

- Education Savings Accounts can be rolled over to another member of the original beneficiary's family if the new beneficiary is under age thirty at the time of the rollover. Only one rollover per year is permitted.

- The balance in an Education Savings Account that is not used must be distributed within thirty days of the beneficiary's thirtieth birthday. This results in taxable earnings. (See above for exceptions made for special needs beneficiaries.)

Financial Aid

Education Savings Accounts are not financial aid friendly. The federal financial aid forms treat them as a student asset (remember the 35 percent rule), and the income is also attributed to the student (remember the 50 percent rule). The institutional methodology, on the other hand, treats the asset as the parents' (subject to the 3 to 5 percent rule) and the income as the student's (the 50 percent rule). Remember, although the income may be tax-free, financial aid forms ask about nontaxable income.

Tax Savings

These accounts were specifically created to provide tax savings to encourage parents to save for college. The tax reform of June 2001 further enhanced the benefits by expanding the definition of qualified education expenses and increasing the contribution limit.

Although the contribution itself is not deductible, the gains are tax-free if the funds are used for qualified education expenses. This allows the investment to compound more rapidly, providing more cash to meet college costs.

Contributions are considered to be gifts of present interest and thus qualify for the annual gift tax exclusion of $11,000. Most times this limit is not important. But if a parent contributes a maximum gift of $11,000 to a Qualified Tuition Plan for the student and then also wants to contribute to an Education Savings Account, the contribution would exceed the gift tax exclusion and would be taxable.

Parents that do not meet the income phaseout limits for contributions to an Education Savings Account might consider gifting the contribution amount to their student, who can then deposit it in the student's own Education Savings Account. Note: This will change the attributes of the plan with respect to ability to qualify for financial aid.

Another gift tax trap to be aware of is that if the Education Savings Account is rolled over to a new beneficiary, and the new beneficiary is of a younger generation than the original beneficiary, gift tax may be due.

Federal estate taxes may be due at the death of the beneficiary. However, because the beneficiary is usually a traditional aged student, this probably is of little consequence.

Control of Money

The custodian controls the investment choices in an Education Savings Account and can move to a different investment at will. However, the beneficiary is the owner of the account and is the person who requests the distributions. The custodian cannot stop the beneficiary from taking a distribution even if it is not to be used for qualified education expenses. Unlike custodial accounts where the custodian cannot change the ownership, there is no language in the regulations that says the custodian of the Education Savings Account cannot change the beneficiary if the original beneficiary decides not to go to college. Parents may wish to consult a tax specialist in their state to clarify when the student gains ownership and full control over the Education Savings Account.

The funds must be distributed by the time the beneficiary reaches age thirty or rolled to a new beneficiary. This also acts to limit some of the control that the custodian might wish to have. New legislation does state that if the beneficiary is a special needs student, this mandatory distribution does not apply.

Creditor Protection

Each state has its own laws to govern creditor protection of Education Savings Accounts.

When to Use an Education Savings Account

As you can see by studying the rules surrounding Education Savings Accounts, families are limited as to the amount they can contribute in any one year. The current high cost of college coupled with the effect of college inflation makes such accounts less useful as a savings tool when used alone. It is extremely difficult to accumulate significant savings.

There are applications, however, where an Education Savings Account can prove effective for families that will not qualify for need-based financial aid. Because the custodian can choose the investment and roll the account from one family of funds to another, an Education Savings Account can be used to counterbalance a conservative Section 529 Plan. From a control-of-money perspective, this can be very attractive. Education Savings Accounts, unlike Section 529 Plans, can be used for private school tuition and other qualified education expenses for grades K–12. Despite the limited contribution amounts, this unique feature makes them worth considering.

Education Savings Accounts are very easy ways for grandparents to contribute to a grandchild's education. The only caution is to make sure that there is coordination within the family to ensure that excess contributions are not made because two sets of grandparents set up accounts and made maximum contributions.

Table 8.4 summarizes key planning attributes for using Education Savings Accounts as a college funding tool.

TABLE 8.4 Summary—Education Savings Accounts Funding Plan

Taxes

Federal income tax	None, if used for qualified education expenses.
State income tax	Varies by state.
Federal estate tax	■ If there is a balance in the account when the beneficiary dies, it is included in the beneficiary's estate.
	■ The account would not be included in the custodian's estate.
Federal gift tax NOTE: Although the maximum annual contribution is $2,000, it is possible to exceed the annual gift tax exclusion. Care must be used if other gifts are being made to the student, especially if a QTP is being used.	■ Donor—none if the contribution does not exceed the annual $11,000 gift tax exclusion. Federal law limits the annual contribution to $2,000. ■ Beneficiary—if the designated beneficiary is changed, there is no gift tax if the new beneficiary is in the same generation as the original beneficiary. If the beneficiary is in a younger generation, the rollover is deemed a gift from the original beneficiary to the new beneficiary.

Financial Aid

Federal methodology	Asset and income are attributed to the student.
Institutional methodology	■ Asset attributed to the parent. ■ Income attributed to the student.

Control Issues

Investment control	Custodian has full control over investment decisions.
Ownership rights	The account is owned by the beneficiary, but the custodian exercises control until the beneficiary reaches majority.
Flexibility	Some flexibility for planning purposes.

Creditor Protection | Varies by state. |

IRA College Savings Plan

The tax act of 1997 brought IRAs into the college savings arena. Beginning in 1998 the Act permitted withdrawals from a *regular IRA* to be used for qualified educational expenses, penalty-free. Taxes would be due on the gain portion. Obviously these accounts are titled to the parent or student, whomever owns the IRA. It is important to remember that IRAs were not designed for college savings. They can be a good backup plan for a crisis situation. But there are better tools for college savings. If parents keep in mind that college is really a subset of the retirement problem, then it is clear that they can be creating a bigger problem if they plan to use IRAs to fund college. See Table 8.5 for college rules for regular IRAs.

TABLE 8.5 The Rules for Using Regular IRAs
as a College Funding Tool

- Regular IRAs New Contribution Amounts:
  - $3,000 for years 2002 through 2003.
  - $4,000 for years 2005 through 2007.
  - $5,000 for years 2008 through 2010.
- For taxpayers who have turned 50 before the end of a tax year, there is an additional $500 contribution allowed for years 2002 through 2005, increasing to $1,000 for tax years beginning 2006 and thereafter.
- Income phaseouts for 2002:
  - Married, filing jointly—$54,000 to $64,000.
  - Single or head of household—$34,000 to $44,000.
  - Married, filing single—$0 to $10,000.
- If distributions are taken for qualified education expenses, there is no penalty.
- On tax-deductible IRAs, the entire distribution is taxable income.
- For nondeductible IRAs, the portion representing the nondeductible contribution is not taxed.
- Qualified education expenses include tuition, fees, books, supplies, and room and board if the student is at least a half-time student.

Financial Aid

From a financial aid standpoint, IRAs as an asset are generally not included in the calculation. However, if a distribution is taken, the income reported on the tax return affects the financial aid calculation for the next school year. If the owner of the IRA is the parent, income is assessed at the parent rate, and if the owner is the student, naturally the assessment is at the student income rate.

Taxes

When considering the tax ramifications of using a regular IRA to pay for college, parents must remember that taxes will be due even when the distribution is used for qualified education expenses. The only break is that the penalty for withdrawal before age fifty-nine and a half is not levied in this situation.

Keep in mind that the taxes due will come at the absolute worst time. Not only are you reducing your retirement assets, but you may have to withdraw additional dollars to pay the taxes, *and* the taxes on the tax withdrawal!

Control of Money

Parents have complete control over these funds in parent-owned IRAs. They choose the investment vehicle and they choose if and when to withdraw the money. Student-owned IRAs do not give parents the control over use of the funds they might like to have. Once the student reaches majority, he or she has full control over investment decisions as well as decisions about when and if to liquidate funds.

Creditor Protection

Each state has its own creditor and bankruptcy laws that govern protection of IRAs.

When to Use a Regular IRA

Table 8.6 gives a summary of key planning attributes for use of a parent-owned IRA as a college funding tool. As indicated, it is not advisable to use this as a tool for saving for college. A reinforcing reminder: *When using IRAs as a college funding mechanism, is the parent creating a retirement problem by paying for college using retirement assets that would grow tax-deferred?* It may be more advantageous to use a PLUS loan and pay it off before retirement than to deplete retirement assets that would continue to grow tax-free or tax-deferred. This strategy of saving for retirement rather than for college is discussed in more depth later in the chapter.

TABLE 8.6 Summary—Parent-Owned Regular IRAs When Used for College

Taxes

Federal income tax	■ No penalty if distributions are used for qualified education expenses.
	■ Taxes are due.
State income tax	Most states levy income tax on distributions from retirement accounts.
Federal estate tax	If the proceeds pass to the spouse of the owner, the marital deduction should be available.
Federal gift tax	Not applicable.

Financial Aid

Federal methodology	■ Asset not included.
	■ Income, though nontaxable, is attributed to the parent.
Institutional methodology	■ Asset not included.
	■ Income, though nontaxable, is attributed to the parent.

Control Issues

Investment control	Complete control.
Ownership rights	Full ownership.
Flexibility	Flexible—can be penalty-free withdrawals, but this is not an advisable college savings plan.

Creditor Protection | Creditor protection varies by state.

Roth IRA College Savings Plan

Roth IRAs were created by the tax act of 1997. They allow taxpayers to make after-tax deposits and withdrawals after age fifty-nine and one-half are tax-free. Prior to age fifty-nine and one-half, withdrawals of contribution amounts are tax-free because they went in on an after-tax basis. This makes the contributions, at the very least, available as a college resource. Like the regular IRAs, the gain portion of withdrawals taken before age fifty-nine and one-half if used for qualified education expenses are penalty free but taxable. See Table 8.7 for rules for use of Roth IRAs as a college funding tool.

Financial Aid

From a financial aid standpoint, the asset would not be counted in the federal calculation. Nevertheless, under the institutional methodology, the treatment is not as clear. In the past, institutions did not try to access *any* retirement funds. However, the lack of penalty and the lack of taxation to the extent the distribution is deemed part of the contribution makes

---

TABLE 8.7 The Rules for Use of Roth IRAs as a College Funding Tool

---

- Contributions are nondeductible.

- Contributions are limited to $2,000 or taxable compensation, whichever is less for 2001.

  For 2002, Roth IRAs have new contribution amounts:

  — $3,000 for years 2002 through 2003.

  — $4,000 for years 2005 through 2007.

  — $5,000 for years 2008 through 2010.

- For taxpayers who have turned fifty before the end of a tax year, an additional $500 contribution is allowed for years 2002 through 2005, increasing to $1,000 for tax years beginning 2006 and thereafter.

- Contributions are limited by income phaseouts:

  — Married, filing jointly—$150,000 to $160,000.

  — Single or head of household—$95,000 to $110,000.

  — Married filing single—$0 to 10,000.

- Growth in a Roth IRA is tax-free.

- Distributions are deemed to come from contributions first, then from earnings—no penalty or income tax applies until total withdrawals exceed total contributions.

- When used for qualified education expenses,

  — Distributions are not subject to penalty.

  — Distributions up to the amount of contributions are tax-free.

  — Distributions that exceed contributions are subject to income taxes.

  — EXCEPTION: Distributions are tax-free if made after a five-year holding period and the taxpayer is at least fifty-nine and one-half.

---

the Roth IRA appear available to pay for college from the college's perspective when determining eligibility for the institution's endowment funds.

Although most colleges still do not include a Roth IRA in their calculation, in 2001 we encountered a college that reduced a financial aid award based on the parents' 401(k) and IRA accounts.

In either case, the reportable income, whether taxable or nontaxable, will reduce financial aid in the subsequent year under both methodologies.

Taxes

When evaluating Roth IRAs as college savings tools through the tax filter, Roths allow us to reclaim our contributions tax-free. But the growth is taxable at the parents' bracket. The exception is that if the parent is over age fifty-nine and one-half and has satisfied the five-year holding period, the growth is tax-free. Taxation reduces the amount available to pay for college.

Control of Money

IRAs do give parents control over the investment choices not available in qualified tuition plans. Parents have complete control over if and when to use the money for college.

Creditor Protection

Creditor protection is governed by individual states' laws.

When to Use a Roth IRA

As a final comment about using IRAs and Roth IRAs as a college funding plan, it is important to state that both IRAs and Roth IRAs were designed as retirement savings tools. Parents that save using these vehicles are making a wise decision. However, we believe that saving in an account such as these with the express intention of using them for college is not wise. There are better savings tools for college. IRAs and Roth IRAs should only be used for college funding in a crisis situation as a stopgap measure. And even then, we are reluctant to see parents invade these accounts at the expense of their retirement goals.

Student-owned IRAs and Roth IRAs as college funding vehicles evoke the same response. If parents want to have their children save some of their own money for college, better tools are available for that purpose. Student IRAs can cause a loss of need-based financial aid. If financial aid is not an issue, there are still better tools for college savings. On the other hand, parents may want to encourage their children to save for their own retirement and benefit from the decades of growth compounding.

TABLE **8.8** Summary—Roth IRA College Plan

Taxes

Federal income tax	■ Nondeductible, nontaxable contributions are deemed to be withdrawn first.
	■ Gains are not penalized if used for qualified education expenses.
	■ Tax would be due on gains.
State income tax	Gain is taxable if the state has an income tax.
Federal estate tax	Tax is generally not included if the direct beneficiary is a spouse and the benefits qualify for the marital deduction.
Federal gift tax	Not applicable.

TABLE 8.8 Summary—Roth IRA College Plan *(Continued)*

Financial Aid	
Federal methodology	■ Asset not included.
	■ Income, though nontaxable is attributed to the parent.
Institutional methodology	■ Asset is generally not included. Some colleges are starting to look at these as assets.
	■ Income, though nontaxable, is attributed to the parent.

Control Issues	
Investment control	Full control.
Ownership rights	Full ownership rights.
Flexibility	Flexible—can be penalty-free withdrawals, but not advisable as a college savings plan.

Creditor Protection	Varies by state.

The Simple Plan™

The Simple Plan™ consists of a portfolio of mutual funds owned by the parents. It is a strategy best suited to a family that is likely to qualify for need-based financial aid. Once it has been determined that the family is likely to qualify for need-based financial aid, an asset-allocated portfolio of mutual funds is created with the parents as owners. Regular financial aid tests should be conducted to ensure that the financial aid situation has not changed for the family.

The Simple Plan™ offers an advisor lots of flexibility to do good work for the client. There are no restrictions on which funds to use or what type of asset allocation is designed. Use of The Attribute Evaluation Worksheet™ offers a superior means of working together with clients to analyze their needs and come up with the appropriate strategy.

For example, one family might be more concerned about financial aid and control of money, while another might place considerably more emphasis on tax savings. Traditional college savings portfolios were designed to be aggressive in the early years and reallocated toward conservative as the student neared college. This might not be the optimum plan for a particular family. Using The Simple Plan™ a financial advisor can design a plan to be tax-managed, aggressive, conservative, growth-oriented, or income-oriented, or any combination that fits. Advisors must remind their clients that investment return and principal value of an investment will fluctuate. An investor's shares, when redeemed, may be worth more or less than the original cost.

Exit strategies are also easier to design in The Simple Plan.™ Based on market conditions and the desired attributes of the family, the planner might decide that it is better to leave the mutual fund portfolio intact and use loans to actually pay college bills. Later the funds can be used to make the loan payments. This can work when market conditions make it less attractive to liquidate; or if the family wants to maximize financial aid, the asset is much less damaging as a parent asset than as parent income created by liquidation of the asset.

Financial Aid

This plan is least damaging from a financial aid standpoint because parent assets are included in the financial aid mix to the tune of 5 to 6 percent. In an account that generates taxable gains every year and in which there is no accumulated gain, financial aid is not affected on the income side of the formula. On the other hand, in accounts that did not generate taxable income annually, a substantial amount of income can be generated when the asset is liquidated.

In order to minimize the income impact on financial aid, the family has two options:

1. Liquidate the account in the student's first semester of the junior year of high school. The income will not be included in the financial aid formula for the freshman year of college.

2. Consider using the Federal PLUS loan during college years, and liquidate the mutual funds after financial aid has been awarded for the senior year.

Taxes

While the money is in the parents' names, taxes may be due annually. Although this can reduce the amount of growth each year, it will not be too damaging in the earlier years when the account is smaller.

Later, if one of the annual financial aid tests done during the accumulation period shows that the family circumstances have changed and the family no longer is likely to qualify for need-based aid, an UGMA/UTMA might allow the family to take advantage of some tax breaks. Once the student reaches age fourteen and the Kiddie Tax is no longer an issue, an UGMA/UTMA account allows the parents to gift the appreciated assets to the student. By transferring their cost basis to the student, the gains are taxed at the student's lower bracket.

Control of Money

However, it is important that the family remember that once the funds are in an UGMA/UTMA account, there has been an irrevocable gift. At this point the parents have relinquished some of the control over the money. At the age of majority, age eighteen in some states, the student has the right to take ownership of the account and use the money for anything they want. Although most students would respect the parents' intention that the account be used to pay for college, it is not always the case. Parents need to be very sure of their children's plans.

While the funds are in the parents' names, the children have full control over the accounts. They can make all investment decisions and choose when and how to use the money.

Creditor Protection

The Simple Plan™ is completely exposed to creditors of the parents. There are no protective wrappers surrounding the plan; it consists of parent-owned mutual funds. If later in the plan years the parents gift the money to the student in the form of an UGMA/UTMA account, the asset would have the protection afforded to a minor. However, once the student reaches majority, the funds are once again exposed. In this case, the student's creditors would have access to the funds.

Portfolio Construction

Building a portfolio for The Simple Plan™ can take several different tacks. Which portfolio is used will depend on which attribute is most important to the parents, financial aid or tax savings. Some portfolio options are

- Traditional college planning portfolios

- Combination of nontraditional portfolios and leveraging with loans

- Tax-managed portfolios

A sample of *traditional college planning portfolios* is found in Figure 8.1. In this case, the family is relatively aggressive in the early years. Once the student enters high school, the family begins a systematic reallocation so that by the time college begins, the funds are extremely liquid.

The *second option,* using a combination of nontraditional portfolios and loans, provides lots of flexibility to the family. Under this scenario the parents do not liquidate the accounts as they did in the traditional portfolio

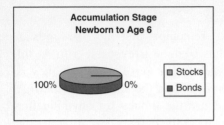

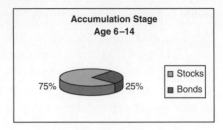

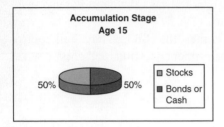

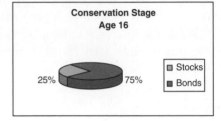

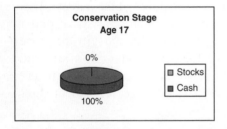

FIGURE 8.1 Sample Traditional College Savings Portfolios

illustration above. Instead they do a financial aid test when the student is age fourteen. If the family is likely to qualify for need-based financial aid, they should hold the account, use loans to pay for college, and liquidate in the student's senior year of college or later. The loans can be a bridge to provide cash flow. Clients should understand that investments could go down and they may have less available to pay off loans.

If, however, the family does a financial aid test when the student is fourteen, and finds they will not qualify for need-based financial aid, then they can gift the appreciated assets to the student, and taxes will be assessed at the student's lower bracket.

The *third option,* tax-managed portfolios, could use investments that would not create taxable income during the accumulation years. Growth funds or tax-exempt funds are examples of this type of investment.

Table 8.9 summarizes the key planning attributes for using The Simple Plan™ as a college funding tool.

TABLE 8.9 Summary—The Simple Plan™

Taxes	
Federal income tax	Parent's bracket—the structure of the portfolio can control taxes.
State income tax	Parent's bracket—the structure of the portfolio can control taxes.
Federal estate tax	Includable in parent's estate at the second death.
Federal gift tax	If funds are put into an UGMA/UTMA account, there is a gift tax due to the extent that the amount in the account exceeds the annual $11,000 exclusion.
Financial Aid	
Federal methodology	Income and assets are attributed to the parents unless there is an UGMA/UTMA account, in which case both income and assets are attributed to the student.
Institutional methodology	Income and assets are attributed to the parents unless there is an UGMA/UTMA account, in which case the income and assets are attributed to the student.
Control Issues	
Investment control	Parents have total control unless the funds are transferred to a UGMA/UTMA account.
Ownership rights	Parents are owners unless funds are transferred to an UGMA/UTMA account.
Flexibility	■ Total flexibility. ■ UGMA/UTMA rules will limit some flexibility.
Creditor Protection	■ Subject to the creditors of the parents. ■ If a UGMA/UTMA account, creditors of the parents cannot access the funds.

Life Insurance College Savings Plan

Use of life insurance as a savings vehicle has its fair share of proponents and detractors. Detractors feel that the internal costs of the insurance reduce the rate of return on the investment portion of the policy, thus making it a poor choice. However, we find that when designed carefully and used with the right client, life insurance can offer significant benefits.

A properly designed life insurance policy can make a very effective college plan. It can have helpful implications regarding all the major attributes we use to evaluate college funding media, including

- Financial aid
- Taxes
- Control of money
- Creditor protection

Generally, a properly designed life insurance policy allows a client to deposit after-tax premium payments, which are invested in the allowable investments as specified in the contract. These investments grow tax-deferred and can be withdrawn tax-free to use for college, retirement, or other uses. Income tax regulations allow nontaxable withdrawals from life insurance contracts under the following situations:

- A policy owner may withdraw cash values from the contract up to the total amount of premiums deposited. These are treated as a tax-free recovery of principal.

- A policy owner may borrow excess cash values from the contract. These loans are interest bearing, but most contracts allow borrowing at a low, net rate of 0 to 1 percent annually.

- If loan balances are accumulated in the contract, they will be repaid from death benefit proceeds before remaining proceeds are paid to a beneficiary. Because life insurance proceeds are income-tax-free, policy loans will be repaid with tax-free dollars.

An important part of the design of a life-insurance-funded college plan is that the policy must be kept in force until the insured dies in order to keep policy withdrawals tax-free. Most insurance carriers have an effective mechanism in place to achieve this result.

Life insurance contracts provide three different classes of investment options. Each of these types of funding media will appeal to different clients' investment needs.

- *Traditional Life* or *Universal Life* offers a conservative investment approach by investing premium dollars in fixed-rate instruments.

- *Variable* or *Variable Universal Life* (VUL) allows the client to invest in a portfolio of mutual funds under the tax-sheltered umbrella of the life insurance wrapper. This tool offers a more aggressive approach that is more likely to keep pace with college inflation. But it carries with it the inherent risks of investing in the stock market.

- *Indexed Life Insurance* is a fixed insurance product that offers its own unique advantages that may be suitable for college planning.

Which type of contract the advisor uses depends on client needs and advisor preferences. Contract design is important regardless of which type of policy is used. Life insurance is normally used to provide a death benefit for a client's family. As such, most contracts attempt to keep the ratio of premiums paid to death benefits low. For college planning, we want to go the other way: We want to maximize the premium dollars going into the contract and minimize the death benefit. Death benefit adds internal costs of the contract that we want to redirect to investment returns. In addition, typical cash values in the early years of a contract are very low. For college funding purposes, it also helps to boost cash values in the early years by reducing or spreading out typical front-end loads. Most insurance companies have riders that can be added to a contract to help maximize cash values.

Because insurance companies are so different, advisors need to explore contract design with each company they consider. The illustrations and examples, which are used in the balance of this chapter, focus on using VUL Insurance as the funding media of choice. The advisor that prefers fixed or indexed life insurance needs to complete a similar analysis of costs and benefits to determine the circumstances under which that product is most effective.

Tables 8.10 and 8.11 are hypothetical ledger illustrations from a properly designed VUL contract assuming a gross rate of return of 8 percent and

TABLE 8.10 Typical VUL College Plan Ledger Illustration for 8 Percent Gross Rate of Return

Assumes Current Cost of Insurance Charges						Gross Earnings Rate Assumption of 8.0%		
Year	Age	Annual Premium	Ann'l Incr. Acc. Value	End of Yr. Acc. Value	End of Yr. Sur. Value	End of Yr. Death Ben	Sur. Value IRR	Death Ben IRR
1	35	$6,000	$5,473	$5,473	$5,367	$157,473	−10.56%	2524.55%
2	36	$6,000	$5,784	$11,257	$11,151	$163,257	−4.79%	374.02%
3	37	$6,000	$6,109	$17,366	$17,260	$169,366	−2.09%	164.80%
4	38	$6,000	$6,440	$23,806	$23,700	$175,806	−0.50%	98.56%
5	39	$6,000	$6,823	$30,629	$30,523	$182,629	0.58%	67.78%
6	40	$6,000	$7,252	$37,882	$37,776	$189,882	1.38%	50.50%
7	41	$6,000	$7,707	$45,589	$45,501	$197,589	2.00%	39.63%
8	42	$6,000	$8,193	$53,781	$53,723	$205,781	2.50%	32.27%
9	43	$6,000	$8,711	$62,792	$62,463	$214,492	2.90%	27.01%
10	44	$6,000	$9,264	$71,757	$71,757	$223,757	3.23%	23.12%
Total		$60,000	$71,756					
11	45	$6,000	$10,280	$82,037	$82,037	$234,037	3.58%	20.17%
12	46	$6,000	$10,977	$93,013	$93,013	$245,013	3.88%	17.87%
13	47	$6,000	$11,719	$104,732	$104,732	$256,732	4.13%	16.03%
14	48	$6,000	$12,508	$117,239	$117,239	$269,239	4.34%	14.55%
15	49	$6,000	$13,331	$130,570	$130,570	$282,570	4.52%	13.34%
16	50	$0	$8,653	$139,223	$139,223	$257,562	4.74%	11.13%
17	51	$0	$9,234	$148,457	$148,457	$264,253	4.91%	10.38%
18	52	$0	$9,840	$158,297	$158,297	$270,668	5.05%	9.73%
19	53	$0	$10,496	$168,793	$168,793	$279,777	5.17%	9.25%
20	54	$0	$11,168	$179,960	$179,960	$290,945	5.28%	8.89%
Total		$90,000	$179,962					

TABLE 8.11 Typical VUL College Plan Ledger Illustration
for 10 Percent Gross Rate of Return

Assumes Current Cost of Insurance Charges					Gross Earnings Rate Assumption of 10.0%			
Year	Age	Annual Premium	Ann'l Incr. Acc. Value	End of Yr. Acc. Value	End of Yr. Sur. Value	End of Yr. Death Ben	Sur. Value IRR	Death Ben IRR
1	35	$6,000	$5,528	$5,528	$5,422	$157,528	−9.64%	2525.47%
2	36	$6,000	$5,951	$11,479	$11,373	$163,479	−3.52%	374.37%
3	37	$6,000	$6,404	$17,884	$17,778	$169,884	−0.62%	165.12%
4	38	$6,000	$6,881	$24,764	$24,658	$176,764	1.09%	98.89%
5	39	$6,000	$7,432	$32,197	$32,090	$184,197	2.26%	68.15%
6	40	$6,000	$8,051	$40,247	$40,141	$192,247	3.12%	50.90%
7	41	$6,000	$8,720	$48,967	$48,880	$200,967	3.79%	40.08%
8	42	$6,000	$9,448	$58,415	$58,357	$210,415	4.33%	32.77%
9	43	$6,000	$10,241	$68,656	$68,627	$220,656	4.76%	27.57%
10	44	$6,000	$11,103	$79,759	$79,759	$231,759	5.11%	23.73%
Total		$60,000	$79,759					
11	45	$6,000	$12,469	$92,228	$92,228	$244,228	5.49%	20.84%
12	46	$6,000	$13,565	$105,793	$105,793	$257,793	5.80%	18.59%
13	47	$6,000	$14,756	$120,549	$120,549	$272,549	6.05%	16.81%
14	48	$6,000	$16,048	$136,597	$136,597	$288,597	6.27%	15.38%
15	49	$6,000	$17,435	$154,032	$154,032	$306,032	6.46%	14.22%
16	50	$0	$13,285	$167,317	$167,317	$309,536	6.67%	13.00%
17	51	$0	$14,444	$181,761	$181,761	$323,534	6.85%	12.27%
18	52	$0	$15,693	$197,454	$197,454	$337,646	6.99%	11.65%
19	53	$0	$17,072	$214,526	$214,526	$351,822	7.11%	11.09%
20	54	$0	$18,539	$233,064	$233,064	$365,911	7.22%	10.60%
Total		$90,000	$233,065					

10 percent, respectively. Although these illustrations were taken from the illustration system of a real insurance carrier, they are not complete and advisors should seek a complete illustration from an insurance carrier. Tables numbered 8.10 through 8.15 are intended to show how the performance of the underlying investment accounts could affect the policy cash and death benefit. They are hypothetical and may not be used to project or predict investment results. They are presented only to illustrate how a properly designed plan should look.

Table 8.12 shows what can happen to a VUL policy when the contract does not perform. This illustration assumes a 0 percent rate of return and maximum insurance charges as opposed to current insurance charges.

The "Variable Universal Life Insurance Funded College Plan" works best with high-tax-bracket clients who have at least ten years to accumulate

TABLE 8.12 VUL College Plan Ledger Illustration
for 0.0 Percent Gross Rate of Return

Assumes Guaranteed Maximum Cost of Insurance Charges   Gross Earnings Rate Assumption of 0.0%

Year	Age	Annual Premium	Ann'l Incr. Acc. Value	End of Yr. Acc. Value	End of Yr. Sur. Value	End of Yr. Death Ben	Sur. Value IRR	Death Ben IRR
1	35	$6,000	$4,607	$4,607	$4,501	$156,607	−24.98%	2510.12%
2	36	$6,000	$4,491	$9,098	$8,992	$161,098	−17.76%	370.57%
3	37	$6,000	$4,371	$13,470	$13,364	$165,470	−14.17%	162.41%
4	38	$6,000	$4,234	$17,704	$17,597	$169,704	−12.03%	96.42%
5	39	$6,000	$4,113	$21,817	$21,711	$173,817	−10.59%	65.68%
6	40	$6,000	$3,913	$25,730	$25,623	$177,730	−9.64%	48.33%
7	41	$6,000	$3,793	$29,522	$29,435	$181,522	−8.90%	37.37%
8	42	$6,000	$3,678	$33,201	$33,142	$185,201	−8.30%	29.89%
9	43	$6,000	$3,558	$36,759	$36,730	$188,759	−7.82%	24.51%
10	44	$6,000	$3,438	$40,198	$40,198	$192,198	−7.44%	20.49%
Total		**$60,000**	**$40,196**					
11	45	$6,000	$3,689	$43,886	$43,886	$195,886	−6.98%	17.40%
12	46	$6,000	$3,597	$47,483	$47,483	$199,483	−6.60%	14.96%
13	47	$6,000	$3,502	$50,985	$50,985	$202,985	−6.29%	12.98%
14	48	$6,000	$3,404	$54,389	$54,389	$206,389	−6.02%	11.36%
15	49	$6,000	$3,282	$57,671	$57,671	$209,671	−5.80%	10.00%
16	50	$0	−$2,415	$55,256	$55,256	$207,256	−5.60%	8.90%
17	51	$0	−$2,499	$52,756	$52,756	$204,756	−5.48%	7.98%
18	52	$0	−$2,612	$50,145	$50,145	$202,145	−5.43%	7.20%
19	53	$0	−$2,718	$47,427	$47,427	$199,427	−5.42%	6.53%
20	54	$0	−$2,875	$44,551	$44,551	$196,551	−5.48%	5.94%
Total		**$90,000**	**$44,551**					

college funds *and* who tend to invest aggressively. Even in a well-designed plan, costs are high, averaging about 3.5 percent over a fifteen-year period. These costs tend to be higher if the investment period is shorter, and lower for longer investment periods. Table 8.13 shows effective after-tax investment yields. The shaded area highlights the range where the tax-free VUL College Plan beats an equivalent yielding taxable investment outright.

It is important to note that the surrender value ("Sur. Value") IRR (internal rate of return) shown in Tables 8.10 and 8.11 represent average returns for the entire period. Returns increase yearly because, despite our careful design efforts, there is still front-end loading that we could not get rid of. Tables 8.14 and 8.15 add one more column, an *Incremental Surrender Value IRR*. This number represents the actual marginal return for

TABLE 8.13 Comparison of VUL Net Tax-Free Returns versus After-Tax Returns

Investment Cost:			3.50%					
Gross Return	5.00%	6.00%	7.00%	8.00%	9.00%	10.00%	11.00%	12.00%
Net Return	1.50%	2.50%	3.50%	4.50%	5.50%	6.50%	7.50%	8.50%

15.00%		4.25%	5.10%	5.95%	6.80%	7.65%	8.50%	9.35%	10.20%
28.00%		3.60%	4.32%	5.04%	5.76%	6.48%	7.20%	7.92%	8.64%
34.00%		3.30%	3.96%	4.62%	5.28%	5.94%	6.60%	7.26%	7.92%
39.60%		3.02%	3.62%	4.23%	4.83%	5.44%	6.04%	6.64%	7.25%

TABLE 8.14 VUL College Plan Ledger Illustration (Showing Incremental Returns versus Average Returns at 8 Percent)

Assumes Current Cost of Insurance Charges   Gross Earnings Rate Assumption of 8.0%

Year	Age	Annual Premium	Ann'l Incr. Acc. Value	End of Yr. Acc. Value	End of Yr. Sur. Value	End of Yr. Death Ben	Sur. Value IRR	Death Ben IRR	Incremental Sur. Value IRR
1	35	$6,000	$5,473	$5,473	$5,367	$157,473	−10.56%	2524.55%	−10.55%
2	36	$6,000	$5,784	$11,257	$11,151	$163,257	−4.79%	374.02%	−1.90%
3	37	$6,000	$6,109	$17,366	$17,260	$169,366	−2.09%	164.80%	0.64%
4	38	$6,000	$6,440	$23,806	$23,700	$175,806	−0.50%	98.56%	1.89%
5	39	$6,000	$6,823	$30,629	$30,523	$182,629	0.58%	67.78%	2.77%
6	40	$6,000	$7,252	$37,882	$37,776	$189,882	1.38%	50.50%	3.43%
7	41	$6,000	$7,707	$45,589	$45,501	$197,589	2.00%	39.63%	3.94%
8	42	$6,000	$8,193	$53,781	$53,723	$205,781	2.50%	32.27%	4.31%
9	43	$6,000	$8,711	$62,792	$62,463	$214,492	2.90%	27.01%	4.59%
10	44	$6,000	$9,264	$71,757	$71,757	$223,757	3.23%	23.12%	4.81%
Total		$60,000	$71,756						
11	45	$6,000	$10,280	$82,037	$82,037	$234,037	3.58%	20.17%	5.50%
12	46	$6,000	$10,977	$93,013	$93,013	$245,013	3.88%	17.87%	5.65%
13	47	$6,000	$11,719	$104,732	$104,732	$256,732	4.13%	16.03%	5.78%
14	48	$6,000	$12,508	$117,239	$117,239	$269,239	4.34%	14.55%	5.88%
15	49	$6,000	$13,331	$130,570	$130,570	$282,570	4.52%	13.34%	5.95%
16	50	$0	$8,653	$139,223	$139,223	$257,562	4.74%	11.13%	6.63%
17	51	$0	$9,234	$148,457	$148,457	$264,253	4.91%	10.38%	6.63%
18	52	$0	$9,840	$158,297	$158,297	$270,668	5.05%	9.73%	6.63%
19	53	$0	$10,496	$168,793	$168,793	$279,777	5.17%	9.25%	6.63%
20	54	$0	$11,168	$179,960	$179,960	$290,945	5.28%	8.89%	6.62%
Total		$90,000	$179,962						

TABLE **8.15** VUL College Plan Ledger Illustration (Showing Incremental
Returns versus Average Returns at 10 Percent)

Assumes Current Cost of Insurance Charges — Gross Earnings Rate Assumption of 10.0%

Year	Age	Annual Premium	Ann'l Incr. Acc. Value	End of Yr. Acc. Value	End of Yr. Sur. Value	End of Yr. Death Ben	Sur. Value IRR	Death Ben IRR	Incremental Sur. Value IRR
1	35	$6,000	$5,528	$5,528	$5,422	$157,528	−9.64%	2525.47%	−9.63%
2	36	$6,000	$5,951	$11,479	$11,373	$163,479	−3.52%	374.37%	−0.43%
3	37	$6,000	$6,404	$17,884	$17,778	$169,884	−0.62%	165.12%	2.33%
4	38	$6,000	$6,881	$24,764	$24,658	$176,764	1.09%	98.89%	3.70%
5	39	$6,000	$7,432	$32,197	$32,090	$184,197	2.26%	68.15%	4.67%
6	40	$6,000	$8,051	$40,247	$40,141	$192,247	3.12%	50.90%	5.38%
7	41	$6,000	$8,720	$48,967	$48,880	$200,967	3.79%	40.08%	5.94%
8	42	$6,000	$9,448	$58,415	$58,357	$210,415	4.33%	32.77%	6.34%
9	43	$6,000	$10,241	$68,656	$68,627	$220,656	4.76%	27.57%	6.63%
10	44	$6,000	$11,103	$79,759	$79,759	$231,759	5.11%	23.73%	6.88%
Total		$60,000	$79,759						
11	45	$6,000	$12,469	$92,228	$92,228	$244,228	5.49%	20.84%	7.54%
12	46	$6,000	$13,565	$105,793	$105,793	$257,793	5.80%	18.59%	7.70%
13	47	$6,000	$14,756	$120,549	$120,549	$272,549	6.05%	16.81%	7.83%
14	48	$6,000	$16,048	$136,597	$136,597	$288,597	6.27%	15.38%	7.94%
15	49	$6,000	$17,435	$154,032	$154,032	$306,032	6.46%	14.22%	8.02%
16	50	$0	$13,285	$167,317	$167,317	$309,536	6.67%	13.00%	8.62%
17	51	$0	$14,444	$181,761	$181,761	$323,534	6.85%	12.27%	8.63%
18	52	$0	$15,693	$197,454	$197,454	$337,646	6.99%	11.65%	8.63%
19	53	$0	$17,072	$214,526	$214,526	$351,822	7.11%	11.09%	8.65%
20	54	$0	$18,539	$233,064	$233,064	$365,911	7.22%	10.60%	8.64%
Total		$90,000	$233,065						

each year. These values are higher. Many planners increase the overall
yield by delaying withdrawals from the contract. To illustrate,

If the client keeps the cash in the contract for sixteen years instead of
withdrawing some to pay college bills, note that the average return has
increased from 4.52 percent to 4.74 percent. But the actual net return
in that year, assuming the 8 percent gross return, is 6.63 percent. If you
refer back to Table 8.13, it shows a client in the 39.6 percent tax bracket
would have to earn a pre-tax 11 percent return to match the return in
the VUL policy.

Parents can delay their withdrawals by paying early college bills through the use of PLUS loans or home equity loans. The financial leverage gained by paying tax-deductible interest while accumulating tax-free growth can be attractive. There are increased risks in effectively borrowing to invest, risks that need to be fully analyzed and communicated to the client.

Do not be too quick, however, to compare this strategy on yield only. The life insurance death benefit can be extremely valuable in its own right. Flexibility and financial aid benefits also add value. In other cases a self-completing disability benefit can be added to the plan that may not otherwise be available. Chapter 10 demonstrates some effective uses of the VUL College Plan in case study form.

The attributes of the VUL College Plan are affected significantly by ownership. For this reason we created two attribute evaluation summaries. They consider the following ownership situations:

- A parent-owned/parent-insured plan (see Table 8.16)

- A grandparent-owned/parent-insured plan (see Table 8.17)

TABLE 8.16 Summary—The VUL Funded College Plan: Parent-Owned/Parent-Insured

Taxes

Federal income tax	■ Contributions are after-tax.
	■ Withdrawals are tax-free if done properly.
State income tax	■ Contributions are after-tax.
	■ Withdrawals are tax-free if done properly.
Federal estate tax	Death benefit would be in the estate of the parent.
Federal gift tax	Not applicable.

Financial Aid

Federal methodology	Not included.
Institutional methodology	Generally not included, but individual colleges might ask. Worst case, the cash value would be attributed to the parent at 3 to 5 percent.

Control Issues

Investment control	Investment choices limited to VUL choices.
Ownership rights	Full ownership rights to parents.
Flexibility	Totally flexible.

Creditor Protection

	■ Varies by state.
	■ Often life insurance proceeds payable to a named beneficiary are given some protection.

TABLE 8.17 Summary—The VUL Funded College Plan: Grandparent-Owned/Parent-Insured

Taxes

Federal income tax	■ Contributions are after-tax.
	■ Withdrawals are tax-free if done properly.
State income tax	■ Contributions are after-tax.
	■ Withdrawals are tax-free if done properly.
Federal estate tax	Death benefit would be in the estate of the parent.
Federal gift tax	Not applicable.

Financial Aid

Federal methodology	Not included.
Institutional methodology	Not included.

Control Issues

Investment control	Investment choices limited to VUL choices.
Ownership rights	Full ownership rights to grandparents.
Flexibility	Totally flexible.

Creditor Protection

	■ Varies by state.
	■ Often life insurance proceeds payable to a named beneficiary are given some protection.

Retirement Plan College Savings Plan

The Introduction discusses the dilemma faced by many parents over whether to save for college or for retirement. Many families find they can only save for one eventuality. Because college is really a subset of the retirement problem as we discussed earlier, saving for retirement makes the most sense. Saving for college at the expense of retirement is actually a short-term solution that still will leave the parents with a problem at a point in their lives that they can least afford to deal with it. *Remember, there is no financial aid for retirement!*

The way this plan works is that the parents put all available resources into the various retirement savings plans they have available to them. Instead of liquidating the retirement funds to pay for college, parents use loans to pay for college. Then, if the retirement plans are truly well-funded enough to meet their retirement goals, the parents stop saving in their retirement plans and redirect those dollars to paying the college loans. As long as retirement is funded, parents can afford to redirect their savings to paying off loans after college. The logic is simple. By maximizing 401(k) contributions for example, a parent not only gets the tax-deferred growth, but often there is an employer match. It is a rare college savings plan that offers a match. The Louisiana QTP is the only one we have uncovered to date that does offer a match. Furthermore, the contributions to the 401(k) are pre-tax, so there is a bit more of a bang for the contribution buck. Payroll deduction makes it easy to make the regular contributions, and it is unlikely that the parents would stop them in the event of a cash crunch. This account will just keep compounding until the parents need to tap into it for retirement. The ability to take a long-term approach to saving provides the opportunity to obtain better returns.

The federal PLUS loan is a good source of loan money. Parents can borrow up to the full cost of college, and the program caps interest at 9 percent. The interest rate for PLUS loans from July 1, 2001, to June 30, 2002, is 6.79 percent! Home equity is also another good source of loan money. The interest on both types of loans can be tax-deductible. Education loan interest, however, does have income phaseouts.

To illustrate how the plan works, consider the Stone family. Mr. and Mrs. Stone, aged thirty-three, have one child who will enter college in fifteen years. They have been saving in their 401(k) plan but recognize they need to save for college as well. Unfortunately, they cannot do both. Mr. Stone has a pension that will cover basic needs, but they also want to have $1,000,000 at retirement to supplement the pension. They carefully analyzed their budget and decided whatever they do, they can only afford to save $4,000 per year.

When we looked at their 401(k) plan, we found that they already have $22,500 saved. The company matches 50 percent to a maximum of $6,000 annually. The Stones are in a 28 percent tax bracket. The long savings horizon allows them to be aggressive with their investment and target an 8.5 percent growth rate. Allowing for the tax savings of contributing pre-tax dollars to the 401(k), we developed the following table to show the effect of overfunding their retirement plan and using loans to pay for college. Table 8.18 shows that if they save $5,550 in the 401(k) until the start of college, the account will grow to $1,234,863 at age sixty-five.

To recap what makes this plan work,

- The employer match increases the effective return on investment.

- By being able to use pre-tax dollars, more can actually be contributed while still meeting the net savings goal of $4,000 annually.

- The long investment horizon allows a more aggressive investment strategy to achieve a higher rate of return.

- Availability of loans with reasonable interest rates makes it possible to redirect the retirement savings dollars to repay the loans. To be absolutely

TABLE 8.18 Retirement Plan College Savings Plan Example

Assumptions:

Client Tax Bracket	28.00%
Growth Rate	8.50%
College Period Start	45
College Period Stop	49
Retirement Start	65
Start Age	33
Current Retirement Balance	$22,500
Planned Annual Contribution	$5,550
Net After Tax Cost	$3,996
Employer Match	50.00% up to $6,000

Age	Annual Savings	Employer Match	Growth	Account Balance
				$22,500
33	$5,550	$2,775	$1,913	$32,738
34	$5,550	$2,775	$2,783	$43,845
35	$5,550	$2,775	$3,727	$55,897
36	$5,550	$2,775	$4,751	$68,973
37	$5,550	$2,775	$5,863	$83,161
38	$5,550	$2,775	$7,069	$98,555
39	$5,550	$2,775	$8,377	$115,257
40	$5,550	$2,775	$9,797	$133,379
41	$5,550	$2,775	$11,337	$153,041
42	$5,550	$2,775	$13,008	$174,374
43	$5,550	$2,775	$14,822	$197,521
44	$5,550	$2,775	$16,789	$222,635
45	$0	$0	$18,924	$241,559
46	$0	$0	$20,533	$262,092
47	$0	$0	$22,278	$284,370
48	$0	$0	$24,171	$308,541
49	$0	$0	$26,226	$334,767
50	$0	$0	$28,455	$363,222
51	$0	$0	$30,874	$394,096
52	$0	$0	$33,498	$427,595
53	$0	$0	$36,346	$463,940
54	$0	$0	$39,435	$503,375
55	$0	$0	$42,787	$546,162
56	$0	$0	$46,424	$592,586
57	$0	$0	$50,370	$642,955
58	$0	$0	$54,651	$697,607
59	$0	$0	$59,297	$756,903
60	$0	$0	$64,337	$821,240
61	$0	$0	$69,805	$891,045
62	$0	$0	$75,739	$966,784
63	$0	$0	$82,177	$1,048,961
64	$0	$0	$89,162	$1,138,123
65	**$0**	**$0**	**$96,740**	**$1,234,863**

clear, this means that instead of continuing to put savings into the retirement plans, the parents now use that cash to make loan payments.

Financial Aid

Currently the financial aid system tries not to include retirement assets in the Expected Family Contribution calculation. The Free Application for Federal Student Aid (FAFSA) explicitly says not to include retirement assets on the form. The institutional methodology, which uses the PROFILE form, also does not expect parents to list their retirement accounts among their assets. However, we should caution planners that more and more colleges are asking for retirement account balances. As yet, we have only seen one college that actually reduced the amount of financial aid offered to a student based on the retirement account values of her parents. But as college inflation increases and students need more and more financial aid, it is likely that colleges will take retirement accounts into consideration.

Tax Savings

The Tax Relief Act of 2001, which provided the ability to save more in qualified plans, makes this an interesting option. Table 8.19 lists these changes.

TABLE 8.19 Retirement Savings Limits

Regular and Roth IRAs New Contribution Amounts

- $3,000 for years 2002 through 2003.
- $4,000 for years 2005 through 2007.
- $5,000 for years 2008 through 2010.
- For taxpayers who have turned fifty before the end of a tax year, an additional $500 contribution is allowed for years 2002 through 2005, increasing to $1,000 for tax years beginning 2006 and thereafter.

401(k) Plans, 403(b) Plans, 457 Plans, SAR-SEPs

- $11,000 for tax years beginning 2002.
- For 2003 through 2006, the limit will continue to rise by $1,000, to a maximum of $15,000.
- After 2006, the limit will be indexed for inflation in increments of $500.

Simple IRAs and Simple 401(k) Plans

- The limit has been increased to $7,000 for 2002.
- For years 2003 through 2005, this limit will increase by $1,000 each year, to a maximum of $10,000.
- After 2005, the limit will be indexed for inflation in increments of $500.

These changes will make it easier to direct savings to qualified retirement plans. In addition, depending on where the family saves their retirement dollars, there can be the added bonus of tax deferrals on growth, tax-free growth in a Roth IRA, and deductible contributions that reduce the tax burden on the family.

Control of Money

When considering control of money, retirement accounts do offer a significant amount of control to the owner in the case of Regular and Roth IRAs. Employer-sponsored plans like 401(k) plans and 403(b) plans limit the choice of investment products. But the employee does have the choice of allocation percentages. Pension plans usually do not give the employee any control.

Creditor Protection

Creditor protection is governed by individual states' laws.

When to Use Retirement Plans

Parents who are wrestling with whether to save for college *or* retirement should start first with their 401(k) plan and contribute at least up to the match amount. Table 8.20 summarizes they key planning attributes for using retirement accounts as a college funding tool.

TABLE 8.20 Summary—Retirement Plan College Savings Plan

Taxes	
Federal income tax	■ If education loans are used, loan interest may be deductible.
	■ Home equity loan interest will be deductible in most cases.
State income tax	Not applicable.
Federal estate tax	Retirement plan assets would be included in the parents' estate.
Federal gift tax	Not applicable.
Financial Aid	
Federal methodology	Retirement plan assets are not included in the calculation.
Institutional methodology	■ Retirement plan assets are not included on the basic input form.
	■ Individual colleges may ask about balances.

(continues)

TABLE 8.20 Summary—Retirement Plan College Savings Plan *(Continued)*

Control Issues	
Investment control	■ Investment choice may be limited by the options within the employer-sponsored plan.
	■ IRAs will allow full control over investment choice.
Ownership rights	Assets are parent-owned.
Flexibility	There is some flexibility. A crisis situation might call for the retirement funds to be used. But legislation surrounding retirement plans does place limitations on exit strategies.
Creditor Protection	Varies by state.

Direct Tuition Payments to the College by Grandparents

Some might question why direct tuition payments are being addressed in a book about long-term college savings plans. This subject is better suited to crisis college planning. However, often we meet families where the grandparents are wealthy and want to help pay for college. But they want to keep control of the money for one reason or another. The unlimited gift tax exclusion available through direct tuition payments is a very attractive solution.

However, it is not necessarily a good planning practice for parents to rely on a promise of a future payment and abandon their own efforts to save. So this section is included in order to make the pros and cons of this strategy clear.

Financial Aid

From a financial aid perspective, these payments are going to reduce financial aid on a dollar-for-dollar basis. Colleges equate direct tuition payments by a third party to be the same as a scholarship. So this strategy is best suited for a student who will not qualify for need-based financial aid.

Taxes

For the grandparent, there is no federal income tax benefit; the payments are being made with after-tax dollars. The same situation holds true for state taxes. The real benefit to the grandparents arises from the gift and estate tax savings. The tax code considers a direct tuition payment to the college on behalf of a student by another party to be a "qualified transfer" and therefore not a gift for gift tax purposes. Grandparents in this situation find that the funds paid directly to a qualified institution for tuition are immediately removed from their estate. Furthermore, the IRS issued Technical Advice Memorandum 199941013 that treated tuition payments made in advance for future years as qualified transfers if the payments were nonrefundable.

Again, this is an opportunity to reduce an estate. Four years of tuition are paid for in one fell swoop.

As noted above, this transfer would not trigger a gift tax for the donor. What is interesting is the issue of the educational tax credits, the Hope Credit and the Lifetime Learning Credit. In cases in which a direct payment was made by a third party, the student is treated as receiving the payment from the grandparent and then in turn paying the college. Consequently, the student is permitted to take an education tax credit if he or she is not claimed as a dependent on someone's income tax return. If the student is claimed as a dependent, then the taxpayer who claims the dependent gets to take the tax credits.

Control of Money

Grandparents have complete control over the money when using this strategy. They control the investment during the accumulation period. When making the distribution, they can decide if, when, and how much to pay directly to the college.

Creditor Protection

These funds would be completely available to the creditors of the grandparents. However, payments made for future years would not be accessible to creditors.

When to Use Direct Tuition Payment to the College by Grandparents

In summary, if the student will qualify for need-based financial aid, this strategy would have a devastating effect unless the grandparents are paying the full freight. On the other hand, if the family will not qualify for need-based aid, this strategy can be a great plan for grandparents and parents alike.

So in cases in which the grandparents are highly affluent and the parents of the student are not, it would be better for the grandparents to simply help with gifts to the parents and students during the college years to avoid the financial aid trap. This does not necessarily get large sums out of the estate up front, so grandparents will have to weigh the decision carefully.

Another alternative would be for the grandparents to open a Qualified Tuition Plan for the student and make the gifts to the plan. Some fairly substantial gifts can be made every year. Furthermore, most state plans allow the custodian to name a successor custodian so control can pass from the grandparents to the parents should the need arise.

In our next chapter, we examine Qualified Tuition Plans, perhaps better known as Section 529 Plans. Because of the complexities of these plans, we devote an entire chapter to them.

Understanding and Using Qualified Tuition Plans

Because of the complexity of Qualified Tuition Plans (QTPs), an entire chapter is needed to explore the attributes, benefits, and best uses of them. QTPs, or Section 529 Plans as they are often called, are not new. In the mid-1980s, prepaid tuition plans made their debut. The Tax Reform Act of 1997 further clarified the tax treatment of these plans and also gave birth to a new type of program that allowed savings in market-rate investments. Suddenly states were rushing to create their own plan for these very attractive savings plans.

Understanding QTPs and how they fit into a college savings plan is much more complex than it may seem. The complexity arises from the fact that

- Federal legislation governs the basic structure of these plans.

- From there each individual state then builds its own plan around this structure and adds another level of complication as each tries to distinguish itself competitively.

- Finally, entry of investment companies as the plan managers layers on another coat of complexity.

What all this means is that financial advisors must not only be educated about the regulations surrounding educational savings plans but also have a system in place that will keep them abreast of federal and state legislative changes to ensure that they make the best recommendation to their clients at a given time.

To some extent, as more and more investment companies enter the arena as plan managers, competition will dictate that the investment companies will be strongly motivated to keep advisors as informed as possible about their product. This is especially true in situations where the advisors can be compensated for selling a plan.

We begin our examination of QTPs with the basics. QTPs fall into two categories:

- Prepaid Plans
- Savings Plans

Prepaid Plans

Prepaid Plans guarantee that if the parent deposits a certain amount of money now, or on a contractual basis monthly or annually, when the student enters college the full tuition and fees at the state college will be covered. The rate of return on these accounts is approximately the college inflation rate for the particular state's public college tuition. In times of high college inflation, this is not a bad deal. Some states actually charge a premium or a discount for a college tuition unit in order to be able to earn enough to meet their guarantees. In that case, earnings will approximate bond interest rates for the period, which may or may not match college inflation.

Initially participants were restricted to using the funds at in-state schools. But now most states allow the funds to be used at private colleges and out-of-state colleges as well. However, the guarantee of tuition and fees will only be for the equivalent of the state college tuition and fees of the state in which the plan is situated.

Many states have severe penalties for withdrawing funds from the pre-paid plan when the funds are not used for qualified education expenses. At the extreme, some go so far as to only return the principal amount, less an administrative charge. In other words, you forfeit all interest.

It is not necessary to fund all four years; a family can contract for one year if they wish. Furthermore, many states allow participants to choose between contracts for two-year colleges and four-year colleges. A recent addition to the Pennsylvania prepaid plan gives families the choice of funding for various levels of college. The plan even has an Ivy League category among its choices.

Savings Plans

In 1997 Congress created Qualified Tuition Savings Programs (later called Qualified Tuition Plans) in response to the demand of parents who wanted to be able to take advantage of soaring market returns. The tax act defined the tax treatment of these plans, and the states were off and running to establish their own savings plans. *Savings Plans* allow a donor to open an account that will be invested in market-return investments. Additional differences from other educational savings plans include

- Unlike Education Savings Accounts, there is no *federal* restriction on the annual donation amount.

- There is no income-based restriction on contribution amounts. State laws, on the other hand, do establish restrictions on maximum contribution amounts to plans for each student.

- Furthermore, federal regulations do not require that the funds be distributed once the beneficiary turns thirty as in the Coverdell Education Savings Account. It appears that federal regulations put no age restriction on the plans. However, understand that if the money eventually winds up in the hands of the next generation, a generation-skipping tax may be assessed.

- States, on the other hand, might place restrictions based on age in their plan—for example, no contributions accepted after the beneficiary reaches a certain age, withdrawals for qualified education expenses must begin by a certain age, etc.

- Federal law requires that once funds are deposited in a QTP, the custodian must "relinquish all investment decisions." However, a recent ruling from the IRS made in September 2001 indicated it would have no problem with a QTP that allows custodians to change their portfolio from one investment portfolio approach within the plan to another in the same plan once a year. Custodians cannot, however, design their own portfolio.

- After December 31, 2001, gains are not taxed if the withdrawal is used for qualified education expenses. These expenses include
  - Tuition
  - Fees
  - Books
  - Supplies
  - Equipment
  - Room and board
  - Special need costs
  - Transportation
  - Special needs as defined in the Education Savings Account section

Rules and Requirements for QTPs

Table 9.1 summarizes the rules and requirements for QTPs. The states have the role of

- Choosing the investment manager
- Determining the investment allocations by dictating the portfolio design options
- Setting the minimum and maximum contribution amounts
- Setting the state tax treatment
- Determining limitations on whom may participate
- Choosing various other features as long as they do not countermand the federal rules

So we find some states that allow

- State tax deductions on some or all of the contribution amounts
- Tax-free growth in the account if used for qualified education expenses
- All-equity portfolios
- All-bond portfolios
- Asset allocation portfolios based on the age of the student
- Rules on where the funds are permitted to be used, and so on

The variety makes choosing the appropriate state plan much more complex.

TABLE 9.1 The Rules for Qualified Tuition Plans

- Qualified education expenses include tuition, fees, books, supplies, equipment, and room and board.
- Income is tax-free if used for qualified education expenses.
- Accounts can be rolled over for the same beneficiary once every twelve months to another state plan without penalty.
- Custodians are now permitted to select a different portfolio option within a plan once every year.
- The custodian can change the beneficiary on the plan to another member of the family. If the new beneficiary is in a generation younger than the original beneficiary, there may be generation skipping taxes due.

TABLE 9.1 The Rules for Qualified Tuition Plans *(Continued)*

- The custodian is considered the owner of the account and retains full rights, including
  - Ability to change beneficiary
  - Ability to request distributions and ability to choose not to distribute funds
  - Ability to move the account to another state plan
- Prepaid plan distributions are treated as an outside resource of the student's, and financial aid is reduced dollar-for-dollar.
- Savings plans are considered the asset of the custodian by the institutional methodology.
- Each state establishes the rules for its own plan within the bounds of the federal legislation. For example, federal law set the rules governing what qualifies a plan to be treated under Section 529 of the IRS Code. However, the states choose the investment manager, determine the types of portfolios that will be available, establish state income tax treatment, determine who can participate in the plan, etc.
- Contributions to the plan are considered a completed gift. Donors may elect to contribute up to $55,000 in one year to a beneficiary and use their annual gift tax exclusion for the next five years. If the donor dies prior to the end of the five-year period, the remaining gift tax exclusion must be put back into the estate of the donor.
- Withdrawals for nonqualified education expenses or for other non-education reasons are subject to the tax due on the gain as well as a 10 percent penalty. This is a federal tax penalty. The June 2001 tax act intended this penalty to replace the state-imposed penalty. However, in a prepaid plan, this penalty is *in addition to* the penalty that is imposed by the state through reduction of the refund amount for cancellations and refunds as stated in the terms of the plan contract.
- If the student receives a scholarship, the custodian is permitted to withdraw the amount of the scholarship from the QTP without penalty. Taxes would be payable on the gain portion of the withdrawal.
- The new tax law of June 2001 established a coordination of qualified tuition plans and use of education tax credits. Beginning in 2002, a taxpayer can claim a Hope Scholarship Credit or Lifetime Learning Credit for a taxable year *and* exclude distributions from a qualified tuition program only if the distribution is not used for the same expenses for which the tax credits are being claimed.
- The same coordination is established for withdrawals from an Education Savings Account and a qualified tuition plan.
- In the event of the death or disability of the beneficiary of a QTP, the account can be rolled over to a new beneficiary, or the funds may be withdrawn without penalty. Taxes would still be due if the funds are simply withdrawn.

Key Planning Attributes

Returning to the issues raised in Chapter 7, we evaluate the merit of using QTPs based on the benefits we want to build in to the college savings plan. First, we explore how QTPs are treated for need-based financial aid purposes.

Financial Aid

QTPs are not financial aid friendly. In the case of *prepaid plans,* these are considered an outside resource available to the student. The U.S. Department of Education requires that they be treated as a student resource, so they act more like a scholarship. This results in a dollar-for-dollar reduction in financial aid.

Conversely, with a *savings plan* the asset is considered that of the custodian. This means that if the parent is the custodian on the account, it will be included in financial aid formulas for up to 6 percent of the account value. If a grandparent, aunt, or uncle owns the account, the asset will not count at all.

However, the real problem with the *savings plans* can arise with the issue of income. Despite the fact that the growth in the accounts will not be counted for federal income tax purposes, currently the financial aid formulas require parents and students to report *all* income, whether taxable or nontaxable. A question about this to the College Board at the time of writing gave us this response:

> . . . No one has officially addressed the issue of whether these distributions should then be reported as the untaxed income of the student. Right now, this income is not being requested on the PROFILE, nor [*sic*] on the FAFSA. The implications of the new tax laws are still being sorted out, so not all of the decision [*sic*] on how things will be treated in the student aid program have been asked and answered. I think you will see the debate continue over the next year.

Should the determination be made that the gain is to be reported as untaxed income, keep in mind the financial aid rules of thumb: Student income is assessed at 50 percent. This will affect financial aid awards for the student's sophomore, junior, and senior years. However, there is always the worst-case scenario that finds the savings plans getting the same financial aid treatment as prepaid plans—dollar-for-dollar reduction.

Because of the uncertainty surrounding financial aid treatment of the QTP savings plans, when deciding whether a QTP is appropriate for a particular family, financial advisors need to remember the parable of the UGMA. States instituted these accounts and advisors and parents jumped on them as the ultimate tax-savings strategy. They became the college savings account of choice. Then Congress enacted the "Kiddie Tax," and parents found themselves paying the taxes once again and they were locked into accounts because they had made irrevocable gifts to their children.

Most states say that state financial aid is not affected by QTPs. Although this is a benefit to consider, the fact of the matter is that state financial aid is not a large segment of the financial aid pie. Furthermore, states may put restrictions on who is eligible for state aid that mean some students would not have gotten state aid anyway. For example, New Jersey requires that a student attend a New Jersey college in order to receive state aid. So a needy student from New Jersey who attends a college in Pennsylvania or Delaware cannot receive a New Jersey Tuition Aid Grant.

Taxes

When evaluating whether to use a QTP from a tax perspective, they are quite attractive. *Federal tax law* states that after December 31, 2001, withdrawals from a QTP that are used for qualified education expenses will be free of federal income tax. Finally, the effects of the power of compounding will be fully available to pay for college. This is a powerful tool. Keep in mind, however, that the laws passed in June 2001 will revert to the original rules in 2010 unless Congress amends or re-enacts them.

State tax treatment varies. Many states offer a deduction on all or part of the contribution amount. One issue to note here is that a state might demand recapture of the tax deduction on the contribution if the account is rolled into a different state's plan. Specifically, the Virginia savings plan will expect the deductible contributions to be added back to income when an account is moved to another state plan.

Some states also offer tax-free growth on qualified distributions; some are still only tax-deferred. Some experts believe that the states will follow suit on the federal tax treatment within a short period of time. It appears that some states are structured such that they will automatically follow federal 1040 treatment. Others may need specific legislation to effect the change.

Custodians are given an interesting opportunity to do some *estate tax planning* with QTPs. The law allows that contributions are gifts of present interest and thus subject to the $11,000 annual gift tax exclusion. (Beginning in 2002, the annual gift tax exclusion increases to $11,000 per year due to inflation adjustments.) Interestingly though, the custodian still retains all control over the account and can take back the money for any reason. The gift taxes may be due and income taxes would be due, along with the 10 percent penalty. But the flexibility this gives to grandparents is a bona fide benefit.

Now let us expand on the concept. Federal law allows a donor to lump five years of gifts in one year when contributed to a QTP. Donors who choose then to contribute $55,000 to an account in one year have used their annual gift tax exclusion for the next five years.

It follows, then, that a grandfather and grandmother can each contribute $55,000 to an account for each one of their grandchildren. If they have six grandchildren, this immediately removes $660,000 from their estate. Bear in mind that in the event that the donor dies before the end of the five-year period, the remaining "gifts" are added back to the estate. But the estate planning implications are monumental.

Control of Money

Control-of-money issues can cast a shadow over QTPs. Federal law mandates that the custodian may not exercise control over investment decisions once funds are contributed to the plan. The intention is that custodians not be able to get involved in market timing. *Thou shalt not day-trade in a QTP!*

We find that many states have established portfolios based on the age of the beneficiary that are designed to become more conservative as the student nears college age. Although the concept of moving funds that will be needed in a short period of time to less volatile investments is a time-honored strategy of basic financial planning, overall these portfolios are often not aggressive enough to counteract the effect of college inflation. For this reason, many custodians might find it disadvantageous to use a QTP.

But things are not really as bleak as it may seem. Here are some ways that Uncle Sam is ceding some control back to the custodian.

- As noted earlier, a recent IRS ruling indicated that the IRS would not fault a state plan that allowed a custodian to move from one portfolio within the plan to another portfolio, once a year.

- More and more states are adding all-equity portfolio and all-income portfolio investment options to their plans. This offers a custodian the chance to exercise a little more control. For example, the percentages in each investment can be controlled by the size of the annual contribution allocated to each. So while a bit more complicated, there is a small amount of investment control in the hands of the custodian.

  □ A custodian can set up one account using the all-equity portfolio and another account using a money-market portfolio. Then each year by changing the amount contributed into each account, the custodian can control the investment allocation.

☐ Another possibility is a QTP that allows the custodian to designate the percentage to be contributed among several portfolio options in the plan. Once the money is in the portfolio, however, the custodian can only redistribute the funds once a year.

■ Another opportunity for a bit of investment control was introduced with the tax changes of June 2001. The ability to roll a QTP to another state plan once in a twelve-month period without penalty allows a custodian to change to a more attractive plan if he or she becomes unhappy with the performance of a plan or the investment manager.

But custodians need to be careful about the ease of moving an account from one state plan to another. Some things to watch for are

☐ If the original state plan offered a state tax deduction on contributions, the state might try to recapture the tax when the account is moved.

☐ There might be costs associated with moving the account. For example, if either the old plan or the new plan paid commissions to the advisor, this needs to be factored into the plan costs.

☐ The new plan might have a waiting period before funds can be withdrawn for qualified education expenses.

Advisors and parents need to be sure to understand all the features of a plan before moving into it.

Each state still retains the ability to change the investment manager. The contracts are usually for a specific period of time, often five years, but many have a clause that allows a change in the interim if the state desires. The states also establish and have the right to change the investment options. Again, the custodian has the option of the penalty-free annual rollover. He or she can move the account to a more favorable state plan if dissatisfied with the current plan. See the paragraphs above for more options available to the custodian.

QTPs offer more control than custodial accounts when it comes to use of the funds. UGMA/UTMA accounts eventually revert to the student when the student reaches the age of majority in the student's particular state. This means that a child who decides not to go to college has the right and ability to use the money for anything he or she wants. Conversely, the custodian on a QTP account retains the rights to determine how and when to use the money in the account. So a beneficiary who decides not to go to college cannot access the funds in the QTP without the cooperation of the custodian. The custodian can change the beneficiary to another student or even take the funds back for the custodian's own use and pay the taxes and penalties that would be due.

Creditor Protection

Because each QTP is designed individually on a state-by-state basis, issues of creditor protection also vary on a state-by-state basis. Federal laws state that a QTP cannot be used as security for a loan. Yet although a custodian is prohibited from using the assets of a QTP as collateral for a loan, at the state level there is not a standard of law that prevents nonconsensual claimants, or judgment creditors, to get to plan assets.

As recently as March 2001, only eleven states had incorporated express statutory language in their plans that protect their plans from judgment creditors. Surprisingly there was actually an opinion rendered in Nevada that stated fund assets can be reached in the absence of specific statutory limitations. In light of this, it is incumbent on a financial advisor to check a state plan for creditor protection issues before recommending it to a client.

On a cautionary note, grandparent custodians also need to be very aware of an issue pertaining to Medicaid. Because the federal laws clearly state that the account is owned by the custodian, a grandparent could be compelled to liquidate fund assets and use them up before being able to qualify for Medicaid benefits and other programs like this.

There are two other situations that might threaten the assets of a QTP: divorce and bankruptcy of the custodian. Although a state might specifically protect a QTP from creditors, it would be foolhardy to assume that the protection would be automatically extended to alimony and child support claims. Immediate family needs versus future education could very possibly convince a court to invade a plan for the benefit of the children.

The second scenario, bankruptcy of the custodian, offers another risk to an account. There is precedent in one bankruptcy court that ruled that assets in a *prepaid plan* established before IRC Section 529 were part of the bankruptcy estate. Although legislation has been introduced that would protect these plan assets from bankruptcy court, it has been vetoed because of other unrelated, undesirable features. Until such laws are signed, a financial advisor must consider the risks, especially if a client is exposed to the possibility of bankruptcy.

When to Use QTPs

Tables 9.2 and 9.3 give a summary of the key planning attributes for using QTPs—Prepaid Plans and Savings Plans, respectively—as college funding tools.

TABLE 9.2 Summary—Qualified Tuition Plans: Prepaid Plans

Taxes

Federal income tax	Gains are tax-free if used for qualified education expenses.
State income tax	■ Will vary from state-to-state.
	■ Some are tax-free, others are tax-deferred if used for qualified education expenses.
Federal estate tax	■ Due if distributed to the beneficiary's estate upon the death of the beneficiary.
	■ If donor dies before the end of the five-year gift tax proration period, the remaining amounts are included in the donor's estate.
Federal gift tax	■ Due if gift exceeds the annual gift tax exclusion and the donor does not elect to use the five-year proration period.
	■ May be due if the account is rolled over in favor of a beneficiary of a younger generation.

Financial Aid

Federal methodology	Treated as a student asset—reduces financial aid dollar-for-dollar.
Institutional methodology	Asset attributed to the custodian.
	Income attributed to the student.

Control Issues

Investment control	Very limited—by choice of state.
Ownership rights	Attributed to the custodian.
Flexibility	Very limited.

Creditor Protection | Varies by state.

TABLE 9.3 Summary—Qualified Tuition Plans: Savings Plans

Taxes

Federal income tax	None if used for qualified education expenses.
State Income tax	Varies by state.
Federal estate tax	■ Due if distributed to the beneficiary's estate upon the death of the beneficiary.
	■ If donor dies before the end of the five-year gift tax proration period, the remaining amounts are included in the donor's estate.
Federal gift tax	■ Due if gift exceeds the annual gift tax exclusion and the donor does not elect to use the five-year proration period.
	■ May be due if the account is rolled over in favor of a beneficiary of a younger generation.

Financial Aid

Federal methodology	■ Asset attributed to the custodian.
	■ Income attributed to the student.
Institutional methodology	■ Asset attributed to the custodian.
	■ Income attributed to the student. *(continues)*

TABLE 9.3 Summary—Qualified Tuition Plans: Savings Plans *(Continued)*

Control Issues	
Investment control	Limited.
Ownership rights	Custodian owns.
Flexibility	Limited.
Creditor Protection	Varies by state—if not protected by state law, as an asset of the custodian it is subject to creditors of the custodian.

Earlier in this chapter we touched on the fact that QTPs are layered with complexity. Our discussion up to this point has centered on the basics of federal and state treatment of these accounts with respect to the attributes of our analysis framework. However, the differences that arise out of the fact that each state designs its own plan warrant special attention because they are integral to choosing the right plan if it is decided that a QTP is the appropriate tool for a family.

Fifty states and better than fifty different plans create a major task for any advisor. Alaska alone has three savings plans! Furthermore, the reality that competition for the potential billions of savings dollars is going to result in constant refining of plans by states and investment managers means that parents and their advisors need to continually track the changes in the QTP marketplace. The following are some issues to be watched.

UGMA/UTMA Accounts

We have mentioned UGMA and UTMA accounts several times in the last few chapters. To recap, these types of accounts were originally used to take advantage of children's lower tax bracket. The advent of the Kiddie Tax made them much less advantageous. Furthermore, financial aid treatment of UGMA/UTMA accounts made them extremely penalizing to a family that otherwise might have qualified for need-based financial aid. And lastly, the configuration of the law gave the minor total ownership of the funds at the age of majority. Although it may not be a common occurrence, we have seen situations in which a child took the money in the account and bought a car instead of going to college, much to the dismay of his or her parents.

In order to exercise more control, parents often look to QTPs to ensure that the money will be used as they intended, for college. In addition, there is the very attractive income tax treatment to entice them to move the money to a QTP. Instead of being taxed at the child's rate, funds grow tax-free. But this is not a perfect solution, and parents need to understand some of the pitfalls.

- First, UGMA money is UGMA money. When transferring these funds to a QTP, the UGMA rules are still intact. What that means is that the student is still the owner of the funds even though a custodian may be named while the child is still a minor. At majority, the student once again is the owner of the account with all the rights and privileges attached. The result is that once again the student can withdraw the funds at will and use them for whatever the student wishes.

■ If the money is not used for qualified education expenses, the taxes are due as well as the 10 percent penalty.

■ On the other hand, if the student does decide to use the account for college, the financial aid wrinkle kicks in. The account belongs to the student, so now the asset as well as the income is attributed to the student.

■ The next detail parents need to face is that QTPs can only accept cash contributions. Therefore, if they wish to move an UGMA/UTMA account into a QTP, they must liquidate the account and pay any income taxes that might be due before depositing them in the QTP. The timing of paying these taxes might not be opportune.

■ Finally, each state plan will have its own treatment of UGMA/UTMA money. Parents and advisors must be careful to read the plan document carefully before making any decisions.

Plan Costs

When choosing from the myriad QTPs available, parents and financial advisors need to be aware of the costs of the plans. Once again the fact that each individual state sets its own rules can result in fees and costs that are all over the board. Here are some things to check.

1. Is there an application fee?

2. Is there an annual administration or maintenance fee from the state?

3. What are the management fees for each underlying investment? Compare them to management fees for similar investments outside the plan.

4. Are there other fees for things such as change of beneficiary or an account owner or beneficiary who lives out-of-state, and so forth?

5. In some cases where commissions are paid to the advisor, there may be loads or surrender charges to take into account.

Other Considerations

It would be foolish to try to list all the possible differences between every state plan. Yet it is critical to be aware of the possibilities. Now that more and more states are giving financial advisors the opportunity to be compensated for selling their QTP to clients, suitability issues mandate that advisors be especially careful when choosing a plan for a client. The following are some idiosyncrasies that we have uncovered in reviewing many of the state plans. Many provide benefits, but many can be traps, so we cannot stress enough that an advisor must be familiar with the plans they recommend.

- Virginia allows an annual $2,000 state income tax deduction for contributions to their plan. However, for residents over the age of seventy, the cap is removed, and they can deduct their entire contribution.

- Many states that allow an advisor to be compensated for selling their plan restrict the compensation to nonresident accounts. Residents must come into the plan at Net Asset Value (NAV).

- Maximum allowable contributions vary by state. Some limit the maximum to the total account value of all accounts for that student and tie it to the average estimated cost of four years of college in that state. Others cap the actual contribution amount.

- The Pennsylvania prepaid plan has a series of tuition indexes the custodian can choose from when setting up the account. They even offer an Ivy League private school tuition index.

- In general, prepaid plans have many different ways of charging for accounts that are not used for college. Some only refund the actual contribution amount, others might give back a minimum interest amount as well.

- New York's savings plan requires that the funds be invested for thirty-six months before they can be withdrawn.

- Also in New York, a nonqualified withdrawal is included in New York state income tax, in full—not just the growth portion. So a custodian who deposited $11,000 into a plan to maximize the gift tax exclusion, and took a $5,000 state income tax deduction for the contribution, will find him- or herself paying tax on the entire $11,000, not just the $5,000 on which the custodian took the deduction.

- Not all states allow the custodian to name a successor custodian in the event of his or her death. Some plans dictate that at the death of the custodian the beneficiary becomes the owner. Financial aid rules will then consider the asset to be the student's.

- Prepaid plans often have an enrollment period. Alabama's only lasts one month, others match the academic year, and still others run from January through October. Poor timing could mean the loss of a year's investing.

- Residency requirements vary. Some states require that the custodian be a resident, others require the beneficiary to be a resident, and still others make it an either-or requirement. Some are fully open to all nonresidents.

- In Utah, beneficiaries who have been in their savings plan for at least eight years and then move to another state can still be eligible for in-state tuition at Utah state colleges.

- On the other hand, if a refund of the account value is requested in Utah before the account has been open for more than two years, the earnings are forfeited.

- Louisiana has a match built in to their plan. The percentage of the match is based on the adjusted gross income of the depositor. In addition, in June of 2001 they have added a 2 percent match for employers who establish an account for an employee's child who is a resident of the state.

- Some states have more than one savings plan. Alaska has a prepaid plan and two savings plans, one managed by T. Rowe Price and one by Manulife using multiple fund managers.

Private Prepaid Tuition Plans

The tax act signed into law in June of 2001 also expanded the definition of a QTP to include eligible education institutions. Prior to the change, the law defined the programs as being established and maintained by a state or agency or other instrumentality that permitted an individual taxpayer to purchase tuition credits or certificates, or to make contributions to an account to fund the higher education of a beneficiary.

Now the law allows private institutions to design and maintain their own prepaid tuition plans. The program must

- Receive a ruling that it meets the requirements for a QTP

- Hold the assets in a qualified trust

Participants may purchase tuition credits or certificates, but unlike state-sponsored QTPs, they may not contribute to a savings plan.

Summary

Once a financial advisor has determined that a QTP is the appropriate savings tool for a client, the following methodology will help to ensure that the best plan is chosen for the client.

1. The first plan to evaluate is always that of the resident state of the custodian. State tax deductions for contributions give an added boost to savings dollars.

2. If the custodian's resident state does not offer a tax deduction or does not have a state income tax, then look at the resident state of the

beneficiary if it is different. Grandparents might wish to give the contribution to the parents of the beneficiary if they can get a deduction on the contribution.

3. If the beneficiary's family is likely to relocate several times before the student enters college, a state income tax deduction on the contribution might not be beneficial if that particular state recaptures the tax when the account is moved.

4. If state income taxes are not an overriding concern, then you may wish to review other state plans and compare them with the state plan of the custodian's resident state and that of the beneficiary, if different. Things to look for are

   a. Who is the investment manager?

   b. What are the portfolio options?

   c. What are the plan costs?

   d. Is there creditor protection?

   e. Is there a waiting period before funds can be used?

It is prudent to offer a comment on the issue of advisor compensation at this point in the discussion. Some investment companies that manage QTPs give financial advisors the opportunity to earn a commission on accounts they set up. Advisors should be aware that many states that offer a national plan, meaning that anyone can participate regardless of residency, stipulate that residents be allowed to enter the plan at NAV. *A financial advisor who recommends a plan on which he or she expects to earn a commission must be extremely careful that it is the best plan possible for the client's circumstances.* If that client could have invested in the client's own state plan at NAV and also gotten a state income tax deduction, the advisor may need to document and support his reasons for recommending a commission plan.

Using the Tool Comparison Chart

In Chapters 8 and 9, we have explained a plethora of college savings tools. Table 9.4 summarizes those tools. We have assigned an arbitrary ranking for each tool for the attributes we have laid out. Financial advisors will have to do a careful analysis of their clients' financial goals as well as their feelings and concerns about risk and reward. Remember that *the problem is not isolated to college; retirement is the overriding concern.*

When it comes time to choose a tool, the main concerns of the client will dictate the choice, for example,

- If financial aid is paramount, The Simple Plan,™ parent-owned VUL, and the Retirement/College plan are all options worth consideration.

- When estate taxes are driving the plan, clients will want to consider the Education Savings Account and more likely, a QTP.

- Creditor protection concerns will guide parents to select QTPs or perhaps a Life Insurance College Plan.

TABLE 9.4 Summary of College Savings Tools, with Attributes and Ranking

College Savings Plan Tool/Strategy	Tax Benefits				Financial Aid Friendly	Control of Money		Creditor Protection	Flexibility of Exit Strategies
	Fed	State	Estate	Gift		Inv.	Asset		
U.S. Savings Bonds	A	A	C	N/A	D	D	A	D	A
Education Savings Accounts	A	B	A	C	D	A	D	B	C
Regular IRA College Plan	D	D	N/A	N/A	D	A	A	B	C
Roth IRA College Plan	A	A	N/A	N/A	D	A	A	B	C
The Simple Plan™	D	D	N/A	N/A	B	A	A	D	A
Parent-Owned Life Insurance College Plan	A	A	C	B	A	B	B	A	A
Retirement/College Plan	A	A	B	N/A	A	B	B	B	C
Direct Tuition Payment by Grandparent	N/A	N/A	B	A	F	A	D	N/A	A
Qualified Tuition Plan (Prepaid Plan)	A	A	B	A	F	D	B	Depends on the state	D
Qualified Tuition Plan (Savings Plan)	A	A	A	A	D	B	B	Depends on the state	B-C

RANKING SYSTEM:

A = Highly Preferable

B = Preferable

C = Neutral

D = Not Preferable

F = Plan Killer

PART

III

Putting the Plan Together

CHAPTER

10

Implementing the Plan: Case Studies

The College Savings Plan Checklist

After reading the first nine chapters, you have all the data you need to begin designing plans for your clients. Now you need to identify your client's needs and apply the appropriate tools. Many clients come to us with a preconceived idea of what they want in a college savings plan. For example, "I want to set up an Education IRA." Or "I want to invest in one of these new Section 529 Plans." What they really mean is "I want to set up a college savings plan for my children or my grandchildren." Too many advisors take the easy way out and implement what the client first asks for without going through a thorough analysis.

There is a four-step process to help you assist your client. Step 1 involves fact-finding and testing. Step 2 involves quantifying the plan. Step 3 develops the funding tools to get the job done. Step 4 involves implementing the plan.

Step 1: Analyze the client's needs.

- What are the client's realistic college goals?

  — Determine the type of college or college cost classification that is appropriate for the client.

  — Complete the college cost forecast.

  — Use The College Savings Calculator™ to test the client's goals to determine whether they are realistic.

- Do you need to consider financial aid implications in the college plan?

  — Use The Financial Aid Test™ to test for potential aid eligibility.

  — Check for pockets of aid—periods when two or three students may be in college at one time, making a non-aid family an aid candidate.

  — Check to see if cost sharing with the student is a feasible way to reduce the parent saving's burden. Do parents philosophically want to do this? Will the student be able to borrow?

- What is the college funding time framework?

  — Can we prefund the entire college burden?

  — Do we need to consider using income during the college years in a "pay-as-you-go" plan?

  — Will postfunding be required?

- What is the client's income tax and estate tax situation?

  — To what extent will the client benefit from income tax savings in a college savings plan?

  — How important are estate tax considerations?

- What are the client's attitudes regarding "control of money"?

  — What are the client's perceptions of risk/return for college investments?

  — Does the client have preferences regarding money managers or money management style?

Step 2: Map out the numeric portion of the college plan using The College Funding Integrator.™

- How much initial cash or other resources can the client commit to the plan?

- How much can the client take from current income during the college years, and how much will the client need to borrow?

- How will the client liquidate college debt and over what time period?

Step 3: Analyze the tools and products available.

- Use The Attribute Evaluation Worksheet™ to help you choose the right tools.

- Will retitling plan assets and tools enhance tool attributes, making them more effective?

- What appropriate exit strategies can be built into the plan to handle contingencies?

Step 4: Implement the plan.

Case Studies

Over the years we have had the opportunity to help thousands of parents implement college funding plans. The following are some typical and some not-so-typical cases. We have tried to lay out how we handled them so that you can get some ideas. There are often many solutions to the same problem. Advisor preferences and client preferences need to be considered. Every situation poses individual problems and opportunities. This book has explored a number of tools and options. There is lots of room, however, for planner creativity.

Case #1: Planning for the Probable Financial Aid Candidate

Parents whose students have a high probability of qualifying for financial aid represent a high percentage of the population. Although this group is not the typical client of most financial planners, they often represent the children of some of our better clients. We need to be able to help them. Here is a typical example:

Milt and Dawn Hart have a daughter Denise who they feel is a very hard-working student. Denise is eight years old. The Harts feel that a private college would probably best suit their daughter. Denise seems to excel in smaller classes and in an environment when she has direct access to her teachers. Milt and Dawn have an earned income of $75,000 annually. They expect their income to keep pace with inflation but not to exceed it. They expect no inheritances and no real help from Denise's grandparents.

Step 1: We used The College Savings Calculator™ (Figure 10.1) to help the Harts establish their college funding goals and to assess the Harts' commitment to college savings. According to Figure 10.1

- A private college such as Lycoming College currently costs $29,080.

- Four years of future costs at Lycoming are anticipated to total $205,702.

- It would require monthly savings of $792 at 8 percent after tax for the Harts to fully prefund college.

The Harts were very concerned that college would cost so much, but they felt that a mid-priced college like Lycoming was still the right type of

The College Savings Calculator™
Version: 2002(Book).b

College Money

Client Data:	11/08/01
Name:	The Harts
Plan Start year	2001
First Year of College:	2011
Type of College:	3
Geographic Region:	1

Geographic Region	Northeast
Type of College	Medium
Benchmark College	Lycoming College
Current Total Cost	$29,080

Target Growth Rate: 8.00%

Projected Future College Costs:

Freshman Year	2011	$46,068
Sophomore Year	2012	$49,467
Junior Year	2013	$53,120
Senior Year	2014	$57,048
Total Cost		$205,702

Approximate Monthly Savings Required	Rate	Savings
Beginning Sept.	7.00%	$839
Through The End	8.00%	$792
Of College	9.00%	$747

Copyright: College Money, 2001

Purpose:
The purpose of this program is to forecast future college costs and to determine the approximate monthly savings required to meet them. Savings begin in September of the current year and continue through August of the last year of college. The College Savings Calculator™ is a trademark of College Money.

Raw Data Sources:

CPI Data: U.S. Department Of Labor, Bureau of Labor Statistics, Washington, D.C. 20212
Consumer Price Index, All Urban Consumers - (CPI-U), U.S. city average,
All items, 1982-84=100 (Year Ending June 30)

College Inflation: The College Board, New York, NY

Current College Costs: Direct from college websites or college admission departments. Costs include tuition, room, board, fees, books, and miscellaneous cost. Added is "pizza money" an allowance for extra costs parents claim they incur.

The College Savings Calculator™

College Cost Data Valid Through: 12/31/02   www.collegemoney.com

FIGURE 10.1 Hart Family Example 1—Savings Required
for Medium-Priced College

college to incorporate in their plan design. They figured that they could save about $250 monthly and might be able to increase savings slightly each year. In addition, they were willing to commit $10,000 of their existing savings to the college plan.

Step 2: Use The Financial Aid Test™ software to establish the Harts' financial aid probability. Completing The Financial Aid Test™ also helps the advisor gather the data needed to build a plan. This data is collected right on the Main Page data input section of The Financial Aid Test.™ You will note that it is an excellent data-gathering tool. Figure 10.2 shows the Harts' current financial circumstances and their expected family contribution (EFC) as if Denise were attending college today.

The results of The Financial Aid Test™ show that the Harts would be highly probable financial aid candidates at a school like Lycoming. In fact, their EFC under the Institutional Methodology (the most likely methodology) of $16,818 would make them eligible for $12,262 of financial aid for the first year or 42 percent of the college bill. See Table 10.1.

TABLE 10.1 Financial Aid Summary for the Hart Family

	$	% Total Cost
Cost of Lycoming (2001–2002)	$29,080	
EFC (institutional methodology)	$16,818	57.8%
Financial need	$12,262	42.2%

Step 3: Use The College Funding Integrator™ to see how the Harts would fare. Assuming that the Harts

- Saved $250 each month during the first year

- Increased savings by 5 percent yearly

- Committed $10,000 of their existing savings to the college fund

- Paid $5,000 annually out of pocket during each of the four college years

This plan would leave the Harts considerably short according to the "Integrator" results shown in Figure 10.3. The major concern is that they would need to accumulate college loans with an annual payment of $27,990 or total college loan payments of $139,950 over the five-year period between college and retirement to complete the plan. Obviously this caused great concern.

Factoring in estimated financial aid made a significant difference. From the table above (Table 10.1), we know that the Harts may receive as much as 42 percent of their college bill in first-year financial aid. The first-year cost at Lycoming for Denise in 2011 is projected to be $46,068. This amount came from The College Savings Calculator™ in Figure 10.1. The College Funding Integrator™ can handle estimated financial aid by increasing "annual payments during college" by the amount of expected financial aid. In this case we took the Harts' $5,000 commitment and added $19,000 (42 percent

The Financial Aid Test™

Version: 2002-Book.f
08-Nov-01

Family Data:

Parent's Name (in report form)	Hart
Student's Name (in report form)	Denise
Street Address	123 Main
City, State, ZIP	Voorhees, NJ 08053
Home Telephone:	856-596-1234
Business Telephone:	
State of Residence (All Caps, eg. NJ)	NJ
1 Age of Older Parent	46
2 Number of Parents in Family	2
3 Number of Dependent Children in Family	1
4 Number of students in college for plan year	1
5 Total ages of all pre college children	0

Student Financial Data:

23 Student Assets	$0
24 Student's Income	
a From Work	$0
b From Investments	$0
25 Student Income Tax Paid	$0
26 Assets in Siblings Names (IM only)	$0

Parent Financial Data:

6	Father's Wages	$50,000
7	Mother's Wages	$25,000
8	Other Taxable Income	$2,500
9	Non taxable income	$0
10	Untaxed Benefits	$0
11	Losses from Business, Farm, Capital Loss	$0
12	Adjustments to income	$0
13	Child Support Paid	$0
14	Tuition Tax Credits	$0
15	Taxable Student aid	$0
16	Medical & Dental Expense	$0
17	Federal Income Taxes Paid	$5,500
18	Net Home Equity (include farm - if you live on it)	
	a Market Value	$150,000
	b Sum of all Mortgages	$75,000
19	Net Equity of Other Real Estate	
	a Market Value	$0
	b Sum of all Mortgages	$0
20	Business/Farm Net Value (Your Share)	
	a Business net value	$0
	b Farm net value - if not used as residence	$0
21	Parent Cash	$25,000
22	Parent Investments	
	a Qualified Retirement Plans	$400,000
	b Other	$0
*	Debts other than mortgages	$0

The Financial Aid Test™ - Quick Calc

Federal Methodology

Parent Expected Cont./Student	$15,172
Student Expected Contribution	$0
Expected Family Contribution/Student	$15,172

Key Counseling Numbers
Federal Methodology

	Assets	Income
% EPC From:	0.00%	100.00%
% ESC From:	0.00%	0.00%
Par. Marg.Cont.:	5.64%	47.00%
Stud. Marg. Cont:	35.00%	50.00%

Institutional Methodology

Parent Expected Cont./Student	$15,668
Student Expected Contribution	$1,150
Expected Family Contribution/Student	$16,818

Key Counseling Numbers
Institutional Methodology

	Assets	Income
% EPC From:	17.75%	82.25%
% ESC From:	0.00%	100.00%
Par. Marg. Cont:	5.00%	46.00%
Stud. Marg. Cont:	25.00%	50.00%

This analysis provides estimated financial aid data for planning purposes only. Actual financial aid awards are determined by each college at the time of admission. The validity of the input data can dramatically affect financial aid values. Which assets must be counted and how each asset is valued may be treated differently by the government and each individual college. Calculations are based on:

Federal Methodology   2001–02

Institutional Methodology 2001–02

Financial Aid Formulas Become Outdated After: 02/28/02
The College Financial Aid Test™ is a trademark of College Money.

www.collegemoney.com

FIGURE 10.2 Hart Family Financial Aid Test

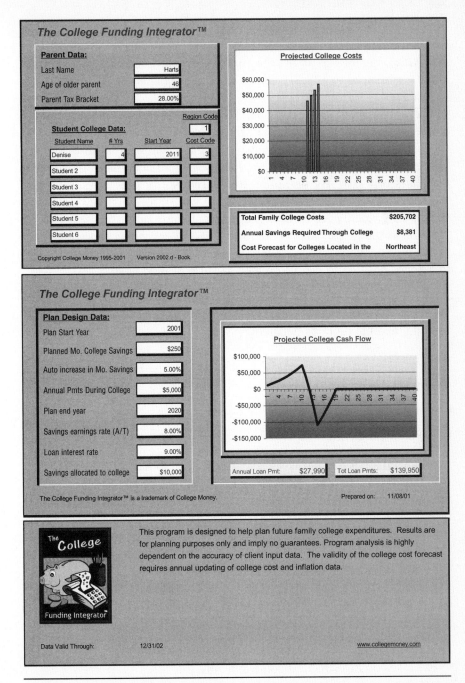

FIGURE 10.3 Hart Family Example 2—College Plan Integrating Lump Sum and Monthly Savings, Loans, and Out-of-Pocket Payments During College

of $46,068 = $19,348 rounded down) of expected aid. This produced $24,000 each year during college to pay college bills before having to draw on savings. Figure 10.4 shows the effect on the Harts' need to borrow. Total loans are reduced to $29,173 or five annual payments of $5,835. This is a workable plan for the Harts.

It is important to understand that the Harts' assumption of financial aid is not guaranteed. If financial aid rules change and the Harts cannot get this aid, they would have to change their plans and have Denise attend a less expensive school. In this case, however, there is no more money that the Harts can save. By designing the Harts' plan in this way, they were motivated to save money. They could see a way of meeting their goal even though they would need to stretch significantly during the recovery period. Most importantly, they had a plan to meet their goal and an alternative plan for Denise to attend a less expensive school if necessary, and they will be in a better position to handle college because of it.

Step 4: Using The Attribute Evaluation Worksheet,™ evaluate the key attributes that the Harts require in a college funding medium. Choosing the right funding medium requires balancing:

- Taxes

- Financial aid

- Control

- Creditor protection

Financial aid is a major issue. The Harts stand to pick up about $76,000 in financial aid over the four-year college period. We can easily ascertain the importance of creditor protection and control by talking to the Harts. In this case, the Harts really are not concerned about being sued. So we can minimize this factor. They also trust Denise; but if she decides not to attend college, the Harts want access to the funds. As for investment control, they are leaning on you, their trusted advisor, for help. Taxes are important, but they need to see if the potential tax savings of any funding option can approach the huge potential impact that financial aid is likely to have.

Table 10.2 spreadsheets three tax options for the Harts:

- Pay taxes on investment income annually

- Defer taxes until withdrawal

- Generate tax-free growth for college

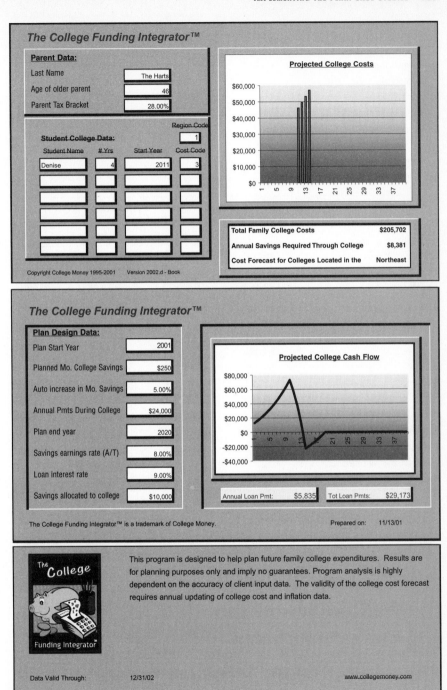

FIGURE 10.4 Hart Family Final Plan—Integrates Financial Aid

TABLE 10.2 Income Tax Analysis for the Harts

Assumptions:

Monthly Savings:	$250
Initial Savings	$10,000
Increase in Savings	5.00%
Annual Growth Rate	8.00%
Tax Bracket	28.00%
Years to Accumulate	10
Savings Deposited @ Start of Year	

Years	Annualized Savings	Accum Tax Current	Accum Tax Deferred	Accum Tax Free
Initial Savings	$10,000	$10,000	$10,000	$10,000
1	$3,000	$13,749	$14,040	$14,040
2	$3,150	$17,872	$18,565	$18,565
3	$3,308	$22,400	$23,623	$23,623
4	$3,473	$27,363	$29,263	$29,263
5	$3,647	$32,795	$35,542	$35,542
6	$3,829	$38,734	$42,521	$42,521
7	$4,020	$45,217	$50,264	$50,264
8	$4,221	$52,286	$58,845	$58,845
9	$4,432	$59,985	$68,339	$68,339
10	$4,654	$68,362	$78,833	$78,833
Total Savings	$47,734			
Investment Gain		$20,628	$31,099	$31,099
Taxes Due at Withdrawal		$0	$8,708	$0
Net After-Tax Gain		$20,628	$22,391	$31,099

Both the tax-deferred option and the tax-free option do save taxes over a fully taxable investment vehicle and thus increase the after-tax value of the Harts' college fund. If funds can accumulate income-tax-free, the Harts will have almost $9,500 more in their college account. But even though that is a significant amount, it is dwarfed by the almost $76,000 potential financial aid benefit. Financial aid is the dominant benefit in this case. With all of this in mind, the advisor needs to complete The Attribute Evaluation Worksheet.™ Although completing this worksheet is somewhat arbitrary, it is effective in helping advisors compare actual funding options in order to help the Harts choose the right option. We completed a sample worksheet for the Harts in Table 10.3.

Step 5: The Harts and their advisor are now ready to choose the funding vehicle for their college plan. There are a number of possible options. In

TABLE 10.3 The Attribute Evaluation Worksheet™

Prepared for *The Hart Family*

Prepared on _____

Attribute	Why Important?	Attribute Ranking
Taxes		
Federal income tax	*Controlling taxes can help increase the accumulation in the college account.*	2
State income tax	*Controlling taxes can help increase the accumulation in the college account.*	2
Federal estate tax	*Not an issue in this case.*	
Federal gift tax	*Not an issue in this case.*	
Financial Aid		
Federal methodology	*Not an issue in this case.*	
Institutional methodology	*Probably the dominant methodology— May mean $76,000 in college funding.*	1
Control Issues		
Investment control	*Would like to give advisor maximum flexibility to control taxes and get the best return subject to risk constraints.*	4
Ownership rights	*The Harts want the funds if Denise does not attend college.*	3
Flexibility		
Creditor Protection	*Not expected to be a problem.*	

evaluating choices we went back to Chapters 8 and 9 and compared the attributes of the strategies and tools listed there against Table 10.3, The Attribute Evaluation Worksheet™ for the Harts.

Our choice was a portfolio of parent-owned mutual funds (The Simple Plan™). The main reasons for this choice were based on financial aid and control issues, with some thoughts toward taxes. The rationale for our choice includes:

- The portfolio could be set up to control taxes in the early years by choosing mutual funds that are tax managed. By this we mean that minimal taxes are paid each year, accumulating the majority of the tax liability until the funds are liquidated. This strategy gives the Harts two exit options that are discussed below. A client-owned portfolio gives the advisor maximum investment options because the client has complete control.

- The advisor can structure the portfolio for the best risk/reward relationship for the client again because the client has control.

- Because the parent owns the portfolio, it is considered a parent asset for financial aid purposes. The 6 percent rule applies, and therefore this approach will minimize any negative effects on the Harts' ability to qualify for financial aid.

- Because the Harts own the account, they can use the money any way they wish if Denise does not attend college.

Step 6: The advisor and the Harts need to consider exit strategies for this plan if things change.

- If the plan holds up and financial aid is significant, the Harts will need to plan the liquidation of their investments so that deferred taxes such as unrealized capital appreciation do not increase their income for financial aid purposes. This can usually be accomplished by liquidating the portfolio no later than the first semester of the high school junior year. Any capital appreciation would appear on the Harts' income tax form two years before college and would not be considered as income for financial aid purposes.

- But what if the Harts' financial circumstances change and they find they will not get financial aid? The Harts can still generate some income tax savings by gifting the appreciated mutual fund portfolio to their daughter and letting her liquidate the portfolio. In this case she takes on her parents' basis in the funds and she pays the tax, likely in a lower tax bracket. However, they need to be aware that this will transfer control of the funds to Denise at majority.

Step 7: The advisor needs to choose the specific set of mutual funds for the Harts and develop an appropriate asset allocation to generate the risk/return and tax mix required by the Harts. Choosing appropriate funds is beyond the scope of this book, but planners need to think fairly aggressively when investing college funds. Remember that college inflation almost always runs significantly ahead of consumer price index (CPI).

A creative financial planner may come up with other options for the Harts. Our purpose here was to demonstrate the process and give you one working option and the accompanying rationale for our choice. Thinking through the options, using the evaluation tools, and most importantly thinking through the exit strategies are critical to the process.

Case #2: Grandparent Plan—Mixed Financial Aid Needs

Chuck and Ann have two children and two grandchildren. Their son Michael is in business for himself and is doing extremely well. Chuck's observation is that "Michael will soon be either a multi-millionaire or be totally bankrupt." According to Ann, their daughter Julie "is happily married, has a comfortable life, but will probably never have much money." There are two grandchildren. Julie and her husband have a son, Charley, aged three. Michael and his wife have a daughter, Elizabeth, aged six. Chuck and Ann want to set up a college fund for each.

The following information came from a discussion with them:

- Estate planning is not a major issue with Chuck and Ann. They are very comfortable, but not rich.

- They would like to maintain control over their money to make sure that the grandchildren use it appropriately.

- They also want to be able to do something for unborn grandchildren but are not sure how much more money they will be able to contribute.

- Chuck and Ann are willing to contribute a total of $1,000 monthly to help fund a college education for their grandchildren.

- Chuck and Ann are in a 39.6 percent marginal tax bracket.

Chuck and Ann really need to develop two separate college funding plans because their children's circumstances are so different. Michael's main needs revolve around tax savings and maybe creditor protection. Julie, on the other hand, needs to maximize financial aid. One common plan probably will not do it. Chuck and Ann need to be concerned about income taxes, and because planned gifts are relatively small, gift taxes are not an issue. In this case, a particular college choice is not important. Chuck and Ann are not trying to fully fund college. They do want to help and they would probably like some feedback on how helpful they will be if they contribute toward a college education for their grandchildren.

As a planner, you need to take several steps:

1. Do a Financial Aid Test™ on each of the children. This is primarily to make sure that financial aid assumptions are valid, but it is also a great way to get an introduction to Michael's and Julie's families and assess their financial circumstances to see if they might make good clients in their own right. We did not reproduce financial aid test results here; however, for design purposes, Michael is not likely to qualify, but Julie is a highly probable candidate.

2. Use either The College Funding Integrator™ or The College Savings Calculator™ to show Chuck and Ann the impact they will have on a plan.

3. Choose the funding medium for each plan.

In this case we completed two Attribute Evaluation Worksheets,™ one for Michael and one for Julie. They appear below as Tables 10.4 and 10.5.

The next step was to use The College Funding Integrator™ for each family to determine the savings needed at the appropriate rate of return to achieve their targeted goals. In Julie's case, we suspected that we would use The Life Insurance College Plan funded by Variable Universal Life, based on The Attribute Evaluation Worksheet,™ so we projected a lower

---

TABLE 10.4 The Attribute Evaluation Worksheet™

Prepared for *Michael's Children*
Prepared on _____

Attribute	Why Important?	Attribute Ranking
Taxes		
Federal income tax	■ *Michael is in a high bracket.* ■ *Chuck and Ann are in a high bracket.*	1
State income tax	■ *Michael is in a high bracket.* ■ *Chuck and Ann are in a high bracket.*	1
Federal estate tax	*Not an issue.*	
Federal gift tax	*Not an issue.*	
Financial Aid		
Federal methodology	*Not an issue.*	
Institutional methodology	*Not an issue.*	
Control Issues		
Investment control	*Neither Michael nor Chuck and Ann want to control investment money management.*	
Ownership rights	*Chuck and Ann wish to ensure that the money is used for college.*	3
Flexibility		
Creditor Protection	*May be important.*	2

rate of return. On the other hand, we felt that a QTP would probably be the likely tool for Michael's family, so we projected a higher rate of return. Figures 10.5 and 10.6 show the results.

To design a plan for Julie's children, we compared her Attribute Evaluation Worksheet™ to several options from Chapters 8 and 9. We felt that the VUL College Plan will meet her needs as well as Chuck and Ann's goals. A summary page from the VUL College Plan appears in Table 10.6. It shows Chuck and Ann depositing $6,000 annually into the plan and withdrawing $34,168 in each of the plan years 15, 16, 17, and 18 when Charley will be in college. Note that there is still money in the contract to pay the life insurance costs. This is designed to keep the contract in force, thus protecting the tax-free status of the withdrawals.

TABLE 10.5 The College Funding Tool Attribute Evaluation Form™

Prepared for *Julie's Children*
Prepared on _____

Attribute		Why Important?	Attribute Ranking
Taxes			
	Federal income tax	*Important to Chuck and Ann but not to Julie.*	2
	State income tax	*Important to Chuck and Ann but not to Julie.*	2
	Federal estate tax	*Not an issue.*	
	Federal gift tax	*Not an issue.*	
Financial Aid			
	Federal methodology	*Major importance.*	1
	Institutional methodology	*Major importance.*	1
Control Issues			
	Investment control	*Neither Julie nor Chuck and Ann wish to exert control over the investment strategy.*	
	Ownership rights	*Chuck and Ann wish to ensure that the money is used for college.*	3
	Flexibility		
Creditor Protection		*Not an issue.*	

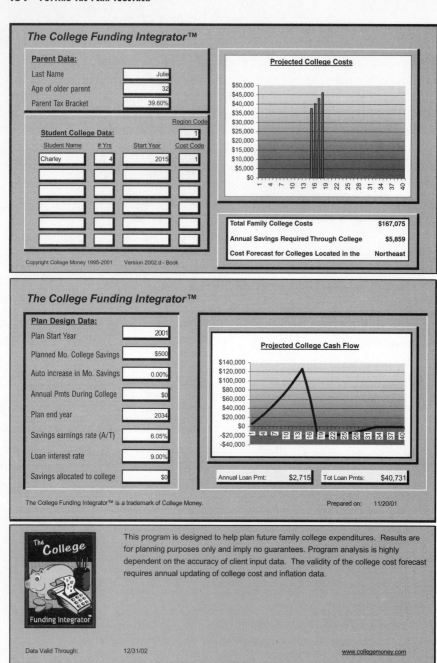

FIGURE 10.5 College Savings Plan for Julie

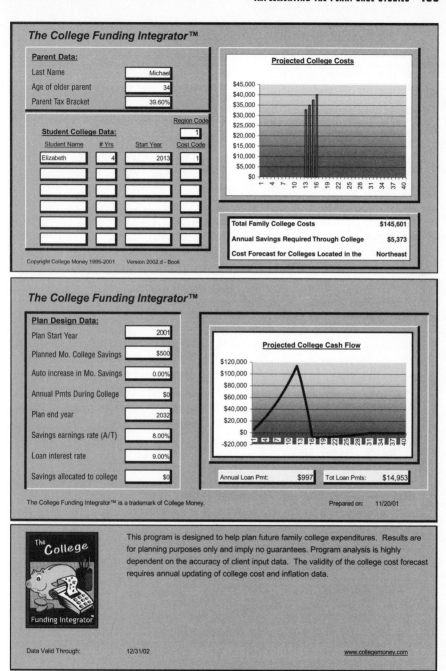

FIGURE 10.6 College Savings Plan for Michael

TABLE 10.6 VUL College Plan—Julie

Assumes Current Cost of Insurance Charges   Gross Earnings Rate Assumption of 10.0%

Year	Age	Annual Premium	Withdrawal	Net Loan	End of Yr. Acc. Value	End of Yr. Sur. Value	End of Yr. Death Ben	Sur. Value IRR	Death Ben IRR	Incremental Sur. Value IRR
1	32	$6,000	$0	$0	$551	$5,415	$172,511	−9.75%	2775.18%	−9.75%
2	33	$6,000	$0	$0	$11,389	$11,293	$178,388	−3.98%	397.55%	−1.07%
3	34	$6,000	$0	$0	$17,661	$17,566	$184,661	−1.22%	173.85%	1.58%
4	35	$6,000	$0	$0	$24,366	$24,270	$191,365	0.45%	103.77%	2.99%
5	36	$6,000	$0	$0	$31,551	$31,455	$198,550	1.58%	71.38%	3.91%
6	37	$6,000	$0	$0	$39,276	$39,180	$206,275	2.42%	53.23%	4.61%
7	38	$6,000	$0	$0	$47,567	$47,485	$214,566	3.07%	41.84%	5.10%
8	39	$6,000	$0	$0	$56,495	$56,441	$223,495	3.59%	34.13%	5.53%
9	40	$6,000	$0	$0	$66,117	$66,090	$233,116	4.02%	28.65%	5.84%
10	41	$6,000	$0	$0	$76,492	$76,492	$243,491	4.37%	24.58%	6.11%
Total		$60,000	$0							
11	42	$6,000	$0	$0	$88,687	$88,687	$255,686	4.85%	21.55%	7.51%
12	43	$6,000	$0	$0	$101,956	$101,956	$268,956	5.24%	19.18%	7.68%
13	44	$6,000	$0	$0	$116,391	$116,391	$283,391	5.57%	17.31%	7.81%
14	45	$6,000	$0	$0	$132,093	$132,093	$299,092	5.85%	15.81%	7.93%
15	46	$0	$34,168	$0	$106,065	$106,065	$273,065	6.05%	14.69%	−19.70%
16	47	$0	$34,168	$0	$77,735	$77,735	$244,734	6.16%	13.82%	−26.71%
17	48	$0	$15,664	$18,504	$46,818	$46,818	$231,818	6.20%	13.11%	−39.77%
18	49	$0	$0	$34,168	$13,110	$13,110	$180,110	6.17%	12.54%	−72.00%
19	50	$0	$0	$0	$13,609	$13,609	$180,608	6.16%	12.04%	3.81%
20	51	$0	$0	$0	$14,097	$14,097	$181,097	6.14%	11.60%	3.59%
Total		$84,000	$84,000	$52,672						

There are several reasons why we opted for this solution for Julie.

- Chuck and Ann could own the plan. They keep complete control over the money. They can use it any way they wish, with no restrictions.

- Chuck and Ann would not incur any income tax liability for investment returns during the accumulation period.

- Julie's husband is the insured on the plan. This solved an additional concern that Chuck and Ann had. Since Julie and her husband did not make a lot of money, Chuck and Ann were concerned that they might have some financial responsibility for Julie and Charley if Julie's husband died. The VUL College Plan created a $172,000 death benefit on Julie's husband.

- Furthermore, by maintaining the ownership, Chuck and Ann can ensure that the account can be used for additional children should there be a brother or sister for Charley.

■ When Charley is ready for college, Julie's family will apply for financial aid based on their own financial circumstances. The VUL College Plan does not enter into the calculations in any way.

■ After Charley receives his financial aid package, Chuck and Ann will withdraw $34,168 from the VUL College Plan. This is a tax-free withdrawal for Chuck and Ann.

■ Chuck and Ann make gifts totaling $34,168 to Charley, Julie, and Julie's husband, dividing the gifts as necessary to avoid gift taxes.

■ If Chuck or Ann dies before gifts are made, the survivor becomes the contract owner. No estate taxes are due because of the unlimited marital deduction. If both die, taxes are minimal because of Chuck and Ann's limited estate and the fact that only the cash surrender value of the account goes into the estate, not the death benefit.

Although the rate of return in the life insurance contract is lower than that projected for Michael's plan, by preserving Julie's financial aid eligibility, the plan will actually work better.

For Michael's daughter, Elizabeth, Chuck and Ann decided on another approach, a Qualified Tuition Savings Plan, or Section 529 Plan. When we refer back to The Attribute Evaluation Worksheet,™ we saw that the priorities were

■ Federal tax savings

■ State tax savings

■ Ownership rights—Chuck and Ann want to ensure that the money is used for college. They also felt that the QTP would alleviate any concerns about creditors or bankruptcy issues for Michael.

Our next step was to select the appropriate plan. The first plan we reviewed was the Michigan plan. Because Chuck and Ann resided in Michigan, it was the obvious place to begin.

■ The federal tax savings are a moot issue because they apply to all QTPs.

■ But we also found that the Michigan plan offered a maximum $5,000 state tax deduction for annual contributions.

■ The investment manager of the plan is TIAA-CREF (Teachers Insurance and Annuity Association-College Retirement Equities Fund), a well-known and reputable investment manager.

■ The plan has no enrollment fee and no annual maintenance fee.

We briefly considered the New Jersey plan where Michael and his wife live. However, Chuck and Ann would not be able to deduct their contributions using the New Jersey plan. Furthermore, Chuck was not comfortable with the investment manager, which in this case is the state treasury. Both Chuck and Ann were very happy with the decision to use the Michigan plan.

Again, Chuck and Ann will own the account, thus maintaining the control they need to be sure the funds will be used as they intended. Furthermore, this gives them the flexibility to make sure additional children in Michael's family will have access to the college savings.

Case Study #3: Grandparents with a Large Estate

Myra and Harry Black have five grandchildren. The Blacks come from a family that has traditionally sent their children to Columbia University in New York City. They have two sons, Howard and Arthur, who both attended Columbia, and five young grandchildren, aged two, four, five, six and eight. The Blacks are doing some estate planning and wish to fully fund the undergraduate education of their five grandchildren at Columbia if they can later qualify for admission. As part of their estate plan, they have been giving $10,000 each annually to each of their sons, their son's spouses, and to their grandchildren.

The following other important issues have come to light in reviewing the Blacks' situation:

- Financial aid is not an issue because the grandparents are fully funding college. Also a Financial Aid Test™ (not shown) indicates that Howard and Arthur are financially well off and not likely to qualify for financial aid.

- Estate reduction is of major importance to the Blacks.

- Income taxes are important to the Blacks and to Howard and Arthur.

- Creditor protection may or may not come into play, but it is not a major concern.

- For the year 2002 the annual gift exclusion increases to $11,000 per person per donor.

- Myra and Harry live in New York City.

- Arthur and his two children live in Syracuse, New York.

- Howard and his family live in Manhasset, New York.

There are three parts to organizing this case:

1. Complete an Attribute Evaluation Worksheet™ for the Blacks. (Table 10.7)

2. Use The College Funding Integrator™ to determine the funding requirements. (Figure 10.7)

3. Choose the appropriate funding media.

The Attribute Evaluation Worksheet™ details the priorities Myra and Harry have placed on their plan. Taxes are an overriding concern, with estate reduction being the most important and avoidance of gift taxes following. The ability to reduce federal and state income taxes would also make them happy.

The Blacks are not interested in exercising much control over the investment, but they do want to ensure that the funds are used to pay for their grandchildren's college educations.

TABLE 10.7 The Attribute Evaluation Worksheet™

Prepared for *Myra and Harry Black*
Prepared on _____

Attribute	Why Important?	Attribute Ranking
Taxes		
Federal income tax	*Myra and Harry are wealthy. They pay income taxes at the highest tax bracket. Arthur and Harry are also in high tax brackets.*	3
State income tax	*New York City residents pay very high state and local taxes.*	3
Federal estate tax	*Estate reduction is the Blacks' major goal.*	1
Federal gift tax	*The Blacks want to avoid gift taxes.*	2
Financial Aid		
Federal methodology	*Financial aid is not a factor.*	
Institutional methodology	*Financial aid is not a factor.*	
Control Issues		
Investment control	*The Blacks do not want to directly manage the college fund account.*	5
Ownership rights	*The Blacks want to make sure that gift funds are not misused.*	4
Flexibility		
Creditor Protection	*Creditor protection is not likely to be a major issue.*	

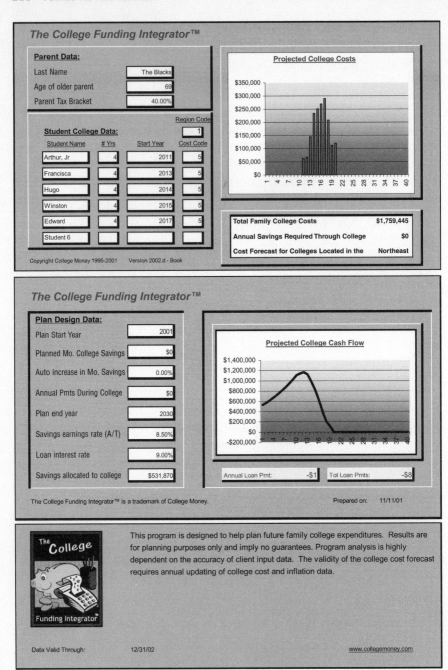

FIGURE 10.7 College Savings Plan for the Blacks' Grandchildren

Our next step was to project college costs and savings needed. We used The College Funding Integrator™ because it gave us the ability to include all five grandchildren at once. If we had used The College Savings Calculator,™ we would have had to run five different scenarios, and it would have been too cumbersome.

The College Funding Integrator™ indicates that if the Blacks deposit $531,870 and get an average 8.5 percent after-tax return, there will be enough money to pay for college. After reviewing the Blacks' needs and the attributes of the various tools available, it appears that a Qualified Tuition Plan (QTP) (Section 529 Plan) is the appropriate choice because

- It appears that a QTP solves their gift and estate tax problem. By depositing funds in a QTP, the Blacks make a completed gift that removes the contributed amount from their estate. Using the special gift tax treatment afforded to QTPs, they can gift five years of annual exclusions ($11,000/year/donee in 2002) for a total of $550,000 gift-tax-free. The Blacks need to understand that if they die within five years of making their gift, a pro rata portion of their gift will be included in their estate.

- The Blacks do not want to pay income tax. Again it appears that QTPs meet their needs because funds will grow within the plan income tax-free. In addition, depending on plan choice, the Blacks may be able to generate a state income tax deduction or credit by using a QTP.

- From an investment control standpoint, the Blacks can choose from a selection of predetermined portfolios offered by the plans. The extent of choice will be dependent on which state plan they choose. They need a fairly aggressive portfolio to meet the 8.5 percent return built into their plan design. Once the initial selection is made, the Blacks have no management responsibilities other than to review overall performance on a periodic basis.

- The Blacks will still maintain effective ownership control over the plan. They can change account beneficiaries, control distributions, and even reclaim money for their own use subject to income taxes, penalties, and potential gift taxes on funds that they reclaim.

The next issue for the Blacks is which QTP or what combination of plans to use. Because all three families live in the state of New York, this is obviously the first plan to evaluate.

- The New York plan offers a state income tax deduction of $5,000 annually on contributions to the account ($10,000 for couples married, filing jointly).

- The investment manager is TIAA-CREF, a well-known and reputable fund manager.

- There will be no federal income taxes generated on the growth in the portfolio if the funds are used for college.

- There will be no state income taxes generated on the growth in the portfolio if the funds are used for college.

- The New York plan allows them to name successor owners, which is something they needed to consider given the young ages of their grandchildren.

- Also, the plan only exposes $10,000 per account to judgment creditors of account owners who are not minors. While they do not expect to have a problem in this area, given their wealth their attorney advised them to check into that issue.

- Although the New York plan puts a thirty-six-month waiting period on an account before funds can be withdrawn for qualified education expenses, again this is not a problem given the ages of the grandchildren.

Harry and Myra were pleased with the proposed college savings plan we presented. They had two choices regarding how to make the contributions.

- Myra and Harry could open the account with the entire $531,870.

- Myra and Harry could open the account with $511,870 and gift $10,000 to each son for deposit into the account. This way all three families could also qualify for the $10,000 New York state tax deduction on the contribution.

Case Study #4: High-Income Parent Sets Up a College Savings Plan

John Long, aged forty, is owner of the Marketing Promotions, LLC. John has two children, Jason, aged three, and Jessica, aged two. His annual income exceeds $300,000. John is a graduate of American University in Washington, D.C. He would like to have the funds available to send his children to his alma mater should they want to go. John lives in New Jersey. John's major concerns are income taxes, control over funds, and investment performance. John does not have time to make daily investment decisions.

Step 1: John's Attribute Evaluation Worksheet™ is shown in Table 10.8.

Step 2: John needs to know how much to save. The College Funding Integrator™ analysis below (Figure 10.8) shows that he needs to save about $1,500 monthly through the end of college.

TABLE 10.8 The Attribute Evaluation Worksheet™

Prepared for *John Long*

Prepared on _____

Attribute	Why Important?	Attribute Ranking
Taxes		
Federal income tax	*John is in a very high tax bracket.*	1
State income tax	*John is in a very high tax bracket.*	1
Federal estate tax	*Not currently an issue.*	
Federal gift tax	*Not currently an issue.*	
Financial Aid		
Federal methodology	*Not currently an issue.*	
Institutional methodology	*Not currently an issue.*	
Control Issues		
Investment control	*John is an aggressive investor who is results-oriented, but he does not want day-to-day management responsibilities.*	3
Ownership rights	*John is a controller. If his children do not attend college, he wants control over the funds.*	2
Flexibility		
Creditor Protection	*John is in business for himself and wants to creditor-proof the college plan to the extent he can.*	4

Step 3: Choose an appropriate funding vehicle for John's plan. A QTP (Section 529 Plan) seems to best fill John's needs:

- It will give him tax-free growth so that he will pay no federal taxes while the money grows or when it is withdrawn to pay qualified education costs.

- John lives in New Jersey, which will not give him a deduction from state income taxes on his contributions but does exempt withdrawals from any state plan if they are used to pay for qualified education expenses.

- John can control the distribution of funds and can control the choice of investments to the extent that he can choose the plan. He cannot manage the portfolio, but he did not want this responsibility anyway.

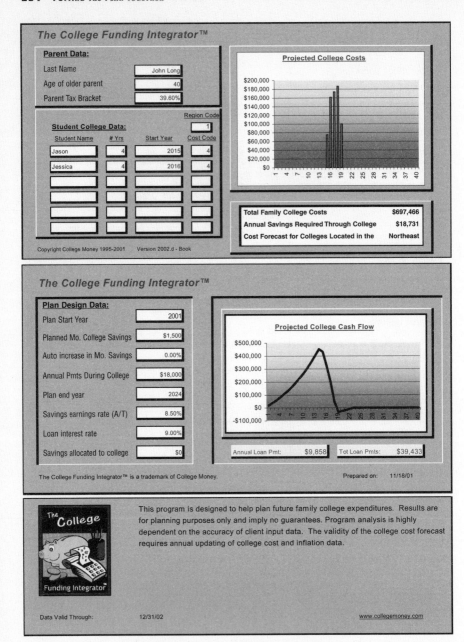

FIGURE 10.8 Long Family College Savings Plan

The next question to answer for John is, "Which state plan should he choose?"

■ John did not feel constrained to use the New Jersey Plan because

— It did not give him a state income tax deduction.

— It did not give him specific creditor protection.

— It did not give him a name-brand money manager.

■ Because the only state that can give a donor a state tax deduction is the state of residence of the donor, John cannot get these benefits unless he moves to another state or until New Jersey grants them.

■ John did find his specific creditor protection and his name-brand money managers in the Colorado State plan, which fortunately allows contributions from residents of other states.

Advisors and clients may have to do substantial research to find the appropriate state plan. Appendix G lists the Web site addresses of plans in existence at this writing. In addition, state tax codes can be extremely important in order to ascertain the tax deductibility of Section 529 Plan contributions for state income tax purposes and to ensure that withdrawals from other state plans do not create taxable income at the state level.

Other Situations of Note

There are several other situations that do not require a full case study but do deserve comment.

Situation #1: Remember That Paying for College Is Really a Retirement Problem

Sometimes we run into parents who are struggling with the conflict of saving for retirement and saving for college. There is not enough money to do both. Saving money is the important thing. Whether it is in an account labeled college or an account labeled retirement does not really matter. It is important to look at the attributes that the family requires and match them to a tool that can fulfill those requirements. Many of the families who do not have enough cash flow to save both for college and for retirement are families who will qualify for financial aid. They are likely to have a 401(k) plan at work with a significant match.

What to Do:

1. Use The Financial Aid Test™ software to verify the probability of financial aid.

2. Have the parent max out his or her 401(k).

3. Plan to borrow to fill college needs—PLUS loans or home equity arrangements.

Typical Results:

In most cases 401(k) values are not considered a resource to pay for college. Therefore, using this strategy will not negatively hurt the financial aid picture. By maximizing a corporate 401(k) match, we boost the client's retirement benefits. We gave a more detailed example of this situation in Chapter 8 that you may wish to refer to.

Warning! If you use this type of plan, do not use 401(k) loans to pay college bills. Loans from qualified plans must be repaid over a period of five years or less. This results in high monthly payments. Default on a 401(k) plan may not adversely affect the client's credit, but it can cause a disastrous premature distribution with an accompanying tax bill and penalty charges.

Situation #2: A Sole Proprietor Saves for College in the Business Name

Ricky Taylor, aged thirty-five, is a self-employed graphic artist who works out of his home. Ricky shows an annual income of $50,000 net after business expenses. He and his wife Susan have a baby girl, Karma, aged three. They wish to set up a college savings plan. Ricky and Susan enjoy their lifestyle. They do not feel they need to make a lot more money. The Taylors can save $200/month for college. Lawsuits are not prevalent in Ricky's business.

What to Do:

- Use The College Savings Calculator™ to explore college costs and types of schools with the Taylors. A state college, for example, will cost about $40,000 in 2016 when Karma is ready to attend. (Figure not shown.)

- Use The Financial Aid Test™ software to determine the financial aid status of the Taylor family. The Taylors would have a Federal EFC of $5,300 and an Institutional EFC of $7,059 if Karma were to attend college today. They are highly likely financial aid candidates at most schools. (Figure not shown.)

- Use The Attribute Evaluator Worksheet™ to itemize the Taylors' needs. In this case, financial aid is the dominant concern. (Figure not shown.)

- Use The College Funding Integrator™ to show the Taylors how their program will work. (Figure not shown.)

Plan Design:

Because financial aid is important, The Simple Plan™ would work well for the Taylor family. Setting up the college savings plans titled as a business asset can enhance future financial aid benefits because of the business discount that the financial aid system applies to parent assets. You can review details about this concept in Chapter 8.

There is no major disadvantage to saving in the business name. Because Ricky is a sole proprietor, any creditor problems would likely pierce his personal assets anyway, and Ricky did not see this as a major issue. Unless there are state or local business taxes to consider, Ricky's income tax picture will be the same. Ricky will simply report any dividends or capital gains on his Schedule C instead of on his personal Schedule B.

Situation #3: Client Already Has a UGMA Account or Savings Bonds

Sometimes advisors find existing college plans that are not structured correctly for the client. Advisors need to recommend how to undo them. Typically this involves money in UGMA or UTMA accounts, but it could also involve savings bonds.

> Rachel Rich is a widow. Two years ago when her husband died, she took $40,000 from her husband's life insurance proceeds and made two $20,000 deposits to UGMA accounts to fund college for each of her twin sons, Tom and Ray, aged four. Rachel is well set financially and pays high taxes. Rachel suspects that a QTP might be a better choice but is unsure about dealing with the irrevocable gifts she made to her sons.

> Rachel has two choices:

- If the gains in the UGMA account are not too great, she can liquidate the accounts, pay the taxes due, and open UGMA accounts in a QTP of her choice. The UGMA ownership status flows through to the QTP. At the age of majority, her sons will control the QTP, and it will be their asset for financial aid purposes. The tax status of the accounts will, however, change from taxable subject to the Kiddie Tax rules to the tax-free status of a QTP.

- A second option is to keep the UGMA accounts but change the investments within them to a tax-managed strategy, deferring as much of the tax burden as possible so that Rachel does not need to pay tax in her high bracket. When her sons reach age fourteen and the Kiddie Tax is no longer applicable, she can liquidate the accounts at her sons' lower tax bracket. *Warning:* Deferring the taxes can actually result in a larger total tax being paid even at the lower rates if the growth in the account is substantial.

––––––––

Nora Notsorich is a widow with a similar problem but different circumstances. She also has a UGMA account for her daughter. Nora's family, however, is very likely to get financial aid. Transferring funds to a QTP does not really help. Her best solution is to spend her daughter's money on appropriate items for her daughter's benefit. The law (see regulations for specific states) allows parents to spend UGMA money for the benefit of the beneficiary.

Usually allowable expenses include items like the following:

- School tuition
- Educational trips
- School trips
- Home computers
- Car and car expenses for the student

Many parents will spend down UGMA account money and set aside an equal amount in a parent-owned account for college. This trade changes the account attributes to be more financial aid friendly.

––––––––

The Saver family has been buying U.S. Savings Bonds for years, hoping to use the tax-free interest benefit of the bonds for college expenses. However, their family income is edging close to the threshold where the bond interest will no longer be tax-free. A solution is to roll the bonds into a QTP where there is no income threshold. The Savers need to complete the rollover in a year when their taxable income is below the bond income threshold to ensure a tax-free exchange. (See IRS Publication 970 for details.)

––––––––

Situation #4: An Exit Strategy Is Needed for a Family Whose Income Is Increasing Rapidly

Fred and Francine Fasttrack had a major change in their financial circumstances. Fred had been a maintenance worker for a small company when he and Francine started their college plan. They had been saving $200 a month for almost ten years. When they set up their plan, financial aid had been a high probability for their two sons, now aged fourteen and fifteen. But Fred found out by accident that he had a flair for computers. He now has a supervisory position in his company. In the last four years his income has tripled. Financial aid is no longer the issue, but taxes are.

The Fasttracks' college account is currently worth about $60,000, with a cost basis of about $20,000. The growth funds Fred originally purchased were now starting to kick off substantial annual taxable dividends.

What Can Fred Do?

A QTP is now an appropriate solution for Fred. But QTPs can only take cash. Fred can liquidate his appreciated mutual funds and pay the tax in his high bracket, then purchase shares in his favorite QTP. Fred maintains control if he uses this approach but pays tax on a $40,000 gain.

As an alternative Fred and Francine can gift the appreciated investments to their sons using UGMA accounts and spreading the gifts over two years to avoid gift taxes. This is an income-tax-free exchange. The sons take on the parents' cost basis in the investment. Fred as custodian of the UGMA account can then sell the appreciated investments, paying tax at their sons' tax rates. Because their sons are older than fourteen, the Kiddie Tax no longer applies. Fred as custodian invests in his favorite QTP. Fred can generate substantial tax savings using this approach, but there is a cost. When his sons reach age eighteen, they will control the QTP assets.

Situation #5: Divorce and/or Remarriage Often Changes the Focus of a Plan

Advisors need to be attuned to the need for a college savings plan review when parents get divorced or when a single parent gets remarried. Both events signal potential changes in financial aid eligibility and income tax brackets. The main concern in addressing these issues is in making sure that exit strategies are built into the original plans to account for them.

Peggy, a widow for many years, set up her college savings plan to maximize financial aid. Her plan consisted of a portfolio of highly appreciated parent-owned mutual funds. When her son was a senior in high school, she met Mr. Right and fell in love. Mr. Right proposed.

Peggy had the following dilemma:

- If Peggy married Mr. Right, his income and assets would effectively cancel any financial aid eligibility.

- In addition, their combined tax bracket as a married couple would diminish the value of her college account substantially upon liquidation.

- Peggy did not want to burden Mr. Right with her college problem, even though he would have been glad to help.

Peggy came up with two possible options:

- Marry Mr. Right. Gift her son, through a UGMA account, the investments in her portfolio. Let her son liquidate the portfolio and pay the tax at his bracket. And get some help from Mr. Right to compensate for lost aid.

- Don't marry Mr. Right until the senior year of college, hope he will wait, and actuate her college plan as intended.

Peggy took the gutsy approach and opted for option two. She did not want to impose her problem at the start of the new relationship. By the way, her approach paid off. Peggy and Mr. Right are happily married, and her son has graduated from college.

———

Divorce is a difficult obstacle to handle in college planning. Our experience in offering court testimony is that in the case of young children, the courts do not want to deal with college, even when the parents are wealthy. This experience corroborates the comments made in Chapters 9 and 10 that courts might force the liquidation of college funds to meet current support obligations.

Bob and Mary Badmatch came to the conclusion that their divorce was inevitable. One of the few things they both agreed on was that they would keep the college funds for their two children isolated. Bob was currently the custodian for the family's QTP. Because Bob could withdraw money at any time, subject to taxes and penalties, Mary was concerned. QTPs do not allow for joint custodians.

These are some of the options that Bob and Mary considered:

- Name a trusted friend as custodian. This raised two issues. First, as custodian, the friend would have all the rights of ownership, including the right to take the funds out of the account, pay the taxes and penalties, and use it for whatever he wished, contrary to the intentions of Bob and Mary. This right raises the second issue: Would there be a gift tax due?

- Set up a trust and name the trusted friend as trustee. This may involve costs of setting up the trust. In addition, it is necessary to make sure the state plan allows a trust to be custodian of a QTP.

- Set up a custodial account. However, this involves the issue of the student becoming owner of the account at majority. Once again, the student could withdraw the money and use it for non-educational purposes.

- Bob and Mary could split the existing QTP into two separate accounts with one of them a custodian for each account. This would assure Mary that at least half of the fund would be in her control, but the other half would still be in Bob's control.

Their case does demonstrate how the divorce issue can complicate the college plan.

Final Comments

You have probably noticed that in the case studies in this chapter, we have focused on three planning tools:

- The Life Insurance Funded College Plan

- The Qualified Tuition Plan (QTP)

- The Simple Plan™ (a portfolio of parent-owned investments)

We feel that these are the basic tools advisors really need to have in their college planning arsenal. IRAs, Roth IRAs, savings bonds, UGMA and UTMA accounts, and Education Savings Accounts all have a minor role on paying for college. Planners need to understand them, but these tools do not have the same impact as the big three above. We should point out, however, that education savings accounts do have an impact on funding pre-college education, i.e., grades K–12, and should not be ignored.

We have tried to give several examples as prototype plans for advisor use, but advisors need to be creative beyond these examples. Educating children is a noble goal and the last great gift parents give children before they leave home. A properly designed college plan can make this gift a reality, and it can be done without ruining the parents' retirement.

In this book we have tried to give advisors a college planning system that will be useful for some time. The tools we discussed in the first seven chapters—

- The College Savings Calculator,™

- The Financial Aid Test,™

- The College Funding Integrator,™ and

- The Attribute Evaluation Worksheet™

—are the guts of the planning system. Updating these tools regularly will give the advisor the means to collect data from parents about their goals and dreams, map out an effective college plan, and communicate it effectively to clients.

Chapters 8 and 9 talked about current products, tax vehicles, and strategies. These change over time. We have listed a number of useful Web sites, an IRS publication, and other resources in Appendixes F and G to help you keep up to date. Finally, trade associations can be particularly helpful in keeping advisors up-to-date. The Financial Planning Association, the Society of Financial Service Professionals, the Academy of College Financial Planning, and the American Institute of Certified Public Accountants are several organizations that occasionally sponsor programs on planning for college funding.

Appendix A

The College Savings Calculator™: Savings Required for the 20 Benchmark Colleges

Western Region — State (Resident)

The College Savings Calculator™ — Projected College Costs and Savings Required

---

Assumptions:

Planned Savings Starts in September	2002
Planned Withdrawals Begin in September	Freshman Year
Geographic Region (1 = Northeast, 2 = Midwest, 3 = South, 4 = West)	**4 West**
Cost Categories (1 = Low, 2 = Med/Low, 3 = Medium, 4 = Med/High, 5 = High)	**1 State College (Resident)**
Benchmark College:	**U of Washington**
Projected After-Tax Growth Rates on Savings Deposits	8.00% 9.00% 7.00%

Notes:

Assume Funding through August of the Last Year of College

College Costs are total costs based on college budget bill plus misc. costs reported by parents.

Cost Categories—1 Low for State schools (in-state resident), 5 High for Ivy League, 2–4 Medium range for Private

Projected Freshman Year	Projected Freshman Cost	Projected Sophomore Cost	Projected Junior Cost	Projected Senior Cost	Projected Four-Year Cost	Approx. Mo. Savings Req. 8.00%	Approx. Mo. Savings Req. 9.00%	Approx. Mo. Savings Req. 7.00%
2002						n/a	n/a	n/a
2003	$17,118	$17,796	$18,503	$19,240	$72,658	$1,158	$1,152	$1,165
2004	$17,796	$18,503	$19,240	$20,116	$75,656	$964	$954	$975
2005	$18,503	$19,240	$20,116	$21,035	$78,895	$827	$813	$840
2006	$19,240	$20,116	$21,035	$21,998	$82,389	$724	$708	$740
2007	$20,116	$21,035	$21,998	$23,008	$86,157	$645	$627	$663
2008	$21,035	$21,998	$23,008	$24,067	$90,107	$581	$562	$601
2009	$21,998	$23,008	$24,067	$25,718	$94,791	$532	$511	$553
2010	$23,008	$24,067	$25,718	$27,487	$100,280	$493	$471	$516
2011	$24,067	$25,718	$27,487	$29,382	$106,654	$463	$440	$487
2012	$25,718	$27,487	$29,382	$31,413	$114,000	$439	$414	$465
2013	$27,487	$29,382	$31,413	$33,589	$121,870	$419	$393	$446
2014	$29,382	$31,413	$33,589	$35,921	$130,304	$401	$373	$430
2015	$31,413	$33,589	$35,921	$38,421	$139,343	$385	$356	$416
2016	$33,589	$35,921	$38,421	$41,101	$149,031	$371	$341	$403
2017	$35,921	$38,421	$41,101	$43,974	$159,416	$359	$328	$392
2018	$38,421	$41,101	$43,974	$47,055	$170,549	$348	$315	$383
2019	$41,101	$43,974	$47,055	$50,358	$182,487	$338	$304	$374
2020	$43,974	$47,055	$50,358	$53,901	$195,288	$328	$294	$366
2021	$47,055	$50,358	$53,901	$57,702	$209,016	$320	$284	$360
2022	$50,358	$53,901	$57,702	$61,778	$223,740	$313	$276	$354
2023	$53,901	$57,702	$61,778	$66,152	$239,534	$306	$267	$348

Source: College Money © 1997–2001. Version: 2002 (Book).b.

Western Region—State (Nonresident)

The College Savings Calculator™—Projected College Costs and Savings Required

Assumptions:

Planned Savings Starts in September	2002
Planned Withdrawals Begin in September	Freshman Year
Geographic Region (1 = Northeast, 2 = Midwest, 3 = South, 4 = West)	**4 West**
Cost Categories (1 = Low, 2 = Med/Low, 3 = Medium, 4 = Med/High, 5 = High)	**2 State College (Nonresident)**
Benchmark College:	**U of Washington (NR)**
Projected After-Tax Growth Rates on Savings Deposits	8.00% 9.00% 7.00%

Notes:

Assume Funding through August of the Last Year of College

College Costs are total costs based on college budget bill plus misc. costs reported by parents.

Cost Categories—1 Low for State schools (in-state resident), 5 High for Ivy League, 2–4 Medium range for Private

Projected Freshman Year	Projected Freshman Cost	Projected Sophomore Cost	Projected Junior Cost	Projected Senior Cost	Projected Four-Year Cost	Approx. Mo. Savings Req. 8.00%	Approx. Mo. Savings Req. 9.00%	Approx. Mo. Savings Req. 7.00%
2002						n/a	n/a	n/a
2003	$27,283	$28,438	$29,645	$30,904	$116,270	$1,853	$1,843	$1,864
2004	$28,438	$29,645	$30,904	$32,405	$121,392	$1,547	$1,530	$1,564
2005	$29,645	$30,904	$32,405	$33,982	$126,937	$1,330	$1,308	$1,352
2006	$30,904	$32,405	$33,982	$35,639	$132,931	$1,168	$1,143	$1,194
2007	$32,405	$33,982	$35,639	$37,381	$139,408	$1,043	$1,015	$1,072
2008	$33,982	$35,639	$37,381	$39,210	$146,213	$943	$912	$975
2009	$35,639	$37,381	$39,210	$42,033	$154,263	$865	$832	$900
2010	$37,381	$39,210	$42,033	$45,064	$163,687	$805	$769	$842
2011	$39,210	$42,033	$45,064	$48,318	$174,625	$758	$719	$797
2012	$42,033	$45,064	$48,318	$51,814	$187,229	$721	$680	$763
2013	$45,064	$48,318	$51,814	$55,568	$200,764	$689	$647	$735
2014	$48,318	$51,814	$55,568	$59,600	$215,301	$662	$617	$710
2015	$51,814	$55,568	$59,600	$63,932	$230,914	$638	$591	$688
2016	$55,568	$59,600	$63,932	$68,585	$247,686	$617	$567	$670
2017	$59,600	$63,932	$68,585	$73,585	$265,702	$598	$546	$654
2018	$63,932	$68,585	$73,585	$78,956	$285,058	$581	$527	$639
2019	$68,585	$73,585	$78,956	$84,728	$305,854	$566	$509	$627
2020	$73,585	$78,956	$84,728	$90,929	$328,198	$552	$494	$616
2021	$78,956	$84,728	$90,929	$97,594	$352,207	$539	$479	$606
2022	$84,728	$90,929	$97,594	$104,757	$378,008	$528	$465	$597
2023	$90,929	$97,594	$104,757	$112,455	$405,735	$517	$453	$590

Source: College Money © 1997–2001. Version: 2002 (Book).b.

Western Region—Private (Medium Cost)

The College Savings Calculator™—Projected College Costs and Savings Required

Assumptions:

Planned Savings Starts in September	2002
Planned Withdrawals Begin in September	Freshman Year
Geographic Region (1 = Northeast, 2 = Midwest, 3 = South, 4 = West)	**4 West**
Cost Categories (1 = Low, 2 = Med/Low, 3 = Medium, 4 = Med/High, 5 = High)	**3 Private College (Medium Cost)**
Benchmark College:	**University of Denver**
Projected After-Tax Growth Rates on Savings Deposits	8.00% 9.00% 7.00%

Notes:

Assume Funding through August of the Last Year of College

College Costs are total costs based on college budget bill plus misc. costs reported by parents.

Cost Categories—1 Low for State schools (in-state resident), 5 High for Ivy League, 2–4 Medium range for Private

Projected Freshman Year	Projected Freshman Cost	Projected Sophomore Cost	Projected Junior Cost	Projected Senior Cost	Projected Four-Year Cost	Approx. Mo. Savings Req. 8.00%	Approx. Mo. Savings Req. 9.00%	Approx. Mo. Savings Req. 7.00%
2002						n/a	n/a	n/a
2003	$32,833	$34,275	$35,781	$37,355	$140,244	$2,235	$2,222	$2,248
2004	$34,275	$35,781	$37,355	$39,234	$146,645	$1,869	$1,848	$1,889
2005	$35,781	$37,355	$39,234	$41,210	$153,581	$1,609	$1,582	$1,635
2006	$37,355	$39,234	$41,210	$43,289	$161,089	$1,415	$1,384	$1,446
2007	$39,234	$41,210	$43,289	$45,475	$169,208	$1,266	$1,232	$1,301
2008	$41,210	$43,289	$45,475	$47,774	$177,748	$1,146	$1,109	$1,185
2009	$43,289	$45,475	$47,774	$51,303	$187,840	$1,054	$1,013	$1,096
2010	$45,475	$47,774	$51,303	$55,096	$199,648	$981	$938	$1,027
2011	$47,774	$51,303	$55,096	$59,175	$213,347	$925	$879	$974
2012	$51,303	$55,096	$59,175	$63,560	$229,133	$882	$833	$934
2013	$55,096	$59,175	$63,560	$68,275	$246,105	$845	$792	$900
2014	$59,175	$63,560	$68,275	$73,345	$264,355	$813	$757	$872
2015	$63,560	$68,275	$73,345	$78,798	$283,978	$784	$726	$847
2016	$68,275	$73,345	$78,798	$84,661	$305,079	$759	$698	$825
2017	$73,345	$78,798	$84,661	$90,967	$327,772	$737	$673	$806
2018	$78,798	$84,661	$90,967	$97,750	$352,176	$717	$651	$790
2019	$84,661	$90,967	$97,750	$105,044	$378,422	$700	$630	$775
2020	$90,967	$97,750	$105,044	$112,890	$406,652	$684	$611	$763
2021	$97,750	$105,044	$112,890	$121,330	$437,014	$669	$594	$752
2022	$105,044	$112,890	$121,330	$130,409	$469,673	$656	$578	$742
2023	$112,890	$121,330	$130,409	$140,175	$504,804	$644	$563	$734

Source: College Money © 1997–2001. Version: 2002 (Book).b.

Western Region—Private (High Cost)

The College Savings Calculator™—Projected College Costs and Savings Required

Assumptions:

Planned Savings Starts in September   2002

Planned Withdrawals Begin in September   Freshman Year

Geographic Region (1 = Northeast, 2 = Midwest,
   3 = South, 4 = West)   **4 West**

Cost Categories (1 = Low, 2 = Med/Low,
   3 = Medium, 4 = Med/High, 5 = High)   **4 Private (High Cost)**

Benchmark College: **California Inst of Tech**

Projected After-Tax Growth Rates on Savings Deposits   8.00%   9.00%   7.00%

Notes:

Assume Funding through August of the Last Year of College

College Costs are total costs based on college budget bill plus misc. costs reported by parents.

Cost Categories—1 Low for State schools (in-state resident), 5 High for Ivy League,
   2–4 Medium range for Private

Projected Freshman Year	Projected Freshman Cost	Projected Sophomore Cost	Projected Junior Cost	Projected Senior Cost	Projected Four-Year Cost	Approx. Mo. Savings Req. 8.00%	Approx. Mo. Savings Req. 9.00%	Approx. Mo. Savings Req. 7.00%
2002						n/a	n/a	n/a
2003	$37,238	$38,835	$40,504	$42,246	$158,823	$2,531	$2,517	$2,546
2004	$38,835	$40,504	$42,246	$44,324	$165,909	$2,114	$2,091	$2,137
2005	$40,504	$42,246	$44,324	$46,508	$173,582	$1,818	$1,789	$1,848
2006	$42,246	$44,324	$46,508	$48,803	$181,881	$1,598	$1,563	$1,633
2007	$44,324	$46,508	$48,803	$51,216	$190,851	$1,428	$1,389	$1,468
2008	$46,508	$48,803	$51,216	$53,752	$200,279	$1,292	$1,249	$1,335
2009	$48,803	$51,216	$53,752	$57,657	$211,429	$1,186	$1,140	$1,233
2010	$51,216	$53,752	$57,657	$61,853	$224,478	$1,104	$1,055	$1,155
2011	$53,752	$57,657	$61,853	$66,360	$239,622	$1,039	$987	$1,094
2012	$57,657	$61,853	$66,360	$71,202	$257,072	$990	$934	$1,048
2013	$61,853	$66,360	$71,202	$76,405	$275,819	$947	$888	$1,009
2014	$66,360	$71,202	$76,405	$81,996	$295,962	$910	$848	$976
2015	$71,202	$76,405	$81,996	$88,004	$317,607	$877	$812	$947
2016	$76,405	$81,996	$88,004	$94,461	$340,865	$849	$780	$922
2017	$81,996	$88,004	$94,461	$101,400	$365,860	$823	$752	$900
2018	$88,004	$94,461	$101,400	$108,859	$392,723	$800	$726	$881
2019	$94,461	$101,400	$108,859	$116,876	$421,595	$780	$702	$864
2020	$101,400	$108,859	$116,876	$125,494	$452,628	$761	$681	$849
2021	$108,859	$116,876	$125,494	$134,758	$485,986	$744	$661	$836
2022	$116,876	$125,494	$134,758	$144,718	$521,845	$729	$643	$825
2023	$125,494	$134,758	$144,718	$155,425	$560,394	$715	$626	$815

Source: College Money © 1997–2001. Version: 2002 (Book).b.

Western Region—Ivy League

The College Savings Calculator™—Projected College Costs and Savings Required

---

Assumptions:

Planned Savings Starts in September	2002
Planned Withdrawals Begin in September	Freshman Year
Geographic Region (1 = Northeast, 2 = Midwest, 3 = South, 4 = West)	**4 West**
Cost Categories (1 = Low, 2 = Med/Low, 3 = Medium, 4 = Med/High, 5 = High)	**5 Ivy League**
Benchmark College:	**Stanford University**
Projected After-Tax Growth Rates on Savings Deposits	8.00% 9.00% 7.00%

Notes:

Assume Funding through August of the Last Year of College

College Costs are total costs based on college budget bill plus misc. costs reported by parents.

Cost Categories—1 Low for State schools (in-state resident), 5 High for Ivy League, 2–4 Medium range for Private

Projected Freshman Year	Projected Freshman Cost	Projected Sophomore Cost	Projected Junior Cost	Projected Senior Cost	Projected Four-Year Cost	Approx. Mo. Savings Req. 8.00%	Approx. Mo. Savings Req. 9.00%	Approx. Mo. Savings Req. 7.00%
2002						n/a	n/a	n/a
2003	$41,937	$43,801	$45,751	$47,789	$179,278	$2,857	$2,841	$2,873
2004	$43,801	$45,751	$47,789	$50,223	$187,565	$2,390	$2,364	$2,416
2005	$45,751	$47,789	$50,223	$52,784	$196,548	$2,058	$2,025	$2,092
2006	$47,789	$50,223	$52,784	$55,478	$206,275	$1,812	$1,772	$1,852
2007	$50,223	$52,784	$55,478	$58,313	$216,799	$1,622	$1,578	$1,667
2008	$52,784	$55,478	$58,313	$61,296	$227,871	$1,470	$1,421	$1,519
2009	$55,478	$58,313	$61,296	$65,865	$240,952	$1,352	$1,299	$1,405
2010	$58,313	$61,296	$65,865	$70,778	$256,252	$1,260	$1,204	$1,318
2011	$61,296	$65,865	$70,778	$76,064	$274,003	$1,188	$1,129	$1,251
2012	$65,865	$70,778	$76,064	$81,749	$294,456	$1,134	$1,070	$1,200
2013	$70,778	$76,064	$81,749	$87,864	$316,455	$1,087	$1,019	$1,158
2014	$76,064	$81,749	$87,864	$94,442	$340,119	$1,046	$974	$1,121
2015	$81,749	$87,864	$94,442	$101,519	$365,575	$1,010	$935	$1,090
2016	$87,864	$94,442	$101,519	$109,132	$392,958	$978	$899	$1,063
2017	$94,442	$101,519	$109,132	$117,323	$422,417	$950	$868	$1,039
2018	$101,519	$109,132	$117,323	$126,135	$454,110	$925	$839	$1,018
2019	$109,132	$117,323	$126,135	$135,617	$488,208	$903	$813	$1,000
2020	$117,323	$126,135	$135,617	$145,818	$524,893	$882	$789	$985
2021	$126,135	$135,617	$145,818	$156,795	$564,365	$864	$767	$971
2022	$135,617	$145,818	$156,795	$168,606	$606,836	$847	$747	$959
2023	$145,818	$156,795	$168,606	$181,316	$652,535	$832	$728	$948

Source: College Money © 1997–2001. Version: 2002 (Book).b.

Midwest Region—State (Resident)

The College Savings Calculator™—Projected College Costs and Savings Required

Assumptions:

Planned Savings Starts in September	2002
Planned Withdrawals Begin in September	Freshman Year
Geographic Region (1 = Northeast, 2 = Midwest, 3 = South, 4 = West)	**2 Midwest**
Cost Categories (1 = Low, 2 = Med/Low, 3 = Medium, 4 = Med/High, 5 = High)	**1 State College (Resident)**
Benchmark College:	**Ohio State Univ**
Projected After-Tax Growth Rates on Savings Deposits	8.00% 9.00% 7.00%

Notes:

Assume Funding through August of the Last Year of College

College Costs are total costs based on college budget bill plus misc. costs reported by parents.

Cost Categories—1 Low for State schools (in-state resident), 5 High for Ivy League, 2–4 Medium range for Private

Projected Freshman Year	Projected Freshman Cost	Projected Sophomore Cost	Projected Junior Cost	Projected Senior Cost	Projected Four-Year Cost	Approx. Mo. Savings Req. 8.00%	Approx. Mo. Savings Req. 9.00%	Approx. Mo. Savings Req. 7.00%
2002						n/a	n/a	n/a
2003	$17,109	$17,793	$18,506	$19,249	$72,657	$1,158	$1,152	$1,165
2004	$17,793	$18,506	$19,249	$20,133	$75,681	$965	$954	$975
2005	$18,506	$19,249	$20,133	$21,059	$78,947	$827	$814	$841
2006	$19,249	$20,133	$21,059	$22,031	$82,472	$725	$709	$741
2007	$20,133	$21,059	$22,031	$23,051	$86,274	$646	$628	$664
2008	$21,059	$22,031	$23,051	$24,120	$90,261	$582	$563	$602
2009	$22,031	$23,051	$24,120	$25,785	$94,987	$533	$512	$554
2010	$23,051	$24,120	$25,785	$27,569	$100,526	$494	$472	$517
2011	$24,120	$25,785	$27,569	$29,481	$106,956	$464	$441	$488
2012	$25,785	$27,569	$29,481	$31,531	$114,367	$441	$416	$466
2013	$27,569	$29,481	$31,531	$33,728	$122,309	$420	$394	$448
2014	$29,481	$31,531	$33,728	$36,083	$130,823	$402	$375	$431
2015	$31,531	$33,728	$36,083	$38,608	$139,950	$387	$358	$417
2016	$33,728	$36,083	$38,608	$41,316	$149,735	$373	$343	$405
2017	$36,083	$38,608	$41,316	$44,220	$160,227	$361	$329	$394
2018	$38,608	$41,316	$44,220	$47,334	$171,478	$349	$317	$385
2019	$41,316	$44,220	$47,334	$50,675	$183,545	$339	$306	$376
2020	$44,220	$47,334	$50,675	$54,259	$196,489	$330	$296	$369
2021	$47,334	$50,675	$54,259	$58,104	$210,373	$322	$286	$362
2022	$50,675	$54,259	$58,104	$62,230	$225,268	$315	$277	$356
2023	$54,259	$58,104	$62,230	$66,657	$241,250	$308	$269	$351

Source: College Money © 1997–2001. Version: 2002 (Book).b.

Midwest Region—State (Nonresident)

The College Savings Calculator™—Projected College Costs and Savings Required

---

Assumptions:

Planned Savings Starts in September	2002
Planned Withdrawals Begin in September	Freshman Year
Geographic Region (1 = Northeast, 2 = Midwest, 3 = South, 4 = West)	**2 Midwest**
Cost Categories (1 = Low, 2 = Med/Low, 3 = Medium, 4 = Med/High, 5 = High)	**2 State College (Nonresident)**
Benchmark College:	**Ohio State Univ (NR)**
Projected After-Tax Growth Rates on Savings Deposits	8.00% 9.00% 7.00%

Notes:

Assume Funding through August of the Last Year of College

College Costs are total costs based on college budget bill plus misc. costs reported by parents.

Cost Categories—1 Low for State schools (in-state resident), 5 High for Ivy League, 2–4 Medium range for Private

Projected Freshman Year	Projected Freshman Cost	Projected Sophomore Cost	Projected Junior Cost	Projected Senior Cost	Projected Four-Year Cost	Approx. Mo. Savings Req. 8.00%	Approx. Mo. Savings Req. 9.00%	Approx. Mo. Savings Req. 7.00%
2002						n/a	n/a	n/a
2003	$26,717	$27,851	$29,036	$30,273	$113,877	$1,815	$1,805	$1,825
2004	$27,851	$29,036	$30,273	$31,747	$118,907	$1,515	$1,499	$1,532
2005	$29,036	$30,273	$31,747	$33,296	$124,352	$1,303	$1,281	$1,324
2006	$30,273	$31,747	$33,296	$34,924	$130,241	$1,144	$1,119	$1,169
2007	$31,747	$33,296	$34,924	$36,635	$136,603	$1,022	$994	$1,051
2008	$33,296	$34,924	$36,635	$38,433	$143,288	$924	$894	$955
2009	$34,924	$36,635	$38,433	$41,205	$151,196	$848	$816	$882
2010	$36,635	$38,433	$41,205	$44,182	$160,453	$789	$754	$825
2011	$38,433	$41,205	$44,182	$47,379	$171,197	$743	$705	$782
2012	$41,205	$44,182	$47,379	$50,812	$183,577	$707	$667	$749
2013	$44,182	$47,379	$50,812	$54,501	$196,873	$676	$634	$720
2014	$47,379	$50,812	$54,501	$58,463	$211,155	$649	$605	$696
2015	$50,812	$54,501	$58,463	$62,719	$226,496	$626	$579	$675
2016	$54,501	$58,463	$62,719	$67,292	$242,976	$605	$556	$657
2017	$58,463	$62,719	$67,292	$72,206	$260,681	$586	$536	$641
2018	$62,719	$67,292	$72,206	$77,485	$279,703	$570	$517	$627
2019	$67,292	$72,206	$77,485	$83,158	$300,142	$555	$500	$615
2020	$72,206	$77,485	$83,158	$89,255	$322,104	$542	$484	$604
2021	$77,485	$83,158	$89,255	$95,807	$345,706	$529	$470	$595
2022	$83,158	$89,255	$95,807	$102,849	$371,070	$518	$457	$586
2023	$89,255	$95,807	$102,849	$110,419	$398,330	$508	$445	$579

Source: College Money © 1997–2001. Version: 2002 (Book).b.

Midwest Region—Private (Medium Cost)

The College Savings Calculator™—Projected College Costs
and Savings Required

Assumptions:

Planned Savings Starts in September	2002
Planned Withdrawals Begin in September	Freshman Year
Geographic Region (1 = Northeast, 2 = Midwest, 3 = South, 4 = West)	**2 Midwest**
Cost Categories (1 = Low, 2 = Med/Low, 3 = Medium, 4 = Med/High, 5 = High)	**3 Private College (Medium Cost)**
Benchmark College:	**Cornell College (IA)***
Projected After-Tax Growth Rates on Savings Deposits	8.00% 9.00% 7.00%

Notes:

Assume Funding through August of the Last Year of College

College Costs are total costs based on college budget bill plus misc. costs reported by parents.

Cost Categories—1 Low for State schools (in-state resident), 5 High for Ivy League,
2–4 Medium range for Private

Projected Freshman Year	Projected Freshman Cost	Projected Sophomore Cost	Projected Junior Cost	Projected Senior Cost	Projected Four-Year Cost	Approx. Mo. Savings Req. 8.00%	Approx. Mo. Savings Req. 9.00%	Approx. Mo. Savings Req. 7.00%
2002						n/a	n/a	n/a
2003	$32,642	$34,080	$35,583	$37,154	$139,458	$2,222	$2,210	$2,235
2004	$34,080	$35,583	$37,154	$39,029	$145,845	$1,858	$1,838	$1,879
2005	$35,583	$37,154	$39,029	$41,001	$152,767	$1,600	$1,574	$1,626
2006	$37,154	$39,029	$41,001	$43,076	$160,260	$1,408	$1,377	$1,439
2007	$39,029	$41,001	$43,076	$45,258	$168,365	$1,260	$1,225	$1,295
2008	$41,001	$43,076	$45,258	$47,554	$176,890	$1,141	$1,103	$1,179
2009	$43,076	$45,258	$47,554	$51,075	$186,964	$1,049	$1,008	$1,091
2010	$45,258	$47,554	$51,075	$54,861	$198,749	$977	$934	$1,022
2011	$47,554	$51,075	$54,861	$58,932	$212,422	$921	$875	$970
2012	$51,075	$54,861	$58,932	$63,309	$228,178	$879	$829	$930
2013	$54,861	$58,932	$63,309	$68,017	$245,119	$842	$789	$897
2014	$58,932	$63,309	$68,017	$73,079	$263,338	$810	$754	$868
2015	$63,309	$68,017	$73,079	$78,524	$282,930	$782	$723	$843
2016	$68,017	$73,079	$78,524	$84,380	$304,000	$757	$696	$822
2017	$73,079	$78,524	$84,380	$90,678	$326,661	$735	$671	$803
2018	$78,524	$84,380	$90,678	$97,452	$351,034	$715	$649	$787
2019	$84,380	$90,678	$97,452	$104,739	$377,249	$698	$628	$773
2020	$90,678	$97,452	$104,739	$112,578	$405,448	$682	$610	$761
2021	$97,452	$104,739	$112,578	$121,010	$435,780	$667	$592	$750
2022	$104,739	$112,578	$121,010	$130,082	$468,410	$654	$577	$740
2023	$112,578	$121,010	$130,082	$139,841	$503,511	$642	$562	$732

Source: College Money © 1997–2001. Version: 2002 (Book).b.

Midwest Region—Private (High Cost)

The College Savings Calculator™—Projected College Costs and Savings Required

---

Assumptions:

Planned Savings Starts in September	2002
Planned Withdrawals Begin in September	Freshman Year
Geographic Region (1 = Northeast, 2 = Midwest, 3 = South, 4 = West)	**2 Midwest**
Cost Categories (1 = Low, 2 = Med/Low, 3 = Medium, 4 = Med/High, 5 = High)	**4 Private (High Cost)**
Benchmark College:	**Kenyon College**
Projected After-Tax Growth Rates on Savings Deposits	8.00% 9.00% 7.00%

Notes:

Assume Funding through August of the Last Year of College

College Costs are total costs based on college budget bill plus misc. costs reported by parents.

Cost Categories—1 Low for State schools (in-state resident), 5 High for Ivy League, 2–4 Medium range for Private

Projected Freshman Year	Projected Freshman Cost	Projected Sophomore Cost	Projected Junior Cost	Projected Senior Cost	Projected Four-Year Cost	Approx. Mo. Savings Req. 8.00%	Approx. Mo. Savings Req. 9.00%	Approx. Mo. Savings Req. 7.00%
2002						n/a	n/a	n/a
2003	$39,104	$40,854	$42,684	$44,598	$167,241	$2,665	$2,650	$2,680
2004	$40,854	$42,684	$44,598	$46,883	$175,020	$2,230	$2,206	$2,254
2005	$42,684	$44,598	$46,883	$49,288	$183,454	$1,921	$1,890	$1,953
2006	$44,598	$46,883	$49,288	$51,819	$192,589	$1,692	$1,655	$1,729
2007	$46,883	$49,288	$51,819	$54,483	$202,474	$1,515	$1,474	$1,557
2008	$49,288	$51,819	$54,483	$57,286	$212,876	$1,373	$1,328	$1,419
2009	$51,819	$54,483	$57,286	$61,575	$225,163	$1,263	$1,214	$1,313
2010	$54,483	$57,286	$61,575	$66,189	$239,532	$1,177	$1,125	$1,232
2011	$57,286	$61,575	$66,189	$71,153	$256,203	$1,111	$1,055	$1,169
2012	$61,575	$66,189	$71,153	$76,494	$275,411	$1,060	$1,001	$1,123
2013	$66,189	$71,153	$76,494	$82,239	$296,075	$1,017	$953	$1,083
2014	$71,153	$76,494	$82,239	$88,422	$318,308	$979	$912	$1,049
2015	$76,494	$82,239	$88,422	$95,073	$342,228	$945	$875	$1,020
2016	$82,239	$88,422	$95,073	$102,230	$367,965	$916	$842	$995
2017	$88,422	$95,073	$102,230	$109,932	$395,657	$890	$813	$973
2018	$95,073	$102,230	$109,932	$118,219	$425,455	$867	$786	$954
2019	$102,230	$109,932	$118,219	$127,137	$457,519	$846	$762	$937
2020	$109,932	$118,219	$127,137	$136,734	$492,023	$827	$740	$923
2021	$118,219	$127,137	$136,734	$147,062	$529,153	$810	$719	$910
2022	$127,137	$136,734	$147,062	$158,177	$569,111	$795	$701	$899
2023	$136,734	$147,062	$158,177	$170,139	$612,113	$781	$683	$890

Source: College Money © 1997–2001. Version: 2002 (Book).b.

Midwest Region—Ivy League

The College Savings Calculator™—Projected College Costs and Savings Required

Assumptions:

Planned Savings Starts in September	2002
Planned Withdrawals Begin in September	Freshman Year
Geographic Region (1 = Northeast, 2 = Midwest, 3 = South, 4 = West)	**2 Midwest**
Cost Categories (1 = Low, 2 = Med/Low, 3 = Medium, 4 = Med/High, 5 = High)	**5 Ivy League**
Benchmark College:	**Northwestern University**
Projected After-Tax Growth Rates on Savings Deposits	8.00% 9.00% 7.00%

Notes:

Assume Funding through August of the Last Year of College

College Costs are total costs based on college budget bill plus misc. costs reported by parents.

Cost Categories—1 Low for State schools (in-state resident), 5 High for Ivy League, 2–4 Medium range for Private

Projected Freshman Year	Projected Freshman Cost	Projected Sophomore Cost	Projected Junior Cost	Projected Senior Cost	Projected Four-Year Cost	Approx. Mo. Savings Req. 8.00%	Approx. Mo. Savings Req. 9.00%	Approx. Mo. Savings Req. 7.00%
2002						n/a	n/a	n/a
2003	$41,815	$43,668	$45,605	$47,631	$178,718	$2,848	$2,832	$2,864
2004	$43,668	$45,605	$47,631	$50,049	$186,953	$2,382	$2,356	$2,408
2005	$45,605	$47,631	$50,049	$52,593	$195,878	$2,051	$2,018	$2,085
2006	$47,631	$50,049	$52,593	$55,269	$205,542	$1,805	$1,766	$1,845
2007	$50,049	$52,593	$55,269	$58,085	$215,996	$1,616	$1,572	$1,661
2008	$52,593	$55,269	$58,085	$61,047	$226,994	$1,464	$1,416	$1,513
2009	$55,269	$58,085	$61,047	$65,587	$239,988	$1,346	$1,294	$1,400
2010	$58,085	$61,047	$65,587	$70,469	$255,188	$1,254	$1,199	$1,312
2011	$61,047	$65,587	$70,469	$75,720	$272,823	$1,183	$1,124	$1,245
2012	$65,587	$70,469	$75,720	$81,367	$293,143	$1,129	$1,065	$1,195
2013	$70,469	$75,720	$81,367	$87,441	$314,997	$1,082	$1,014	$1,152
2014	$75,720	$81,367	$87,441	$93,974	$338,502	$1,041	$970	$1,116
2015	$81,367	$87,441	$93,974	$101,002	$363,784	$1,005	$930	$1,084
2016	$87,441	$93,974	$101,002	$108,561	$390,978	$973	$895	$1,057
2017	$93,974	$101,002	$108,561	$116,693	$420,231	$945	$863	$1,034
2018	$101,002	$108,561	$116,693	$125,442	$451,698	$920	$835	$1,013
2019	$108,561	$116,693	$125,442	$134,854	$485,551	$898	$809	$995
2020	$116,693	$125,442	$134,854	$144,980	$521,970	$877	$785	$979
2021	$125,442	$134,854	$144,980	$155,875	$561,151	$859	$763	$965
2022	$134,854	$144,980	$155,875	$167,597	$603,306	$842	$743	$953
2023	$144,980	$155,875	$167,597	$180,210	$648,662	$827	$724	$943

Source: College Money © 1997–2001. Version: 2002 (Book).b.

Southern Region—State (Resident)

The College Savings Calculator™—Projected College Costs and Savings Required

---

Assumptions:

Planned Savings Starts in September	2002
Planned Withdrawals Begin in September	Freshman Year
Geographic Region (1 = Northeast, 2 = Midwest, 3 = South, 4 = West)	**3 South**
Cost Categories (1 = Low, 2 = Med/Low, 3 = Medium, 4 = Med/High, 5 = High)	**1 State College (Resident)**
Benchmark College:	**Univ. of North Carolina**
Projected After-Tax Growth Rates on Savings Deposits	8.00% 9.00% 7.00%

Notes:

Assume Funding through August of the Last Year of College

College Costs are total costs based on college budget bill plus misc. costs reported by parents.

Cost Categories—1 Low for State schools (in-state resident), 5 High for Ivy League, 2–4 Medium range for Private

Projected Freshman Year	Projected Freshman Cost	Projected Sophomore Cost	Projected Junior Cost	Projected Senior Cost	Projected Four-Year Cost	Approx. Mo. Savings Req. 8.00%	Approx. Mo. Savings Req. 9.00%	Approx. Mo. Savings Req. 7.00%
2002						n/a	n/a	n/a
2003	$14,783	$15,373	$15,988	$16,629	$62,772	$1,001	$995	$1,006
2004	$15,373	$15,988	$16,629	$17,391	$65,379	$833	$824	$842
2005	$15,988	$16,629	$17,391	$18,190	$68,197	$715	$703	$726
2006	$16,629	$17,391	$18,190	$19,028	$71,237	$626	$612	$640
2007	$17,391	$18,190	$19,028	$19,907	$74,516	$558	$543	$573
2008	$18,190	$19,028	$19,907	$20,829	$77,954	$503	$486	$520
2009	$19,028	$19,907	$20,829	$22,266	$82,030	$460	$443	$479
2010	$19,907	$20,829	$22,266	$23,804	$86,807	$427	$408	$447
2011	$20,829	$22,266	$23,804	$25,453	$92,353	$401	$381	$422
2012	$22,266	$23,804	$25,453	$27,221	$98,744	$380	$359	$403
2013	$23,804	$25,453	$27,221	$29,115	$105,594	$363	$340	$386
2014	$25,453	$27,221	$29,115	$31,146	$112,936	$347	$324	$372
2015	$27,221	$29,115	$31,146	$33,323	$120,806	$334	$309	$360
2016	$29,115	$31,146	$33,323	$35,658	$129,243	$322	$296	$350
2017	$31,146	$33,323	$35,658	$38,162	$138,289	$311	$284	$340
2018	$33,323	$35,658	$38,162	$40,847	$147,990	$302	$274	$332
2019	$35,658	$38,162	$40,847	$43,727	$158,394	$293	$264	$325
2020	$38,162	$40,847	$43,727	$46,816	$169,552	$285	$255	$318
2021	$40,847	$43,727	$46,816	$50,131	$181,521	$278	$247	$312
2022	$43,727	$46,816	$50,131	$53,687	$194,360	$271	$239	$307
2023	$46,816	$50,131	$53,687	$57,502	$208,136	$266	$232	$303

Source: College Money © 1997–2001. Version: 2002 (Book).b.

Southern Region—State (Nonresident)

The College Savings Calculator™—Projected College Costs and Savings Required

Assumptions:

Planned Savings Starts in September	2002
Planned Withdrawals Begin in September	Freshman Year
Geographic Region (1 = Northeast, 2 = Midwest, 3 = South, 4 = West)	**3 South**
Cost Categories (1 = Low, 2 = Med/Low, 3 = Medium, 4 = Med/High, 5 = High)	**2 State College (Nonresident)**
Benchmark College:	**U of N Carolina (NR)**
Projected After-Tax Growth Rates on Savings Deposits	8.00% 9.00% 7.00%

Notes:

Assume Funding through August of the Last Year of College

College Costs are total costs based on college budget bill plus misc. costs reported by parents.

Cost Categories—1 Low for State schools (in-state resident), 5 High for Ivy League, 2–4 Medium range for Private

Projected Freshman Year	Projected Freshman Cost	Projected Sophomore Cost	Projected Junior Cost	Projected Senior Cost	Projected Four-Year Cost	Approx. Mo. Savings Req. 8.00%	Approx. Mo. Savings Req. 9.00%	Approx. Mo. Savings Req. 7.00%
2002						n/a	n/a	n/a
2003	$25,354	$26,429	$27,550	$28,722	$108,055	$1,722	$1,713	$1,732
2004	$26,429	$27,550	$28,722	$30,118	$112,819	$1,438	$1,422	$1,454
2005	$27,550	$28,722	$30,118	$31,585	$117,975	$1,236	$1,216	$1,256
2006	$28,722	$30,118	$31,585	$33,126	$123,550	$1,085	$1,062	$1,109
2007	$30,118	$31,585	$33,126	$34,745	$129,574	$970	$943	$997
2008	$31,585	$33,126	$34,745	$36,447	$135,903	$877	$848	$906
2009	$33,126	$34,745	$36,447	$39,072	$143,390	$804	$773	$836
2010	$34,745	$36,447	$39,072	$41,891	$152,155	$748	$715	$783
2011	$36,447	$39,072	$41,891	$44,918	$162,328	$704	$669	$741
2012	$39,072	$41,891	$44,918	$48,169	$174,050	$670	$633	$710
2013	$41,891	$44,918	$48,169	$51,661	$186,638	$641	$601	$683
2014	$44,918	$48,169	$51,661	$55,411	$200,158	$615	$573	$660
2015	$48,169	$51,661	$55,411	$59,440	$214,681	$593	$549	$640
2016	$51,661	$55,411	$59,440	$63,768	$230,280	$573	$527	$623
2017	$55,411	$59,440	$63,768	$68,419	$247,038	$556	$508	$608
2018	$59,440	$63,768	$68,419	$73,415	$265,042	$540	$490	$594
2019	$63,768	$68,419	$73,415	$78,784	$284,386	$526	$474	$583
2020	$68,419	$73,415	$78,784	$84,553	$305,170	$513	$459	$573
2021	$73,415	$78,784	$84,553	$90,753	$327,504	$501	$445	$564
2022	$78,784	$84,553	$90,753	$97,416	$351,505	$491	$433	$556
2023	$84,553	$90,753	$97,416	$104,577	$377,298	$481	$421	$548

Source: College Money © 1997–2001. Version: 2002 (Book).b.

Southern Region—Private (Medium Cost)

The College Savings Calculator™—Projected College Costs and Savings Required

Assumptions:

Planned Savings Starts in September	2002
Planned Withdrawals Begin in September	Freshman Year
Geographic Region (1 = Northeast, 2 = Midwest, 3 = South, 4 = West)	**3 South**
Cost Categories (1 = Low, 2 = Med/Low, 3 = Medium, 4 = Med/High, 5 = High)	**3 Private College (Medium Cost)**
Benchmark College:	**University of Richmond**
Projected After-Tax Growth Rates on Savings Deposits	8.00% 9.00% 7.00%

Notes:

Assume Funding through August of the Last Year of College

College Costs are total costs based on college budget bill plus misc. costs reported by parents.

Cost Categories—1 Low for State schools (in-state resident), 5 High for Ivy League, 2–4 Medium range for Private

Projected Freshman Year	Projected Freshman Cost	Projected Sophomore Cost	Projected Junior Cost	Projected Senior Cost	Projected Four-Year Cost	Approx. Mo. Savings Req. 8.00%	Approx. Mo. Savings Req. 9.00%	Approx. Mo. Savings Req. 7.00%
2002						n/a	n/a	n/a
2003	$34,336	$35,851	$37,435	$39,091	$146,713	$2,338	$2,325	$2,351
2004	$35,851	$37,435	$39,091	$41,067	$153,443	$1,955	$1,934	$1,977
2005	$37,435	$39,091	$41,067	$43,145	$160,738	$1,683	$1,656	$1,711
2006	$39,091	$41,067	$43,145	$45,332	$168,635	$1,481	$1,449	$1,514
2007	$41,067	$43,145	$45,332	$47,632	$177,176	$1,326	$1,290	$1,363
2008	$43,145	$45,332	$47,632	$50,052	$186,162	$1,201	$1,161	$1,241
2009	$45,332	$47,632	$50,052	$53,762	$196,779	$1,104	$1,061	$1,148
2010	$47,632	$50,052	$53,762	$57,752	$209,199	$1,028	$983	$1,076
2011	$50,052	$53,762	$57,752	$62,043	$223,609	$970	$921	$1,021
2012	$53,762	$57,752	$62,043	$66,656	$240,213	$925	$873	$979
2013	$57,752	$62,043	$66,656	$71,618	$258,069	$886	$831	$944
2014	$62,043	$66,656	$71,618	$76,954	$277,271	$852	$794	$914
2015	$66,656	$71,618	$76,954	$82,693	$297,921	$823	$762	$888
2016	$71,618	$76,954	$82,693	$88,866	$320,131	$797	$733	$866
2017	$76,954	$82,693	$88,866	$95,506	$344,019	$774	$707	$846
2018	$82,693	$88,866	$95,506	$102,648	$369,713	$753	$683	$829
2019	$88,866	$95,506	$102,648	$110,331	$397,351	$735	$662	$814
2020	$95,506	$102,648	$110,331	$118,595	$427,080	$718	$642	$801
2021	$102,648	$110,331	$118,595	$127,487	$459,061	$703	$624	$790
2022	$110,331	$118,595	$127,487	$137,052	$493,465	$689	$607	$780
2023	$118,595	$127,487	$137,052	$147,343	$530,477	$676	$592	$771

Source: College Money © 1997–2001. Version: 2002 (Book).b.

Southern Region—Private (High Cost)

The College Savings Calculator™—Projected College Costs and Savings Required

---

Assumptions:

Planned Savings Starts in September	2002
Planned Withdrawals Begin in September	Freshman Year
Geographic Region (1 = Northeast, 2 = Midwest, 3 = South, 4 = West)	**3 South**
Cost Categories (1 = Low, 2 = Med/Low, 3 = Medium, 4 = Med/High, 5 = High)	**4 Private (High Cost)**
Benchmark College:	**Univ of Miami**
Projected After-Tax Growth Rates on Savings Deposits	8.00% 9.00% 7.00%

Notes:

Assume Funding through August of the Last Year of College

College Costs are total costs based on college budget bill plus misc. costs reported by parents.

Cost Categories—1 Low for State schools (in-state resident), 5 High for Ivy League, 2–4 Medium range for Private

Projected Freshman Year	Projected Freshman Cost	Projected Sophomore Cost	Projected Junior Cost	Projected Senior Cost	Projected Four-Year Cost	Approx. Mo. Savings Req. 8.00%	Approx. Mo. Savings Req. 9.00%	Approx. Mo. Savings Req. 7.00%
2002						n/a	n/a	n/a
2003	$39,831	$41,582	$43,412	$45,326	$170,150	$2,711	$2,696	$2,727
2004	$41,582	$43,412	$45,326	$47,609	$177,929	$2,267	$2,242	$2,292
2005	$43,412	$45,326	$47,609	$50,011	$186,357	$1,952	$1,920	$1,984
2006	$45,326	$47,609	$50,011	$52,537	$195,482	$1,717	$1,680	$1,755
2007	$47,609	$50,011	$52,537	$55,194	$205,350	$1,536	$1,495	$1,579
2008	$50,011	$52,537	$55,194	$57,989	$215,730	$1,391	$1,346	$1,438
2009	$52,537	$55,194	$57,989	$62,277	$227,996	$1,279	$1,230	$1,330
2010	$55,194	$57,989	$62,277	$66,887	$242,346	$1,191	$1,138	$1,246
2011	$57,989	$62,277	$66,887	$71,844	$258,996	$1,123	$1,067	$1,182
2012	$62,277	$66,887	$71,844	$77,173	$278,180	$1,071	$1,011	$1,134
2013	$66,887	$71,844	$77,173	$82,905	$298,808	$1,026	$962	$1,093
2014	$71,844	$77,173	$82,905	$89,068	$320,990	$987	$920	$1,058
2015	$77,173	$82,905	$89,068	$95,696	$344,842	$953	$882	$1,028
2016	$82,905	$89,068	$95,696	$102,824	$370,492	$922	$848	$1,002
2017	$89,068	$95,696	$102,824	$110,490	$398,078	$895	$818	$979
2018	$95,696	$102,824	$110,490	$118,736	$427,746	$871	$790	$959
2019	$102,824	$110,490	$118,736	$127,605	$459,655	$850	$766	$942
2020	$110,490	$118,736	$127,605	$137,145	$493,976	$830	$743	$927
2021	$118,736	$127,605	$137,145	$147,407	$530,892	$813	$722	$913
2022	$127,605	$137,145	$147,407	$158,446	$570,602	$797	$702	$902
2023	$137,145	$147,407	$158,446	$170,322	$613,320	$782	$685	$891

Source: College Money © 1997–2001. Version: 2002 (Book).b.

Southern Region—Ivy League

The College Savings Calculator™—Projected College Costs and Savings Required

Assumptions:

Planned Savings Starts in September	2002
Planned Withdrawals Begin in September	Freshman Year
Geographic Region (1 = Northeast, 2 = Midwest, 3 = South, 4 = West)	**3 South**
Cost Categories (1 = Low, 2 = Med/Low, 3 = Medium, 4 = Med/High, 5 = High)	**5 Ivy League**
Benchmark College:	**Duke University**
Projected After-Tax Growth Rates on Savings Deposits	8.00% 9.00% 7.00%

Notes:

Assume Funding through August of the Last Year of College

College Costs are total costs based on college budget bill plus misc. costs reported by parents.

Cost Categories—1 Low for State schools (in-state resident), 5 High for Ivy League, 2–4 Medium range for Private

Projected Freshman Year	Projected Freshman Cost	Projected Sophomore Cost	Projected Junior Cost	Projected Senior Cost	Projected Four-Year Cost	Approx. Mo. Savings Req. 8.00%	Approx. Mo. Savings Req. 9.00%	Approx. Mo. Savings Req. 7.00%
2002						n/a	n/a	n/a
2003	$42,425	$44,314	$46,290	$48,355	$181,384	$2,890	$2,874	$2,907
2004	$44,314	$46,290	$48,355	$50,821	$189,780	$2,418	$2,392	$2,445
2005	$46,290	$48,355	$50,821	$53,416	$198,882	$2,083	$2,049	$2,117
2006	$48,355	$50,821	$53,416	$56,146	$208,738	$1,833	$1,794	$1,874
2007	$50,821	$53,416	$56,146	$59,019	$219,402	$1,642	$1,597	$1,687
2008	$53,416	$56,146	$59,019	$62,041	$230,622	$1,487	$1,438	$1,537
2009	$56,146	$59,019	$62,041	$66,671	$243,877	$1,368	$1,315	$1,422
2010	$59,019	$62,041	$66,671	$71,649	$259,380	$1,275	$1,218	$1,334
2011	$62,041	$66,671	$71,649	$77,005	$277,366	$1,203	$1,142	$1,266
2012	$66,671	$71,649	$77,005	$82,766	$298,091	$1,148	$1,083	$1,215
2013	$71,649	$77,005	$82,766	$88,963	$320,383	$1,100	$1,032	$1,172
2014	$77,005	$82,766	$88,963	$95,630	$344,363	$1,059	$986	$1,135
2015	$82,766	$88,963	$95,630	$102,802	$370,160	$1,022	$946	$1,103
2016	$88,963	$95,630	$102,802	$110,518	$397,912	$991	$911	$1,076
2017	$95,630	$102,802	$110,518	$118,819	$427,768	$962	$879	$1,052
2018	$102,802	$110,518	$118,819	$127,751	$459,890	$937	$850	$1,031
2019	$110,518	$118,819	$127,751	$137,362	$494,450	$914	$823	$1,013
2020	$118,819	$127,751	$137,362	$147,703	$531,635	$894	$799	$997
2021	$127,751	$137,362	$147,703	$158,830	$571,645	$875	$777	$983
2022	$137,362	$147,703	$158,830	$170,803	$614,697	$858	$757	$971
2023	$147,703	$158,830	$170,803	$183,688	$661,024	$843	$738	$961

Source: College Money © 1997–2001. Version: 2002 (Book).b.

Northeast Region—State (Resident)

The College Savings Calculator™—Projected College Costs and Savings Required

---

Assumptions:

Planned Savings Starts in September	2002
Planned Withdrawals Begin in September	Freshman Year
Geographic Region (1 = Northeast, 2 = Midwest, 3 = South, 4 = West)	**1 Northeast**
Cost Categories (1 = Low, 2 = Med/Low, 3 = Medium, 4 = Med/High, 5 = High)	**1 State College (Resident)**
Benchmark College:	**Rutgers**
Projected After-Tax Growth Rates on Savings Deposits	8.00% 9.00% 7.00%

Notes:

Assume Funding through August of the Last Year of College

College Costs are total costs based on college budget bill plus misc. costs reported by parents.

Cost Categories—1 Low for State schools (in-state resident), 5 High for Ivy League, 2–4 Medium range for Private

Projected Freshman Year	Projected Freshman Cost	Projected Sophomore Cost	Projected Junior Cost	Projected Senior Cost	Projected Four-Year Cost	Approx. Mo. Savings Req. 8.00%	Approx. Mo. Savings Req. 9.00%	Approx. Mo. Savings Req. 7.00%
2002						n/a	n/a	n/a
2003	$20,049	$20,876	$21,739	$22,640	$85,305	$1,360	$1,352	$1,367
2004	$20,876	$21,739	$22,640	$23,712	$88,968	$1,134	$1,122	$1,146
2005	$21,739	$22,640	$23,712	$24,837	$92,928	$974	$958	$990
2006	$22,640	$23,712	$24,837	$26,019	$97,208	$854	$836	$873
2007	$23,712	$24,837	$26,019	$27,259	$101,827	$762	$741	$783
2008	$24,837	$26,019	$27,259	$28,562	$106,677	$688	$666	$711
2009	$26,019	$27,259	$28,562	$30,580	$112,419	$631	$606	$656
2010	$27,259	$28,562	$30,580	$32,744	$119,145	$586	$560	$613
2011	$28,562	$30,580	$32,744	$35,066	$126,952	$551	$523	$580
2012	$30,580	$32,744	$35,066	$37,558	$135,948	$524	$494	$554
2013	$32,744	$35,066	$37,558	$40,232	$145,601	$500	$469	$533
2014	$35,066	$37,558	$40,232	$43,102	$155,959	$480	$447	$514
2015	$37,558	$40,232	$43,102	$46,182	$167,075	$462	$427	$498
2016	$40,232	$43,102	$46,182	$49,489	$179,005	$446	$410	$484
2017	$43,102	$46,182	$49,489	$53,038	$191,811	$432	$394	$472
2018	$46,182	$49,489	$53,038	$56,848	$205,557	$419	$380	$461
2019	$49,489	$53,038	$56,848	$60,940	$220,314	$407	$367	$452
2020	$53,038	$56,848	$60,940	$65,333	$236,158	$397	$355	$443
2021	$56,848	$60,940	$65,333	$70,050	$253,171	$388	$344	$436
2022	$60,940	$65,333	$70,050	$75,117	$271,439	$379	$334	$429
2023	$65,333	$70,050	$75,117	$80,558	$291,057	$3711	$3251	$423

Source: College Money © 1997–2001. Version: 2002 (Book).b.

Northeast Region—State (Nonresident)

The College Savings Calculator™—Projected College Costs and Savings Required

Assumptions:

Planned Savings Starts in September	2002
Planned Withdrawals Begin in September	Freshman Year
Geographic Region (1 = Northeast, 2 = Midwest, 3 = South, 4 = West)	**1 Northeast**
Cost Categories (1 = Low, 2 = Med/Low, 3 = Medium, 4 = Med/High, 5 = High)	**2 State College (Nonresident)**
Benchmark College:	**Rutgers (Nonresident)**
Projected After-Tax Growth Rates on Savings Deposits	8.00% 9.00% 7.00%

Notes:

Assume Funding through August of the Last Year of College

College Costs are total costs based on college budget bill plus misc. costs reported by parents.

Cost Categories—1 Low for State schools (in-state resident), 5 High for Ivy League, 2–4 Medium range for Private

Projected Freshman Year	Projected Freshman Cost	Projected Sophomore Cost	Projected Junior Cost	Projected Senior Cost	Projected Four-Year Cost	Approx. Mo. Savings Req. 8.00%	Approx. Mo. Savings Req. 9.00%	Approx. Mo. Savings Req. 7.00%
2002						n/a	n/a	n/a
2003	$24,473	$25,507	$26,588	$27,715	$104,283	$1,662	$1,653	$1,671
2004	$25,507	$26,588	$27,715	$29,059	$108,870	$1,387	$1,372	$1,403
2005	$26,588	$27,715	$29,059	$30,471	$113,834	$1,192	$1,173	$1,212
2006	$27,715	$29,059	$30,471	$31,955	$119,201	$1,047	$1,025	$1,070
2007	$29,059	$30,471	$31,955	$33,514	$124,999	$935	$910	$961
2008	$30,471	$31,955	$33,514	$35,151	$131,091	$846	$818	$874
2009	$31,955	$33,514	$35,151	$37,679	$138,299	$776	$746	$807
2010	$33,514	$35,151	$37,679	$40,392	$146,736	$721	$689	$755
2011	$35,151	$37,679	$40,392	$43,306	$156,529	$679	$645	$715
2012	$37,679	$40,392	$43,306	$46,436	$167,814	$646	$610	$684
2013	$40,392	$43,306	$46,436	$49,796	$179,931	$618	$579	$658
2014	$43,306	$46,436	$49,796	$53,406	$192,945	$593	$553	$636
2015	$46,436	$49,796	$53,406	$57,283	$206,922	$572	$529	$617
2016	$49,796	$53,406	$57,283	$61,448	$221,935	$553	$508	$600
2017	$53,406	$57,283	$61,448	$65,923	$238,061	$536	$489	$586
2018	$57,283	$61,448	$65,923	$70,730	$255,385	$520	$472	$573
2019	$61,448	$65,923	$70,730	$75,895	$273,997	$507	$456	$562
2020	$65,923	$70,730	$75,895	$81,445	$293,994	$494	$442	$552
2021	$70,730	$75,895	$81,445	$87,409	$315,480	$483	$429	$543
2022	$75,895	$81,445	$87,409	$93,818	$338,568	$473	$417	$535
2023	$81,445	$87,409	$93,818	$100,707	$363,380	$463	$406	$528

Source: College Money © 1997–2001. Version: 2002 (Book).b.

Northeast Region—Private (Medium Cost)

The College Savings Calculator™—Projected College Costs and Savings Required

Assumptions:

Planned Savings Starts in September	2002
Planned Withdrawals Begin in September	Freshman Year
Geographic Region (1 = Northeast, 2 = Midwest, 3 = South, 4 = West)	**1 Northeast**
Cost Categories (1 = Low, 2 = Med/Low, 3 = Medium, 4 = Med/High, 5 = High)	**3 Private College (Medium Cost)**
Benchmark College:	**Lycoming College**
Projected After-Tax Growth Rates on Savings Deposits	8.00% 9.00% 7.00%

Notes:

Assume Funding through August of the Last Year of College

College Costs are total costs based on college budget bill plus misc. costs reported by parents.

Cost Categories—1 Low for State schools (in-state resident), 5 High for Ivy League, 2–4 Medium range for Private

Projected Freshman Year	Projected Freshman Cost	Projected Sophomore Cost	Projected Junior Cost	Projected Senior Cost	Projected Four-Year Cost	Approx. Mo. Savings Req. 8.00%	Approx. Mo. Savings Req. 9.00%	Approx. Mo. Savings Req. 7.00%
2002						n/a	n/a	n/a
2003	$31,679	$33,068	$34,518	$36,035	$135,300	$2,156	$2,144	$2,168
2004	$33,068	$34,518	$36,035	$37,844	$141,465	$1,803	$1,783	$1,822
2005	$34,518	$36,035	$37,844	$39,747	$148,145	$1,552	$1,526	$1,577
2006	$36,035	$37,844	$39,747	$41,749	$155,375	$1,365	$1,335	$1,395
2007	$37,844	$39,747	$41,749	$43,854	$163,195	$1,221	$1,188	$1,255
2008	$39,747	$41,749	$43,854	$46,068	$171,418	$1,106	$1,069	$1,143
2009	$41,749	$43,854	$46,068	$49,467	$181,137	$1,016	$977	$1,057
2010	$43,854	$46,068	$49,467	$53,120	$192,508	$946	$904	$990
2011	$46,068	$49,467	$53,120	$57,048	$205,702	$892	$847	$939
2012	$49,467	$53,120	$57,048	$61,271	$220,905	$851	$803	$901
2013	$53,120	$57,048	$61,271	$65,811	$237,249	$815	$764	$868
2014	$57,048	$61,271	$65,811	$70,693	$254,822	$783	$730	$840
2015	$61,271	$65,811	$70,693	$75,943	$273,718	$756	$700	$816
2016	$65,811	$70,693	$75,943	$81,588	$294,035	$732	$673	$795
2017	$70,693	$75,943	$81,588	$87,659	$315,884	$711	$649	$777
2018	$75,943	$81,588	$87,659	$94,189	$339,379	$691	$627	$761
2019	$81,588	$87,659	$94,189	$101,211	$364,647	$674	$607	$747
2020	$87,659	$94,189	$101,211	$108,764	$391,823	$659	$589	$735
2021	$94,189	$101,211	$108,764	$116,888	$421,051	$645	$572	$724
2022	$101,211	$108,764	$116,888	$125,626	$452,489	$632	$557	$715
2023	$108,764	$116,888	$125,626	$135,026	$486,304	$620	$543	$707

Source: College Money © 1997–2001. Version: 2002 (Book).b.

Northeast Region—Private (High Cost)

The College Savings Calculator™—Projected College Costs and Savings Required

Assumptions:

Planned Savings Starts in September	2002
Planned Withdrawals Begin in September	Freshman Year
Geographic Region (1 = Northeast, 2 = Midwest, 3 = South, 4 = West)	**1 Northeast**
Cost Categories (1 = Low, 2 = Med/Low, 3 = Medium, 4 = Med/High, 5 = High)	**4 Private (High Cost)**
Benchmark College:	**American Univ.**
Projected After-Tax Growth Rates on Savings Deposits	8.00% 9.00% 7.00%

Notes:

Assume Funding through August of the Last Year of College

College Costs are total costs based on college budget bill plus misc. costs reported by parents.

Cost Categories—1 Low for State schools (in-state resident), 5 High for Ivy League, 2–4 Medium range for Private

Projected Freshman Year	Projected Freshman Cost	Projected Sophomore Cost	Projected Junior Cost	Projected Senior Cost	Projected Four-Year Cost	Approx. Mo. Savings Req. 8.00%	Approx. Mo. Savings Req. 9.00%	Approx. Mo. Savings Req. 7.00%
2002						n/a	n/a	n/a
2003	$38,518	$40,233	$42,027	$43,903	$164,681	$2,624	$2,609	$2,639
2004	$40,233	$42,027	$43,903	$46,143	$172,306	$2,195	$2,171	$2,220
2005	$42,027	$43,903	$46,143	$48,499	$180,572	$1,891	$1,860	$1,922
2006	$43,903	$46,143	$48,499	$50,979	$189,524	$1,665	$1,629	$1,702
2007	$46,143	$48,499	$50,979	$53,588	$199,209	$1,490	$1,450	$1,532
2008	$48,499	$50,979	$53,588	$56,333	$209,399	$1,350	$1,306	$1,396
2009	$50,979	$53,588	$56,333	$60,537	$221,437	$1,242	$1,194	$1,292
2010	$53,588	$56,333	$60,537	$65,059	$235,518	$1,158	$1,106	$1,211
2011	$56,333	$60,537	$65,059	$69,923	$251,853	$1,092	$1,037	$1,150
2012	$60,537	$65,059	$69,923	$75,155	$270,675	$1,042	$983	$1,104
2013	$65,059	$69,923	$75,155	$80,784	$290,921	$999	$937	$1,064
2014	$69,923	$75,155	$80,784	$86,839	$312,701	$961	$896	$1,031
2015	$75,155	$80,784	$86,839	$93,353	$336,130	$928	$859	$1,002
2016	$80,784	$86,839	$93,353	$100,361	$361,336	$899	$827	$977
2017	$86,839	$93,353	$100,361	$107,901	$388,453	$874	$798	$955
2018	$93,353	$100,361	$107,901	$116,013	$417,628	$851	$772	$937
2019	$100,361	$107,901	$116,013	$124,742	$449,017	$830	$748	$920
2020	$107,901	$116,013	$124,742	$134,135	$482,792	$812	$726	$906
2021	$116,013	$124,742	$134,135	$144,242	$519,132	$795	$706	$893
2022	$124,742	$134,135	$144,242	$155,117	$558,236	$779	$687	$882
2023	$134,135	$144,242	$155,117	$166,820	$600,314	$766	$670	$873

Source: College Money © 1997–2001. Version: 2002 (Book).b.

Northeast Region—Ivy League

The College Savings Calculator™—Projected College Costs and Savings Required

Assumptions:

Planned Savings Starts in September	2002
Planned Withdrawals Begin in September	Freshman Year
Geographic Region (1 = Northeast, 2 = Midwest, 3 = South, 4 = West)	**1 Northeast**
Cost Categories (1 = Low, 2 = Med/Low, 3 = Medium, 4 = Med/High, 5 = High)	**5 Ivy League**
Benchmark College:	**Univ. of Pennsylvania**
Projected After-Tax Growth Rates on Savings Deposits	8.00% 9.00% 7.00%

Notes:

Assume Funding through August of the Last Year of College

College Costs are total costs based on college budget bill plus misc. costs reported by parents.

Cost Categories—1 Low for State schools (in-state resident), 5 High for Ivy League, 2–4 Medium range for Private

Projected Freshman Year	Projected Freshman Cost	Projected Sophomore Cost	Projected Junior Cost	Projected Senior Cost	Projected Four-Year Cost	Approx. Mo. Savings Req. 8.00%	Approx. Mo. Savings Req. 9.00%	Approx. Mo. Savings Req. 7.00%
2002						n/a	n/a	n/a
2003	$42,885	$44,796	$46,794	$48,883	$183,358	$2,922	$2,905	$2,938
2004	$44,796	$46,794	$48,883	$51,377	$191,849	$2,444	$2,418	$2,471
2005	$46,794	$48,883	$51,377	$54,001	$201,055	$2,106	$2,071	$2,140
2006	$48,883	$51,377	$54,001	$56,763	$211,024	$1,854	$1,813	$1,895
2007	$51,377	$54,001	$56,763	$59,668	$221,810	$1,660	$1,614	$1,706
2008	$54,001	$56,763	$59,668	$62,726	$233,159	$1,504	$1,454	$1,554
2009	$56,763	$59,668	$62,726	$67,408	$246,565	$1,383	$1,330	$1,438
2010	$59,668	$62,726	$67,408	$72,444	$262,246	$1,289	$1,232	$1,349
2011	$62,726	$67,408	$72,444	$77,860	$280,437	$1,216	$1,155	$1,280
2012	$67,408	$72,444	$77,860	$83,687	$301,399	$1,160	$1,095	$1,229
2013	$72,444	$77,860	$83,687	$89,955	$323,946	$1,112	$1,043	$1,185
2014	$77,860	$83,687	$89,955	$96,699	$348,201	$1,070	$997	$1,148
2015	$83,687	$89,955	$96,699	$103,953	$374,294	$1,034	$957	$1,116
2016	$89,955	$96,699	$103,953	$111,758	$402,365	$1,002	$921	$1,088
2017	$96,699	$103,953	$111,758	$120,155	$432,565	$973	$889	$1,064
2018	$103,953	$111,758	$120,155	$129,190	$465,057	$947	$859	$1,043
2019	$111,758	$120,155	$129,190	$138,912	$500,016	$924	$833	$1,025
2020	$120,155	$129,190	$138,912	$149,373	$537,630	$904	$808	$1,009
2021	$129,190	$138,912	$149,373	$160,629	$578,103	$885	$786	$995
2022	$138,912	$149,373	$160,629	$172,741	$621,654	$868	$765	$982
2023	$149,373	$160,629	$172,741	$185,775	$668,517	$852	$746	$972

Source: College Money © 1997–2001. Version: 2002 (Book).b.

Appendix B

How to Install
The College Savings Calculator™

This program was developed using Microsoft® Excel 2000. All functions take place within the Microsoft® framework. Use of the program with an earlier version of Microsoft® Excel might result in some formatting and display anomalies that we cannot support.

To Install:

1. Open Windows Explorer.

2. Highlight the C: drive in the left window.

3. Choose "New" from the file menu. Click "Folder."

4. Type "College Savings Tools" as the new folder name.

5. Place the CD-ROM in the CD-ROM drive and close it. In the left window of Windows Explorer, select the CD-ROM drive and double-click. The files on the CD-ROM should appear in the right window.

6. Click on the first file, hold down the shift key, and then click on the bottom file. All files should be highlighted.

7. Click on the "Copy" button on the toolbar.

8. In the left window, click on the new folder, "College Savings Tools." Then click "Paste" on the toolbar. The files should appear in the right window.

9. Remove the CD-ROM from the drive.

10. Before using any program, while still in Windows Explorer, highlight each program, click the right mouse button, and select "Properties." At the bottom of the Properties window is an "Attributes" section. Click the "Read-only" box to remove the check mark and then click the "Archive" box. This will allow you to save file information.

Now you are ready to use the software. The following notes are intended to help you negotiate the program.

Helpful Tips

1. All programs are write-protected except in the data-input cells. Data can be entered only in cells where the information appears in blue.

2. Use the [Arrow] keys to move from one input cell to the next one.

3. When you position the cursor over an input cell, a window will open to explain the information needed for that cell.

4. In order to access the supporting pages that are shown in Chapter 2, click on the file tabs at the bottom of the worksheet.

5. Reread Chapter 2 for an explanation of the supporting pages and how they are used.

6. It is important to clear all cells before starting a new case to avoid trailing data.

Appendix C

The Financial Aid Test™ Input Form and Instructions

Family Financial Data: The financial aid formulas are based on parent and student financial data. The following are line-by-line instructions to ensure that you provide the best data possible.

Parents: Be sure to note if you are a single parent. The formulas are different for single and married parents. Please also indicate if you are divorced or remarried. The financial aid system mandates that the custodial parent completes the financial aid form and that a step-parent supply financial data even though they may have no legal obligation to pay for college. *Please do not use data from the non-custodial parent.*

ALL QUESTIONS ARE IMPORTANT! For example, birth dates of parents and children are used in making several calculations. Occupations, company name and job titles sometimes give us hints on how to direct parents toward special scholarship opportunities. Please be sure to let us know if you are self-employed or able to control income from your business.

1. Age of older parent—Enter age of oldest parent

2. Number of parents in family—Step-parents in the custodial household should be included.

3. Number of dependent children—Enter the number of dependent children that you claim on your income tax return.

4. Number of children in college for plan year—If you are completing this test when you will have two students in college, enter "2", "3" if you will have three in for the year, otherwise, the entry will always be "1".

5. Total ages of all pre-college children—For example, if you have 4 children aged, 8, 12, 15, 18, then you would add, $8+12+15$ and enter "35" on line 5.

6. Father's wages—Enter father's W-2 (box #3 on Form W-2) income. This may include tips. When combined with mother's income the figure should match line 7 of the income tax form.

7. Mother's wages—Enter mother's W-2 income. This may include tips. When combined with father's income the figure should match line 7 of the income tax form.

8. Other taxable income—List interest, dividends, capital gains, state tax refunds, alimony received, business income (not included in line 6 or 7 above), IRA distributions, gains from real estate rentals, partnership income, estates, trusts, unemployment compensation, taxable pension and annuity benefits, and taxable social security benefits.

9. Nontaxable income—social security, disability, child support, tax-exempt interest.

10. Untaxed benefits—Include 401(k) plan, tax-deferred pension, and/or Keogh, and savings plans contributions (if not included in line 6 or 7), amounts withheld from wages for dependent care and medical spending accounts, Earned Income Credit, housing, food, and other living allowances, and Foreign Income Exclusion.

11. Losses from business, farm, capital losses—Enter any losses used to offset income on your income tax form.

12. Adjustments to income—deductible IRA contributions, student loan interest deduction, moving expenses, alimony paid, self-employed health insurance deductions, one-half of self-employment tax, penalties on early withdrawals from pensions, IRAs, or 401(k) plans.

13. Child support paid—If you deducted child support payments on your income tax form, enter the amount here.

14. Tuition tax credits—Hope and Lifetime Learning credits deducted on your income tax form.

15. Taxable student aid—Some scholarships and grants are taxable. Check with the institution to determine how much is taxable.

16. Medical and dental expense—Enter the total amount of medical and dental expenses you had for the year.

17. Federal income tax paid—THIS NUMBER WILL *NOT* BE ZERO FOR MOST FAMILIES. Even if you received a refund, you paid some taxes by having money withheld from your paycheck. Enter the number from line 52 of the 1040, line 34 from the 1040A, or line 11 of the 1040EZ for tax year 2001.

18. Net home equity—List the *Market Value* of your primary residence. This is the amount for which you could sell your home to ensure a reasonable "quick sale." On line b, list the balance of all mortgages, home equity loans, etc., on your home. THIS SHOULD NOT BE THE MONTHLY MORTGAGE PAYMENT.

19. Net equity of all other real estate—List the market value of all other real estate and enter the total mortgage amounts on line b.

20. Business/farm net value (your share)—This number should be your share of *Assets* minus *Liabilities.* Do not include goodwill. For a farm, the amount would be your share of the real value minus any indebtedness.

21. Parent cash—Include cash, checking, savings, CDs, and money market funds. Use the average amount you have on hand during the average month.

22. Parent investments—PLEASE SEPARATE YOUR INVESTMENTS BETWEEN *QUALIFIED RETIREMENT PLANS AND OTHER INVESTMENTS. Investments are defined as stocks, bonds, mutual funds, etc. Enter qualified retirement funds on line a, and non-retirement investments on line b.

---

*These items are not used in the Federal Methodology to award financial aid; however, many colleges now ask for these values to award their private funds. Please include this data so we can help you plan.

---

23. Debts other than mortgages—This section relates to *debt value* of car loans, credit cards, medical bills, or other debts you have at this time. We are not interested in the monthly payment, only the value.*

STUDENT DATA: It is important to list data on *all* of your children. The calculations use their ages in the formulas. Many times parents get turned down for financial aid when only one student is in college; however, they are eligible for substantial aid when there are two or more students in college.

These sections pertain to ALL children in the family.

Section C: Please indicate the number of years and the type of undergraduate school the student plans to attend. The key for this section is:

ISC—In-state college
OSC—Out-of-state college
High—High-priced private college
Med—Medium-priced private college
Low—Lower-priced private college

Section D: Please indicate the number of years and type of graduate school the student plans to attend.

Section E: Please indicate the current cost of the private elementary or secondary school each student will or does attend.

Section F: Please indicate the amount of money each child has in savings and investments similar to those of the parents in # 21 and 22 above.

Section G: Please indicate the amount of income each student made from working.

Section H: Please indicate the amount of investment income each student made from their savings and investments.

Section I: Please indicate the amount of federal income taxes each student paid (Line #51 from 1040, line #33 from 1040A, and line #10 from 1040EZ). If the student had no investment income and the earned income was below $4,000, the student most likely had no income tax.

Section 1—Parent Data	Parent #1	Parent #2
Last Name, First Name		
Home Address		
City, State, Zip Code		
Home Phone		
Work Phone		
Company, Occupation, Title		
Date of Birth		
Marital Status—Please indicate: Divorced–Widowed–Separated–Remarried		

Section 2—Family Financial Data		Value	
1	Age of older parent		
2	Number of parents in family		
3	Number of dependent children		
4	Number of children in college for plan year		
5	Total ages of all pre-college children		
6	Father's wages		
7	Mother's wages		
8	Other taxable income		
9	Nontaxable income		
10	Untaxed benefits		
11	Losses from business, farm, capital losses		
12	Adjustments to income		
13	Child support paid		
14	Tuition tax credits		
15	Taxable student aid		
16	Medical and dental expense		
17	Federal income tax paid (line 52 on 1040, line 34 on 1040A, line 11 on 1040EZ)*		
18	Net home equity	Market value	Total of all mortgages
19	Net equity of other real estate	Market value	Total of all mortgages
20	Business/Farm value	Business (assets − liabilities)	Farm (value − indebtedness)
21	Parent cash (checking, savings, money market, etc.		
22	Parent investments	Retirement plans	Other investments
23	Debts other than mortgages		

*Based on 2001 federal tax forms.

Section 3—Student Data

A	B	C	D	E	F	G	H	I
Student First Name Date of Birth	High School Graduation Year	Undergrad School Plans	Graduate School Plans	Current School Costs	Student Savings and Investments	Income Last Year from Work	Income Last Year from Savings and Investments	Income Taxes Paid Last Year
Name: SAMPLE 6 / 27 / 83	2002	4 years High	None	None	$5,000	$2,700	$200	$75
Name: / /								
Name: / /								
Name: / /								
Name: / /								

Section 4—Design Data

1. Do any of your children have special skills or qualifications that may impact college funding such as athletic skills, high SAT scores, or grades, leadership skills, etc.?	
2. Please list any special scholarships or grants for which your student has or will apply.	
3. Are there any obligations to provide college funds to children from previous marriages?	
4. Will any student receive funds for college as part of a divorce or separation agreement?	
5. How much of your present monthly income could you use currently to pay or save for college?	
6. How much of parent cash and investments are allocated for college use?	
7. Do any of your students have any trust funds or olther college resources not included above?	

Appendix D

How to Install
The Financial Aid Test™

This program was developed using Microsoft® Excel 2000. All functions take place within the Microsoft® framework. Use of the program with an earlier version of Microsoft® Excel might result in some formatting and display anomalies that we cannot support.

To Install:

1. Open Windows Explorer.

2. Highlight the C: drive in the left window.

3. Choose "New" from the file menu. Click "Folder."

4. Type "College Savings Tools" as the new folder name.

5. Place the CD-ROM in the CD-ROM drive and close it. In the left window of Windows Explorer, select the CD-ROM drive and double-click. The files on the CD-ROM should appear in the right window.

6. Click on the first file, hold down the shift key, and then click on the bottom file. All files should be highlighted.

7. Click on the "Copy" button on the toolbar.

8. In the left window, click on the new folder, "College Savings Tools." Then click "Paste" on the toolbar. The files should appear in the right window.

9. Remove the CD-ROM from the drive.

10. Before using any program, while still in Windows Explorer, highlight each program, click the right mouse button, and select "Properties." At the bottom of the Properties window is an "Attributes" section. Click the "Read-only" box to remove the check mark and then click the "Archive" box. This will allow you to save file information.

Now you are ready to use the software. The following notes are intended to help you negotiate the program.

Helpful Tips

1. This spreadsheet is locked to ensure that formulas are not inadvertently changed or corrupted. For that reason, you can only enter data in cells that are blue.

2. Use the [Arrow] keys to move from one input cell to the next one.

3. Please review the instructions in Appendix 2 that accompany the input form to be sure of what data should be entered on each line.

4. It is important to clear all cells before starting a new case to avoid trailing data.

5. **Note that you must input the two-letter state abbreviation in ALL CAPS on the state-of-residence line. Otherwise you will get an "ERR" message in the test results.**

6. After all data is entered, use the [Page Down] key to move to the middle of the page. This is where you find the results of The Financial Aid Test.™ Each calculation is broken down into the two components of the EFC, the parent contribution and the student contribution.

7. The EFC is a "per student" calculation. If there is more than one student going to college, a separate financial aid test will have to be run using that student's financial information in order to arrive at the EFC for that student.

8. The area at the right of this section further breaks down the EFC to show what percentage of each calculation is represented by parent income, parent assets, student income, and student assets.

9. To access the supporting pages, click on the file tabs at the bottom of the spreadsheet.

10. "Print Full Report" will display the entire calculation. This is used to evaluate how the various items impact the calculation. This report is not given to the client.

11. "Print Client Page" is a single-page report that is given to the client. It reiterates the data that was input and shows the EFC results for the federal methodology and the institutional methodology.

Special Comments:

The input item on line 11, "Business, farm, capital losses" is somewhat tricky. The Institutional Methodology now adds paper losses back to parent income. If a client has actual cash losses that offset their income, they still have to enter them on that line. The formula will add the losses back to the income.

However, once the EFC information has been sent to the schools the student has chosen, the parents can contact the financial aid officer and explain the nature of the losses. The financial aid officer should have some discretion in deciding whether to allow the losses of offset income or not.

Appendix E

How to Install
The College Funding Integrator™

This program was developed using Microsoft® Excel 2000. All functions take place within the Microsoft® framework. Use of the program with an earlier version of Microsoft® Excel might result in some formatting and display anomalies that we cannot support.

To Install:

1. Open Windows Explorer.

2. Highlight the C: drive in the left window.

3. Choose "New" from the file menu. Click "Folder."

4. Type "College Savings Tools" as the new folder name.

5. Place the CD-ROM in the CD-ROM drive and close it. In the left window of Windows Explorer, select the CD-ROM drive and double-click. The files on the CD-ROM should appear in the right window.

6. Click on the first file, hold down the shift key, and then click on the bottom file. All files should be highlighted.

7. Click on the "Copy" button on the toolbar.

8. In the left window, click on the new folder, "College Savings Tools." Then click "Paste" on the toolbar. The files should appear in the right window.

9. Remove the CD-ROM from the drive.

10. Before using any program, while still in Windows Explorer, highlight each program, click the right mouse button, and select "Properties." At the bottom of the Properties window is an "Attributes" section. Click the "Read-only" box to remove the check mark and then click the "Archive" box. This will allow you to save file information.

Now you are ready to use the software. The following notes are intended to help you negotiate the program.

Helpful Tips:

1. This spreadsheet is locked to ensure that formulas are not inadvertently changed or corrupted. For that reason, you can only enter data in cells that are blue.

2. Use the [Arrow] keys to move from one input cell to the next.

3. It is important to remember to clear all cells before starting a new case to avoid trailing data.

4. When you position the cursor over an input cell, a window will open with a description of the type of data required.

5. If you wish to access the supporting pages, click one of the file tabs at the bottom of the worksheet.

6. Please reread Chapter 5 for an explanation of the supporting pages and how they are used.

Appendix F

Helpful Information Sources for the Planner

Helpful Web Sites

www.state.NJ.us/—This address will take you to the New Jersey Web site. To find another state site, enter the two-letter state abbreviation in place of the "NJ" for the state you wish to locate—e.g., *www.state.CA.us/* for California. This will enable you to visit the site for the state's qualified tuition plans, the treasury for tax forms and instructions, etc.

www.firstgov.gov—Access to numerous federal Web sites. Type in "financial aid" and then select "federal" for federal sites, "state" for state sites.

www.savingforcollege.com—Offers a detailed overview of state prepaid tuition plans and state savings plans.

www.ed.gov/thinkcollege—U.S. Department of Education—explore the resources for getting a college education, applying for financial aid, and returning to school.

www.nast.net/—National Association of State Treasurers.

www.salliemae.com—Sallie Mae provides funds for educational loans, primarily federally guaranteed student loans.

www.academycfp.org—Academy of College Financial Planning is a credentialing organization dedicated to setting and maintaining standards of knowledge about college financial planning among financial services professionals. The Web site has a membership listing that is intended to help families find a competent professional in their area that can help them with college financial planning.

www.irs.treas.gov—This site provides access to all IRS forms, instructions, and publications. See **Publication 970,** Tax Benefits for Higher Education.

www.collegeboard.com—The official Web site of The College Board, this site provides links to most colleges, financial calculators, information about loans, SAT testing, scholarship searches, and much more.

www.petersons.com—Peterson's is a well-known publisher of books on colleges, getting in, and paying for it.

For helpful information on individual state plans, visit the National Association of State Treasurers' Web site at *www.nast.net.* By clicking on "Your State" on the left side of the page you will go to a page with a map of the United States. Click on the state you want to investigate and it will provide a link to their state plan(s).

Appendix G

How to Contact State Departments of Education

ALABAMA

Alabama Commission
on Higher Education
P.O. Box 302000
Montgomery, AL 36130-2000
(334) 242-1998
(800) 843-8534
Toll-Free Restrictions:
AL residents only
FAX: (334) 242-0268
E-Mail: *hhector@ache.state.*
al.us
URL: *http://www.ache.state.al.us/*

ALASKA

Alaska Commission
on Postsecondary Education
3030 Vintage Blvd.
Juneau, AK 99801-7100
(907) 465-2962
(800) 441-2962
TTY: (907) 465-3143
FAX: (907) 465-5316

E-Mail: *customer_service@acpe.*
state.ak.us
URL: *http://www.state.ak.us/acpe/*

ARIZONA

Arizona Commission for
Postsecondary Education
2020 N. Central Ave., Ste. 275
Phoenix, AZ 85004-4503
(602) 229-2591
FAX: (602) 229-2599
E-Mail: *toni@www.acpe.asu.edu*
URL: *http://www.acpe.asu.edu/*

ARKANSAS

Arkansas Department
of Higher Education
114 E. Capitol
Little Rock, AR 72201-3818
(501) 371-2000
FAX: (501) 371-2003
E-Mail: *ronh@adhe.arknet.edu*
URL: *http://www.adhe.arknet.edu/*

CALIFORNIA

California Student Aid
  Commission
P.O. Box 419026
Rancho Cordova, CA 95741-9026
(916) 526-8047
(888) 224-7268
FAX: (916) 526-8002
E-Mail: *custsvcs@csac.ca.gov* or
  jgarcia@csac.ca.gov
URL: *http://www.csac.ca.gov/*

COLORADO

Colorado Commission
  on Higher Education
1380 Lawrence St., Ste. 1200
Denver, CO 80204
(303) 866-2723
FAX: (303) 866-4266
E-Mail: *tim.foster@state.co.us*
URL: *http://www.state.co.us/*
  cche_dir/hecche.html

CONNECTICUT

Connecticut Department
  of Higher Education
61 Woodland St.
Hartford, CT 06105-2326
(860) 947-1833
(800) 842-0229
FAX: (860) 947-1310
E-Mail: *jlyddon@ctdhe.org*
URL: *http://www.ctdhe.org/*

DELAWARE

Delaware Higher Education
  Commission
Carvel State Office Building,
  Fifth Floor
820 N. French St.
Wilmington, DE 19801
(302) 577-3240

(800) 292-7935
FAX: (302) 577-6765
E-Mail: *dhec@state.de.us*
URL: *http://www.doe.state.de.us/*
  high-ed/

DISTRICT OF COLUMBIA

District of Columbia Department
  of Human Services
Office of Postsecondary
  Education, Research, and
  Assistance
2100 Martin Luther King, Jr. Ave.,
  SE, Ste. 401
Washington, DC 20020
(202) 698-2400
FAX: (202) 727-2739

FLORIDA

The Council for Education
  Policy,
Research and Improvement
111 W. Madison St., Ste. 574
Tallahassee, FL 32399-1400
(850) 488-7894
FAX: (850) 922-5388
URL: *http://www.cepri.state.fl.us*

GEORGIA

Georgia Student Finance
  Authority
State Loans and Grants Division
2082 E. Exchange Place,
  Ste. 200
Tucker, GA 30084
(770) 724-9000
(800) 776-6878
FAX: (770) 724-9225
E-Mail: *info@mail.gsfc.state.*
  ga.us
URL: *http://www.gsfc.org/*

HAWAII

Hawaii State Postsecondary
  Education Commission
2444 Dole St., Room 209
Honolulu, HI 96822-2302
(808) 956-8213
FAX: (808) 956-5156
E-Mail: *iha@hawaii.edu*
URL: *http://www.hern.hawaii.
  edu/hern/*

IDAHO

Idaho State Board of Education
P.O. Box 83720
Boise, ID 83720-0027
(208) 334-2270
FAX: (208) 334-2632
E-Mail: *board@osbe.state.id.us*
URL: *http://www.sde.state.id.us/
  osbe/board.htm*

ILLINOIS

Illinois Student Assistance
  Commission
1755 Lake Cook Rd.
Deerfield, IL 60015-5209
(847) 948-8500
(800) 899-4722
TTY: (847) 831-8326
FAX: (847) 831-8549
E-Mail: *isac@wwa.com*
URL: *http://www.isac-online.org/*

INDIANA

State Student Assistance
  Commission of Indiana
150 W. Market St., Ste. 500
Indianapolis, IN 46204-2811
(317) 232-2350
(888) 528-4719
FAX: (317) 232-3260
E-Mail: *grants@ssaci.state.in.us*

IOWA

Iowa College Student Aid
  Commission
200 10th St., Fourth Floor
Des Moines, IA 50309
(515) 281-3501
(800) 383-4222
FAX: (515) 242-3388
E-Mail: *icsac@max.state.ia.us*
URL: *http://www.state.ia.us/
  collegeaid/*

KANSAS

Kansas Board of Regents
700 SW Harrison, Ste. 1410
Topeka, KS 66603-3760
(785) 296-3421
FAX: (785) 296-0983
E-Mail: *kim@kbor.state.ks.us* or
  jbirmingham@kbor.state.ks.us
URL: *http://www.kansasregents.
  org/*

KENTUCKY

Kentucky Higher Education
  Assistance Authority
1050 U.S. Highway 127 S.
Frankfort, KY 40601-4323
(502) 696-7200
(800) 928-8926
TTY: (800) 855-2880
FAX: (502) 696-7496
E-Mail: *webmaster@kheaa.com*
URL: *http://www.kheaa.com/*

LOUISIANA

Louisiana Office of Student
  Financial Assistance
P.O. Box 91202
Baton Rouge, LA 70821-9202
(225) 922-1012
(800) 259-5626

FAX: (225) 922-0790
E-Mail: *custserv@osfa.state.la.us*
URL: *http://www.osfa.state.la.us/*

MAINE

Maine Education Assistance
  Division
Finance Authority of Maine
  (FAME)
5 Community Dr.
Augusta, ME 04332-0949
(207) 623-3263
(800) 228-3734
TTY: (207) 626-2717
FAX: (207) 632-0095
E-Mail: *info@famemaine.com* or
  charliem@famemaine.com
URL: *http://www.famemaine.com/*

MARYLAND

Maryland Higher Education
  Commission
Jeffrey Building
16 Francis St.
Annapolis, MD 21401-1781
(410) 260-4500
(800) 974-1024
Toll-Free Restrictions:
  MD residents only
TTY: (800) 735-2258
FAX: (410) 974-5994
E-Mail: *ssamail@mhec.*
  state.md.us
URL: *http://www.mhec.state.md.us/*

MASSACHUSETTS

Massachusetts Board of Higher
  Education
One Ashburton Place, Room 1401
Boston, MA 02108
(617) 994-6950
FAX: (617) 727-6397

E-Mail: *bhe@bhe.mass.edu*
URL: *http://www.mass.edu/*

Massachusetts Higher Education
  Information Center
Boston Public Library
700 Boylston St.
Boston, MA 02116
(617) 536-0200
(800) 442-1171
Toll-Free Restrictions:
  MA residents only
FAX: (617) 536-4737
E-Mail: *iriarte@teri.org*
URL: *http://www.adinfo.org/*

MICHIGAN

Michigan Higher Education
  Assistance Authority
Office of Scholarships and Grants
P.O. Box 30462
Lansing, MI 48909-7962
(517) 373-3394
(888) 447-2687
FAX: (517) 335-5984
E-Mail: *oir@state.mi.us*
URL: *http://www.MI-*
  StudentAid.org/

MINNESOTA

Minnesota Higher Education
  Services Office
1450 Energy Park Dr., Ste. 350
Saint Paul, MN 55108-5227
(651) 642-0533
(800) 657-0866
TTY: (800) 627-3529
FAX: (651) 642-0675
E-Mail: *info@heso.state.mn.us*
URL: *http://www.mheso.state.*
  mn.us/cfdocs/webdirectory/
  index.cfm

MISSISSIPPI

Mississippi Postsecondary
  Education Financial
  Assistance Board
3825 Ridgewood Rd.
Jackson, MS 39211-6453
(601) 432-6997
(800) 327-2980
Toll-Free Restrictions:
  MS residents only
FAX: (601) 432-6527
E-Mail: *sfa@ihl.state.ms.us*
URL: *http://www.ihl.state.ms.us/*

MISSOURI

Missouri Department of Higher
  Education
3515 Amazonas Drive
Jefferson City, MO 65109-5717
(573) 751-2361
(800) 473-6757
FAX: (573) 751-6635
E-Mail: *cheryl.kesel@mocbhe.gov*
URL: *http://www.missourimost.
  org*

MONTANA

Montana University System
2500 Broadway
P.O. Box 203101
Helena, MT 59620-3103
(406) 444-6570
FAX: (406) 444-1469
E-Mail: *sherry.rosette@state.mt.us*
URL: *http://www.montana.edu/
  wwwoche/*

NEBRASKA

Nebraska Coordinating
  Commission for Postsecondary
  Education
P.O. Box 95005

Lincoln, NE 68509-5005
(402) 471-2847
FAX: (402) 471-2886
E-Mail: *staff@ccpe.state.ne.us*
URL: *http://www.ccpe.state.
  ne.us/*

NEVADA

University of Nevada System
2601 Enterprise Rd.
Reno, Nevada 89512
(775) 784-4901
FAX: (775) 784-1127
URL: *http://www.nde.state.
  nv.us/*

NEW HAMPSHIRE

New Hampshire Postsecondary
  Education Commission
2 Industrial Park Dr.
Concord, NH 03301-8512
(603) 271-2555
TTY: (800) 735-2964
FAX: (603) 271-2696
E-Mail: *kdodge@nhsa.state.
  nh.us*
URL: *http://www.state.nh.us/
  postsecondary/*

NEW JERSEY

Higher Education Student
  Assistance Authority (New
  Jersey)
P.O. Box 540
Quakerbridge Plaza,
  Bldg. 4
Trenton, NJ 08625-0540
(609) 588-3226
(800) 792-8670
TTY: (609) 588-2526
FAX: (609) 588-7389
URL: *http://www.hesaa.org/*

NEW MEXICO

New Mexico Commission on
  Higher Education
1068 Cerrillos Road
Santa Fe, NM 87501
(505) 827-7383
(800) 279-9777
TTY: (800) 659-8331
FAX: (505) 827-7392
E-Mail: *highered@che.state.nm.us*
URL: *http://www.nmche.org/*

NEW YORK

New York State Higher Education
  Services Corporation
99 Washington Ave.
Albany, NY 12255
(518) 473-7087
(888) 697-4372
FAX: (518) 474-2839
URL: *http://www.hesc.com/*

NORTH CAROLINA

North Carolina State Education
  Assistance Authority
P.O. Box 13663
Research Triangle Park, NC
  27709-3663
(919) 549-8614
(800) 700-1775
Toll-Free Restrictions:
  NC residents only
FAX: (919) 549-8481
E-Mail: *emcduffie@ga.unc.edu* or
  mcduffie@ga.unc.edu
URL: *http://www.ncseaa.edu/*

NORTH DAKOTA

North Dakota University System
North Dakota Student Financial
  Assistance Program

600 E. Boulevard Ave.,
  Department 215
Bismarck, ND 58505-0230
(701) 328-4114
FAX: (701) 328-2961
E-Mail: *ndus_office@ndus.
  nodak.edu*
URL: *http://www.nodak.edu/*

OHIO

Ohio Board of Regents
State Grants and Scholarships
  Department
P.O. Box 182452
Columbus, OH 43218-2452
(614) 466-7420
(888) 833-1133
FAX: (614) 752-5903
URL: *http://www.regents.state.oh.
  us/sgs/*

OKLAHOMA

Oklahoma State Regents
  for Higher Education
Oklahoma Guaranteed
  Student Loan Program
655 Research Parkway,
  Ste. 200
Oklahoma City, OK 73104
(405) 225-9100
FAX: (405) 225-9230
E-Mail: *tsimonton@osrhe.edu*
URL: *http://www.okhighered.org/*

OREGON

Oregon Student Assistance
  Commission
1500 Valley River Dr., Ste. 100
Eugene, OR 97401
(541) 687-7400
(800) 452-8807
FAX: (541) 687-7419

E-Mail: *thomas.f.turner@state.or.us*
URL: *http://www.osac.state.or.us/*

Oregon University System
P.O. Box 3175
Eugene, OR 97401
(541) 346-5700
TTY: (541) 346-5741
FAX: (541) 346-5764
E-Mail: *bob_bruce@ous.edu*
URL: *http://www.ous.edu/*

PENNSYLVANIA

Pennsylvania Higher Education
  Assistance Agency
1200 N. Seventh St.
Harrisburg, PA 17102-1444
(717) 720-2800
TTY: (800) 654-5988
E-Mail: *info@pheaa.org* or
  kwoollam@pheaa.org
URL: *http://www.pheaa.org/*

RHODE ISLAND

Rhode Island Higher Education
  Assistance Authority
560 Jefferson Blvd.
Warwick, RI 02886
(401) 736-1100
(800) 922-9855
TTY: (401) 734-9481
FAX: (401) 732-3541
URL: *http://www.riheaa.org/*

Rhode Island Office of Higher
  Education
301 Promenade St.
Providence, RI 02908-5748
(401) 222-6560
TTY: (401) 222-1350
FAX: (401) 222-6111
E-Mail: *ribghe@etal.uri.edu*
URL: *http://www.ribghe.org/*
  riohe.htm

SOUTH CAROLINA

Commission on Higher
  Education
1333 Main St., Ste. 200
Columbia, S.C. 29201
(803) 737-2260
FAX: (803) 737-2297
URL: *http://www.che400.state.*
  se.us

SOUTH DAKOTA

South Dakota Board
  of Regents
306 E. Capitol Ave., Ste. 200
Pierre, SD 57501
(605) 773-3455
FAX: (605) 773-5320
E-Mail: *info@ris.sdbor.edu*
URL: *http://www.ris.sdbor.edu/*

TENNESSEE

Tennessee Higher Education
  Commission
Parkway Towers
404 James Robertson Parkway,
  Ste. 1900
Nashville, TN 37243-0830
(615) 741-3605
FAX: (615) 741-6230
URL: *http://www.state.tn.*
  us/thec/

TEXAS

Texas Higher Education
  Coordinating Board
P.O. Box 12788
Austin, TX 78711
(512) 427-6101
(800) 242-3062
FAX: (512) 427-6420
URL: *http://www.thecb.state.*
  tx.us/

UTAH

Utah State Board of Regents
Three Triad Center
355 W. North Temple, Ste. 550
Salt Lake City, UT 84180-1205
(801) 321-7100
FAX: (801) 321-7199
E-Mail: *heyring@utahsbr.edu*
URL: *http://www.utahsbr.edu/*

VERMONT

Vermont Student Assistance
  Corporation
Champlain Mill
1 Main St., Fourth Floor
P.O. Box 2000
Winooski, VT 05404-2601
(802) 655-9602
(800) 642-3177
TTY: (800) 281-3341
FAX: (802) 654-3765
E-Mail: *info@vsac.org*
URL: *http://www.vsac.org/*

VIRGINIA

State Council of Higher Education
  for Virginia
James Monroe Building
101 N. 14th St., Ninth Floor
Richmond, VA 23219
(804) 225-2600
TTY: (804) 371-8017
FAX: (804) 225-2604
E-Mail: *bradford@schev.edu* or
  nardo@schev.edu
URL: *http://www.schev.edu/*

WASHINGTON

Washington State Higher
  Education Coordinating
  Board
P.O. Box 43430

917 Lakeridge Way
Olympia, WA 98504-3430
(360) 753-7800
TTY: (360) 753-7809
FAX: (360) 753-7808
E-Mail: *info@hecb.wa.gov*
URL: *http://www.hecb.wa.gov/*

WEST VIRGINIA

West Virginia Higher Education
  Policy Commission
1018 Kanawha Blvd., E.
Charleston, WV 25301
(304) 558-2101
FAX: (304) 558-0259
E-Mail: *healey@hepc.wvnet.edu* or
  thralls@hepc.wvnet.edu
URL: *http://www.hepc.wvnet.edu/*

WISCONSIN

Wisconsin Higher Educational
  Aids Board
131 West Wilson St., Room 902
Madison, WI 53707-7885
(608) 267-2206
FAX: (608) 267-2808
E-Mail: *heabmail@heab.state.*
  wi.us
URL: *http://heab.state.wi.us/*

WYOMING

Wyoming Community College
  Commission
Eighth Floor
2020 Carey Ave.
Cheyenne, WY 82002
(307) 777-7763
FAX: (307) 777-6567
E-Mail: *sbutler@commission.*
  wcc.edu
URL: *http://commission.*
  wcc.edu/

TERRITORIES

American Samoa

American Samoa Community
  College
Board of Higher Education
P.O. Box 2609
Pago Pago, AS 96799-2609
(684) 699-1141

Commonwealth of the Northern Mariana Islands

Northern Marianas College
Olympio T. Borja Memorial
  Library
As-Terlaje Campus
P.O. Box 1250 CK
Saipan, MP 96950-1250
(670) 234-3690
FAX: (670) 234-0759
URL: *http://www.nmcnet.edu/*

Puerto Rico

Puerto Rico Council on Higher
  Education
P.O. Box 19900
San Juan, PR 00910
(787) 724-7100
FAX: (787) 725-1275
E-Mail: *sa_espada@ces.prstar.net*

Republic of the Marshall Islands

Republic of the Marshall Islands
RMI Scholarship Grant
  and Loan Board
P.O. Box 1436
3 Lagoon Rd.
Majuro, MH 96960
(692) 625-3108

Virgin Islands

Virgin Islands Joint Boards
  of Education
Charlotte Amalie
P.O. Box 11900
St. Thomas, VI 00801
(340) 774-4546
FAX: (340) 774-3384

Index